Oracle SQL Tuning & CBO Internals

Kimberly Floss

This book is dedicated to my husband Dan - your love and support made it possible for me to write this book. Thank you so much. And, to our newborn son Zachary - we are so lucky to have you in our lives (and thanks for taking those afternoon naps, so mommy could write)

Oracle SQL Tuning & CBO Internals

By Kimberly Floss

Copyright © 2004 by Rampant TechPress. All rights reserved.

Printed in the United States of America.

Published by Rampant TechPress, Kittrell, North Carolina, USA

Oracle In-Focus Series: Book 16

Editors: Linda Webb and John Lavender

Production Editor: Teri Wade

Cover Design: Bryan Hoff

Printing History:

   May 2004 for First Edition

Oracle, Oracle7, Oracle8, Oracle8i, Oracle9i, Oracle Database 10g, Oracle 10g, and Oracle10g are trademarks of Oracle Corporation.

Many of the designations used by computer vendors to distinguish their products are claimed as Trademarks.   All names known to Rampant TechPress to be trademark names appear in this text as initial caps.

The information provided by the authors of this work is believed to be accurate and reliable, but because of the possibility of human error by our authors and staff, Rampant TechPress cannot guarantee the accuracy or completeness of any information included in this work and is not responsible for any errors, omissions, or inaccurate results obtained from the use of information or scripts in this work.

ISBN: 0-9745993-3-6

Library of Congress Control Number: 2004101894

Table of Contents

Table of Contents

Using the Online Code Depot

Your purchase of this book provides you with complete access to the online code depot that contains the sample code scripts.

All of the code depot scripts in this book are located at the following URL:

rampant.cc/cbo.htm

All of the code scripts in this book are available for download in zip format, ready to load and use on your database.

If you need technical assistance in downloading or accessing the scripts, please contact Rampant TechPress at info@rampant.cc.

Advanced Oracle Monitoring and Tuning Script Collection

The complete collection from Mike Ault, the world's best DBA.

Packed with 590 ready-to-use Oracle scripts, this is the definitive collection for every Oracle professional DBA.

It would take many years to develop these scripts from scratch, making this download the best value in the Oracle industry.

It's only $39.95 (less than 7 cents per script!)

To buy for immediate download, go to

www.rampant.cc/aultcode.htm

Conventions Used in this Book

It is critical for any technical publication to follow rigorous standards and employ consistent punctuation conventions to make the text easy to read.

However, this is not an easy task. Within Oracle there are many types of notation that can confuse a reader. Some Oracle utilities such as STATSPACK and TKPROF are always spelled in CAPITAL letters, while Oracle parameters and procedures have varying naming conventions in the Oracle documentation. It is also important to remember that many Oracle commands are case sensitive, and are always left in their original executable form, and never altered with italics or capitalization.

Hence, all Rampant TechPress books follow these conventions:

Parameters - All Oracle parameters will be lowercase italics. Exceptions to this rule are parameter arguments that are commonly capitalized (KEEP pool, TKPROF), these will be left in ALL CAPS.

Variables – All PL/SQL program variables and arguments will also remain in lowercase italics (*dbms_job*, *dbms_utility*).

Tables & dictionary objects – All data dictionary objects are referenced in lowercase italics (*dba_indexes*, *v$sql*). This includes all v$ and x$ views (*x$kcbcbh*, *v$parameter*) and dictionary views (*dba_tables*, *user_indexes*).

SQL – All SQL is formatted for easy use in the code depot, and all SQL is displayed in lowercase. The main SQL terms (select, from, where, group by, order by, having) will always appear on a separate line.

Programs & Products – All products and programs that are known to the author are capitalized according to the vendor specifications (IBM, DBXray, etc). All names known by Rampant TechPress to be trademark names appear in this text as initial caps. References to UNIX are always made in uppercase.

Acknowledgements

This book would not be possible without the work of so many people. To the entire staff at Rampant Publishing, Don, Janet, Andy, Linda, Teri, Kelly, John & company - couldn't have done it without you. Don, thanks for giving me the chance - I am honored.

To all the Oracle Internals Authors - you made this book that much easier to write, because of all your Oracle expertise that you are constantly sharing with the Oracle User Community.

And, to the International Oracle User Group, and our former President Rich Niemiec, your efforts to share knowledge with the Oracle User Community do not go unrecognized, and have inspired me to go to greater lengths to share my knowledge as well, hence, the book. You have helped me to achieve my goals, in more ways than one.

Without the assistance of all of these people, and the support of my family, this book would not be what it is today.

Introduction to SQL Tuning

The Evolution of Oracle SQL

In recent versions, Oracle has added many enhancements to their database software to facilitate improved performance. The purpose of this book will be to explain some of these newer features in more detail – things like plan stability, materialized views, function based indexes, new join types, new analytic functions, and some of the new automated tuning features found in the latest release, Oracle 10g. Some highlights of the new tuning features are discussed below, with the detailed information in subsequent chapters.

We have come a long way from a simple SELECT statement. With each new release, Oracle delivers enhanced functionality to improve performance and make management of the database easier.

We have also come a long way from just reading EXPLAIN PLAN output and access paths. While we certainly still do that, there are many other tools in a DBA's toolbox that should be used.

The intent of this book is to share some key information found in top articles originally published by Oracle Internals Magazine, and to include some additional information, so you can hit the ground running, implementing various new tuning features in your database.

When the cost-based optimizer was first introduced, many folks were reluctant to use it – after all, things were running just fine under the rule-based optimizer. However, over the years, all major optimizer enhancements have gone into the cost-based optimizer (CBO), as opposed to rule-based. In fact, in Oracle 10g, the rule-based optimizer has been de-supported. Recent enhancements have made the CBO much better than its predecessor. However, the trick to using the CBO is to have appropriate statistics in place. For those who didn't have their statistics in order, and attempted to run the CBO, were likely quite unhappy. Since the CBO is basing all of its decisions on those statistics, they need to be present, and they need to be accurate. Later we'll cover use of the *dbms_stats* package, which will generate those statistics.

Statistics

One of the age-old issues has been that of calculating statistics for the cost-based SQL optimizer:

- estimate vs. compute

- frequency of compute

- what if the statistics make things worse

- do you calculate stats regularly, or stop when you have a decent access path and performance is ok

dbms_stats is a package that assists with the calculation of statistics. It handles partitions much better than the old ANALYZE command. But, by far, a huge advantage of using *dbms_stats* is its capability to collect statistics solely on 'stale' objects – although you do need to be sure that monitoring is enabled for the objects in question. *dbms_stats* is covered in detail in Chapter 2. This feature is a key motivator for switching from the old ANALYZE command or *dbms_utility.analyze_statistics* to *dbms_stats*.

Statspack

STATSPACK is one of the most important utilities that Oracle comes with. Most of us have spent hours reviewing output generated from the *utlbstat/utlestat* and trying to figure out what to change to make our systems perform better.

The *utlbstat/utlestat* utilities greatly improve the STATSPACK utility. Not only do we get all the statistics, but we can quickly analyze the top 5 waits, where all the I/O is, if we have latching issues, etc. And, all this data is stored in tables for future reference.

Chapter 3 will cover how to set up the STATSPACK objects, execute a snapshot, and review the report that is created.

Plan Stability

Plan Stability (stored outlines) is a major feature for those tuning packaged applications. Stored outlines allow you to save an SQL execution path and have it automatically reused whenever the SQL executes. This way, if statistics change, indexes change (aside from the one you are using, if you are using indexes), database configuration parameters change, underlying table structures change, or even if the Oracle database is upgraded to a new version, the SQL access path remains the same.

The beauty of plan stability is that you can force an alternate access path for a specific SQL statement, without changing that statement, as is typically the case in a delivered 3rd party application.

When using Plan Stability, you create 'stored outlines' that are stored in the catalog tables. The owner of all stored outlines is the schema owner OUTLN (default password is OUTLN, which you should change). In order to use this feature of the cost based optimizer, you must have the *init.ora/spfile* parameter *use_stored_outlines* set to something other than FALSE – we'll cover the appropriate values shortly.

Materialized Views

Materialized views are typically used as a pre-aggregated summary of a table or group of tables. The term 'view' is misleading because in traditional database systems, a view is an entry in the system catalog and doesn't really take up any storage. Materialized views behave more like tables, in that they do require storage, to store the data. Also, you can build indexes on them to speed access.

Materialized views serve two major purposes. First, they are the replacement to the 'snapshot' functionality in previous Oracle releases. When used in this fashion, a read only version of a table can be created - perhaps from another database or perhaps a collection of tables - and the 'view' is stored as a real object in the database.

The second major use of materialized views is to take advantage of Oracle's 'query rewrite' functionality. In this case, your SQL is coded against the original base tables, but Oracle is smart enough to recognize that a summary table already exists with the data pre-aggregated, so it switches automatically to use the materialized view instead of the base tables.

Queries can be written to operate on the materialized view instead of the original tables, just as we write queries against regular views. The advantage here is that the data is pre-aggregated for you, as this takes place when the materialized view is built. Or, if your materialized view is built across a database link, the data is now stored locally, so it prevents your process from having to incur network traffic to go to another database to get the data.

You can use Materialized Views for pre-summarization or for pre-joining tables together, saving run-time effort.

Introduction to the CBO Optimizer

Oracle 10g introduced many changes to the cost-based optimizer. Below are some highlights, with much of the detail to follow in subsequent chapters. In general, the optimizer is getting smarter, which should make a DBAs job much easier. Noted Oracle expert, Donald K. Burleson, explains below;

Inside the Oracle10g Optimizer – Donald K. Burleson

With the retirement of the ancient rule-based optimizer and the introduction of automated monitoring and tuning, Oracle seized upon the opportunity to ensure that the CBO always had the information it needs to properly determine the access path to data. These remarkable enhancements include:

- Automated statistics collection – The CBO now automatically collects CBO statistics using sophisticated algorithms to determine the optimum sample size (using the *dbms_stats auto_sample_size* parameter). The automated collection mechanism also examines the table data and automatically builds histograms for skewed columns.

- Dynamic sampling – The Oracle10g CBO now uses Artificial Intelligence (AI) to detect when additional information is required and it will dynamically sample the data to ensure an optimal execution plan.

- SQL tuning advisor & SQL access advisor – Oracle10g has automated much of the tedium of SQL tuning with the

---

Database Tuning Pack (DTP). Integral components of the DTP include automatic SQL collection and sophisticated

However, all of this sophistication does not always provide the CBO with enough detailed information about the distribution of the data to always arrive at the optimal plan. Let's take a close look at this issue.

Histograms are not enough

As we may know, Oracle automatically detects indexed columns where the values specified in the SQL statement would influence the best execution plan. For example, a *state_code* index might be best for a query against Rhode Island, but a full-table scan might be best when the query specifies California.

The problem arises when we see a query with multi-column values. One of the most import jobs of the CBO is determining the optimal table join order for multi-table queries. To illustrate, a 5-way table join can be executed with 120 different table join sequences (five factorial=120). The optimal table join order is the one that minimizes the intermediate "baggage" that the CBO must pass between table join steps. For example, a five-way table join might be issued against tables with millions of rows, yet the result set is only ten rows. The optimal join order is usually the one that restricts the result set to ten rows on the first table join. Oracle uses the term cardinality to refer to the size of the intermediate result set.

Unfortunately, histograms are not always enough for the CBO. Consider this query where we have 5,000 students and 6,000 courses in our Oracle database:

```
select
    student_name
from
        student,
```

```
natural join
            grade,
natural join
            course
where
   course.category = 'anthropology'
and
   course.campus = 'brazil'
and
   student.state_residence = 'north carolina'
and
   student.national_origin = 'sweden'
;

Robert Nelson
Sonya Haardson
Swen Jackobsen

3 Rows Returned
```

Here we ask for all three Swedish students living in North
Carolina who are taking an Anthropology course at the campus in
Brazil.

Ultimately, the choice becomes one of inter-column result set
size (cardinality). The CBO knows the *num_rows* for each table,
but it may not be able to accurately predict the number of rows
from multi-column queries.

Returning to our example, consider the following additional
information:

```
select count(*) from course where
   category = 'anthropology' and campus = 'brazil';

900

1 rows returned.
```

```
select count(*) from student where
   state_residence = 'north carolina' and national_origin =
'sweden';

43

1 rows returned.
```

When we see that the there are only 43 Swedish NC students, it becomes clear that the CBO should perform the student-grade join before the course-grade join to minimize the size of the intermediate result set. Even the presence of histograms will not give us the "intersection size" of multi-column query results.

This simple illustration shows why it is impossible for any SQL optimizer to always choose the optimal execution plan for complex queries.

Next, let's look at how Oracle10g SQL Profiles offer a solution to this issue.

Using SQL Profiles

Before Oracle9i the Oracle SQL tuning professional had several ways to alter the execution plans for SQL queries:

- Add Hints – Hints are CBO optimizer directives that are placed inside comments immediately following the select statement. The CBO recognizes these directives and changes the execution plan.

- Change CBO statistics – The CBO statistics can be altered, forcing the CBO to derive a different execution plan.

- Use Stored Outlines – The Optimizer Plan Stability features can be used to freeze and execution plan.

- Adjust optimizer parameters – You could change the default optimizer behavior with commands like alter session set *optimizer_goal*=first_rows_10;

In Oracle10g we see a new option, the SQL Profile. The SQL profile takes a whole new approach to SQL tuning by adjusting the relative costs of a preferred operation without freezing the entire execution plan or requiring changes to CBO statistics.

SQL Profiles are recommended by the SQL Tuning Advisor (STA) after a tuning task has analyzed an SQL statement. During a comprehensive execution analysis, the STA mimics the steps of a human SQL tuning expert:

1. Use row-source sampling - Samples inter-step row sources and compares real costs to initial cost estimates.

2. Mimic original query – The STA re-executes the query with its original bind variables.

3. Intelligent Tuning – The STA add hints and iterates through many executions, comparing various plans with elapsed execution times. The end result is a cost adjustment that can be applied to the query at runtime.

Using this automated approach the STA is far more flexible at hints and stored outlines, never freezing the execution plan. Rather, the SQL Profile lowers the relative costs for the best access method before the decision tree is created. In this fashion, the STA is far more effective and flexible than traditional tuning:

- Allows for the execution plan to change as the CBO statistics change.

- Informs the CBO of the adjusted costs at runtime

- Cost adjustments are based on real-time row-source sampling

Oracle 10g SQL Tuning Advisory Utilities

Oracle 10g introduced major new tuning functionalities – in essence, performing some of the routine analysis for you. A

DBA can jump right into implementing solutions, as opposed to spending so much time analyzing alternatives and generating data.

Oracle 10g came with the Automatic Database Diagnostic Monitor (ADDM), which generates performance diagnostic reports, does problem diagnosis, and helps to identify the cause of performance issues. It stores its data in the Automatic Workload Repository (AWR). Also, there is a new piece of the optimizer called the SQL Tuning Advisor. The SQL tuning Advisor handles statistics analysis, SQL profiling, access path analysis, and analyzes SQL structure.

You can use the SQL Tuning advisor to take any SQL statement and generate tuning suggestions to improve the performance.

ADDM and the SQL Tuning Advisor are covered in detail in Chapter 4.

New SQL Features

And, lastly, in Chapter 5, we'll cover some of the new SQL features - functions like CUBE, ROLLUP and RANK, which are really useful in data warehouse environments. We'll go over some simple tips like dropping a column out of a table, which used to require completely rebuilding the table. We'll also look at tips you can apply to your SQL to make it run faster.

External tables introduce a major new capability for DBAs – that of accessing data which lives outside of Oracle, in flat files, by a SELECT statement. A flat file can be loaded into a table, without using SQL Loader, with just a CREATE TABLE AS SELECT statement, and the data can be manipulated with functions, and such, while the data is on its way in. This eliminates the old two step process of using SQL Loader to load the data, and then writing stored procedures to massage the data – now we can do this all in one step.

Robin Schumacher, performance and tuning expert, illustrates an example of using the new 9i multiple block sizes and their associated data caches.

Exploiting the New 9i Data Caches – Robin Schumacher

In Oracle9i and above, you can create tablespaces with blocksizes that differ from the overall database blocksize. If you choose to do this, then you must also enable one or more of the new *db_nk_cache_size* parameters, so that blocks read in from tablespaces that have a different blocksize than the regular database blocksize have a cache in which to reside.

For example, if you create a tablespace with a 16K blocksize, then you must also set aside RAM for those blocks using the *db_16k_cache_size* parameter. Note that such allocations are in addition to the memory allotments specified by the *db_cache_size* parameter.

This feature allows you to tune your database in ways that were impossible in earlier versions of Oracle. For example, you can use the large (16-32K) blocksize data caches to store data from indexes or tables that are the object of repeated large scans. Does such a thing really help performance? A small but revealing test can answer that question.

For the test, the following query will be used against a 9i database that has a database block size of 8K, but also has the 16K cache enabled along with a 16K tablespace:

```
select
     count(*)
from
     eradmin.admission
where
     patient_id between 1 and 40000;
```

The ERADMIN.ADMISSION table has 150,000 rows in it and has an index built on the PATIENT_ID column. An EXPLAIN of the query reveals that it uses an index range scan to produce the desired end result:

```
Execution Plan
-------------------------------------------------------------
0        SELECT STATEMENT Optimizer=CHOOSE
1            (Cost=41 Card=1 Bytes=4)
   1   0    SORT (AGGREGATE)
   2   1       INDEX (FAST FULL SCAN) OF
'ADMISSION_PATIENT_ID'
             (NON-UNIQUE) (Cost=41 Card=120002 Bytes=480008)
```

Executing the query (twice to eliminate parse activity and to cache any data) with the index residing in a standard 8K tablespace produces these runtime statistics:

```
Statistics
-----------------------------------------------------
        0   recursive calls
        0   db block gets
      421   consistent gets
        0   physical reads
        0   redo size
      371   bytes sent via SQL*Net to client
      430   bytes received via SQL*Net from client
        2   SQL*Net roundtrips to/from client
        0   sorts (memory)
        0   sorts (disk)
        1   rows processed
```

To test the effectiveness of the new 16K cache and 16K tablespace, the index used by the query will be rebuilt into the larger tablespace, while everything else remains the same:

```
alter index
     eradmin.admission_patient_id
     rebuild nologging noreverse tablespace indx_16k;
```

Once the index is nestled firmly into the 16K tablespace, the query is re-executed (again, twice) with the following runtime statistics being produced:

```
Statistics
----------------------------------------------------
          0  recursive calls
          0  db block gets
        211  consistent gets
          0  physical reads
          0  redo size
        371  bytes sent via SQL*Net to client
        430  bytes received via SQL*Net from client
          2  SQL*Net roundtrips to/from client
          0  sorts (memory)
          0  sorts (disk)
          1  rows processed
```

As you can see, the amount of logical reads has been cut in half simply by using the new 16K tablespace and accompanying 16K data cache. Clearly, the benefits of the proper use of the new data caches and multi-block tablespace features of Oracle9i are worth investigating and testing in your own database.

Conclusion

This chapter simply presented an overview of what is to come in subsequent chapters. It just barely scanned the surface of the new key SQL Tuning features of Oracle 10g, as well as many of the tuning options that were available in prior releases of Oracle.

In the next chapter, we'll jump right in – by beginning with an overview of the cost-based optimizer, how it works, and what you can do to influence the access path it selects.

Cost-Based SQL Optimizer

CHAPTER

2

The Cost-Based Optimizer – The Basics

The cost-based optimizer is what makes the decisions regarding the access path inside Oracle. It analyzes all possible access paths (or many of the possible paths, since it needs to make its decision within 1 second). It determines whether to use an index or full table scan, whether to rewrite a query to use a materialized view, or an EXISTS instead of an IN, the sequence of tables for a join, etc. In other words, it is the 'brains' behind this all-important decision making process. The basics of the cost-based optimizer are explained in the following excerpt by Oracle-expert Rick Greenwald:

Cost-Based Optimization: Whys and Hows

One of the founding notions of relational databases is the basic concept that no one needs to define an explicit navigation path to retrieve data. This doesn't mean that no explicit path is used to retrieve data, but rather that the database itself will determine the optimal way to get the data requested by a query.

In most production scenarios, much of the data in an Oracle database can be retrieved by a number of possible paths. The Oracle query optimizer performs the valuable task of determining which potential path should be used to execute a query.

Rule-based Optimization

In its history, the Oracle database has actually had two different optimizers. Oracle's first query optimizer was a rule-based optimizer. As its name implies, the rule-based optimizer used a set of rules to determine the optimal retrieval path. With a limited set of rules, a database developer could count on how the rule-based optimizer would resolve the retrieval path for a particular query.

The bad thing about the rule-based optimizer was that no simple set of rules could effectively resolve all potential query scenarios. In addition, a rule, by its very nature, cannot differentiate between shades of grey in the database. A rule resolves to a binary result — yes or no. But, for instance, the mere presence of an index can mean different things in different situations.

Take the case of a simple join. The join uses two indexes to accomplish the operation. To a rule-based optimizer, each index is equivalent — whether the join is implemented by joining Index A to Index B is irrelevant. But imagine that Index A has 100 entries and Index B has 10,000 entries. It would be much faster to use Index A as the starting point for the join, since this would mean 100 logical reads and then finding the matching row in Index B. If the join were performed with Index B as the starting point, the operation would perform 10,000 logical reads and matches.

In another scenario, an index is being used to select unique rows in a table. It is much faster to use an index to find a specific value. But what if the index only contains a few distinct values? Because retrieval through an index requires twice as many reads — one for the index and one for the associated row — using an index with only a few unique values could take more resources than reading the table directly.

The Cost-Based Optimizer

Both of the scenarios described above point to the same problem — the *cost* of using different retrieval paths can vary wildly. Because of this, Oracle introduced the cost-based optimizer. Once again, as the name implies, the cost-based optimizer takes into account the potential cost of using any particular retrieval path as it determines the optimal path.

The cost-based optimizer takes into account a set of basic statistics that reflect the state of the various tables and indexes within the database. These statistics primarily relate to the size of these database entities and to the cardinality, or uniqueness, of the entries in an index. The greater the percentage of distinct values in an index, the better that index is for selecting specific values. The statistics also reflect the overall depth of the index, which also can affect the cost of using the index for certain operations.

You can also create a histogram for data where values are not evenly distributed. You might have an index with 10,000 entries and 5,000 unique values. With the standard statistics, the cost-based optimizer would assume that there are approximately two entries for each unique value. But the reality could be one value with 5,001 entries and one entry each for the other 4,999 entries. A histogram can help the cost-based optimizer to recognize this situation and react appropriately.

Collecting Statistics

You collect statistics with the ANALYZE SQL command or with one of the procedures in the *dbms_stats* PL/SQL package, which is one of the built-in packages. There are specific procedures to gather statistics on a table, index, schema or the entire database. The *dbms_stats* procedures use the ANALYZE command to collect statistics, but also run these commands in parallel and can perform additional tasks associated with collecting statistics.

When you collect statistics, you can collect statistics on the entire target entity, or on a random sampling of the data in the entity. Collecting statistics on the entire target will be absolutely correct, but could take significantly longer.

You should consider gathering statistics as a part of your regular database maintenance routine. You probably want your statistics to reflect the accurate state of your data, since even the best optimizer is totally dependent on the view of the database offered by the statistics. Keep in mind that whenever the statistics for a particular database object change, any query that references that object will be re-optimized when it is initially executed.

Which Optimizer to Use

Since the Oracle database used the rule-based optimizer for many years, you still have the choice of using either one of the two optimizers.

You can set the optimizer mode as an initialization parameter, which affects the operation of the entire database, or with the ALTER SESSION command for a particular session. For both of these methods, you can set the optimizer mode to RULE to force the use of the rule-based optimizer or CHOOSE, which will use the rule-based optimizer if there are statistics for any table used in the query. The default optimizer mode for Oracle8I is CHOOSE.

So you can use either optimizer, but which one should you use? It makes sense to use the cost-based optimizer, unless you have a compelling reason not to. Oracle has stopped putting support for new features, such as recognizing and using star schemas or materialized views, into the rule-based optimizer. In fact, the Oracle documentation warns that the rule-based approach may not be supported in future versions of the database.

If you are refraining from moving to the cost-based optimizer because you have finely tuned SQL statements based on the rule-based optimizer, you can always use stored outlines, which are described in the final section of this chapter.

Overriding the Decision of the Optimizer

There may be times when the performance of the database leads you to believe that the optimizer has not chosen the proper retrieval path. Before even starting to discuss the topic of overriding the decision of the optimizer, I feel compelled to strongly caution you against ever taking this course of action. There are a few good reasons for accepting the retrieval path suggested by the optimizer:

The optimizer is continually being improved. As mentioned above, new features in the Oracle database are continually being added to the cost-based optimizer, and the cost-based optimizer itself is constantly being refined. Once you override the cost-based optimizer, your query cannot benefit from these changes.

The optimizer reacts to changes in the database environment. If you force your own decision onto a query, Oracle will always follow your direction, regardless of changes in the database. What may have been a better decision today may also turn out to be a poor decision based on the state of the database next month. You could keep revisiting the decisions you force on the database, but this can rapidly become a maintenance headache.

Everyone likes to think that they know how their database works better than any old optimizer. But a comforting thought does not necessarily reflect reality. If you can conclusively determine that the cost-based optimizer is not coming up with the right decision for your particular query, then, and only then, should you proceed to override the decision of the optimizer. Remember, a perceived mistake by the optimizer could be due to a bug in the optimizer, which can be fixed, or it could be due to your less-than absolute understanding of the database.

You should only consider overriding the decision of the optimizer once you have specifically investigated the queries and their paths. But if you have conclusively determined that the optimizer is not making the correct decision for a query, you can add a hint. A hint is essentially a comment within a query that directs the optimizer to use a specific path or technique to optimize a query. Of course, you will also have to test the versions of the query with their hints to guarantee that the new optimization is superior.

You can also use stored outlines to pre-optimize your SQL statements and store the result of the optimization. In effect, a stored outline is saved as a series of hints. When you use stored outlines and the cost-based optimizer encounters an SQL query that matches one of the stored outlines, the optimizer simply retrieves the outline rather than optimize the statement. Stored outlines give you a fixed optimization path, so they will have to be periodically recreated. For an OLTP application, where the same SQL queries are being constantly reused, stored outlines can reduce the overhead of query optimization.

Stored outlines can also be useful when moving to a new version of the database, or when gathering a new set of statistics. Either one of these situations can cause an SQL query to be optimized in a different way. By creating a set of stored outlines, you always have the option of using the "old" optimizations, if the new ones result in reduced performance.

The Oracle8i database gives you a way to check out the affect that a new set of statistics might have on your SQL operations. With some of the procedures in the *dbms_stats* package, you can export statistics to another table in your Oracle database. You can use this table to preserve the previous statistics, while you collect a new set of statistics and determine their effect on your SQL. If it turns out that your applications worked better with the old statistics, you can simply drop the new statistics and import the old ones.

The art and science of query optimization is one of the most complex areas in your Oracle database. This chapter has attempted to give you an overview of your optimization options, so that you can move into your really challenging task — exploring the way that your own Oracle database works with your own set of SQL queries.

Conclusion

Now that the basics have been covered, let's jump in a little deeper – function based indexes, materialized views, stored outlines, bitmap indexes, index organized tables, and such. Pete Cassidy, noted Oracle expert, covers the Internals of the cost-based optimizer as follows:

Internals of the Cost-Based Optimizer – Pete Cassidy

This chapter answers the question, "Why should you use the cost-based optimizer?" The answer is simple. To use the following features, you **must** use the cost-based optimizer:

- Function-based indexes

- Materialized views

- Stored outlines

- Bitmap indexes

- Histograms

- Hash joins

- Hints

- Indexed organized tables

Function-Based Indexes

You can now create function-based indexes in Oracle8i. In previous versions of Oracle, this was impossible. As long as you remember to use the cost-based optimizer (FIRST_ROWS) and activate *query_rewrite_enabled*, the Oracle optimizer may decide to use the function-based index when retrieving rows, as the following example suggests. You can either enter the following ALTER SESSION commands, or you can have the Oracle database administrator make the entries in the *query_rewrite_enabled = true* and *optimizer_mode = first_rows* parameter file.

```
SQL> ALTER SESSION SET
  QUERY_REWRITE_ENABLED = TRUE;
Session altered.

SQL> ALTER SESSION SET OPTIMIZER_MODE = FIRST_ROWS;
Session altered.
```

Now create a function-based index. The following example creates a function-based index on the sum of the two columns SAL and COMM. You would consider creating this index when many queries use SAL+COMM in the WHERE clause.

```
SQL> CREATE INDEX
    INDEX_FB_MANY_EMPS_TOT_SAL
2   ONMANY_EMPS(SAL+COMM)
3   TABLESPACE INDX;
Index created.
```

To view the function-based index you just created, write a query using *user_indexes* similar to the example in Exhibit 1. Notice the INDEX_TYPE column indicates that it is a normal function-based index.

```
SQL> SELECT INDEX_NAME,        INDEX_TYPE,
UNIQUENESS
  2   FROM    USER_INDEXES
  3*  WHERE   TABLE_NAME = UPPER('&TN');
Enter value for tn: MANY_EMPS
INDEX_NAME                       INDEX_TYPE
UNIQUENESS
-------------------------  ---------------------  ---------
INDEX_FB_MANY_EMPS_TOT_SAL FUNCTION-BASED NORMAL   NONUNIQUE
```

Exhibit 1. *Query Using user_indexes*

To view the expression and the columns referenced in a function-based index, you write a query using the data dictionary view *user_ind_expressions*.

```
SQL>  SET    VERIFY          OFF
SQL>  SET    LONG             20
SQL>  COL    INDEX_NAME FORMAT  A26
SQL>  SELECT INDEX_NAME,
  2          COLUMN_EXPRESSION
  3   FROM   USER_IND_EXPRESSIONS
  4*  WHERE  TABLE_NAME = UPPER( '&TN' );

Enter value for tn: MANY_EMPS

INDEX_NAME                  COLUMN_EXPRESSION
------------------          ----------------
INDEX_FB_MANY_EMPS_TOT_SAL   "SAL"+"COMM"
```

To determine if the Oracle optimizer would use the function-based index, use EXPLAIN PLAN on a query referencing SAL+COMM in the WHERE clause.

```
SQL> EXPLAIN PLAN FOR
  2    SELECT * -- 49 Rows Retrieved Out
        Of 28,672
  3    FROM MANY_EMPS-- Oracle May Now Use
        The Function-Based Index
  4    WHERE SAL+COMM = 2751;
Explained.
```

Another nice feature in Oracle8i is that you do not have to write your own SQL scripts to extract data from the table *plan_table*. Instead, Oracle provides you with two new scripts: *utlxpls.sql* and *utlxplp.sql*. Exhibit 2 uses *utlxpls.sql*. Notice Oracle would use the function-based index if you actually executed the SQL statement without using the EXPLAIN PLAN.

```
SQL> @C:\ORACLE8I\RDBMS\ADMIN\UTLXPLS

Plan Table
---------------------------------------------------------------------
|Operation                    | Name       |Rows| Bytes| Cost|Pstart|Pstop|
---------------------------------------------------------------------
|SELECT STATEMENT             |            | 1K| 52K|  40|      |      |
|  TABLE ACCESS BY INDEX ROW  |MANY_EMPS   | 1K| 52K|  40|      |      |
|    INDEX RANGE SCAN         |INDEX_FB_   | 1K|    |   1|      |      |
---------------------------------------------------------------------
```

Exhibit 2. *Extracting Data from the Table plan_table Using utlxpls.sql*

An easier method of invoking EXPLAIN PLAN, involves the use of AUTOTRACE. You must have a table named *plan_table* in your schema before the following will work.

```
SQL>   SET AUTOTRACE TRACEONLY EXPLAIN
SQL>   SELECT * -- 49 Rows retrieved
        Out Of 28,672
  2     FROM MANY_EMPS-- Oracle May Now Use
        The Function-Based Index
  3*    WHERE SAL+COMM = 2751;
```

```
Execution Plan
-------------------------------------------
0   SELECT STATEMENT Optimizer=FIRST_ROWS
       (Cost=40 Card=1639 Bytes=52448)
1 0 TABLE ACCESS (BY INDEX ROWID) OF
       'MANY_EMPS' (Cost=40 Card=1639
       Bytes=52448)
2 1 INDEX (RANGE SCAN) OF 'INDEX_FB_
       MANY_EMPS_TOT_SAL' (NON-UNIQUE)
       (Cost=1 Card=1639)
```

You can also create function-based indexes on columns that are indexed with a btree or bitmap index. The following code creates a function-based index on the SEX column, which already has a bitmap index.

```
SQL>  CREATE INDEX FBI_STATS_SEX
  2          ON STATS(LOWER(SEX));
Index created.
```

The data dictionary shows all four of the indexes currently on the *stats* table.

```
SQL> SELECT INDEX_NAME,
  2          INDEX_TYPE
  3   FROM   USER_INDEXES
  4*  WHERE  TABLE_NAME = 'STATS';

INDEX_NAME          INDEX_TYPE
----------------    --------------------
BMI_STATS_SEX       BITMAP
FBI_STATS_SEX       FUNCTION-BASED NORMAL
I_STATS_REGION      NORMAL
I_STATS_SNAME       NORMAL
```

Materialized Views

For very large tables in a data warehousing application, materialized views (MVs) are used to drastically improve performance. The MVs are really tables that are refreshed on a regular basis. The following example is an MV on an 880,000-row

---

table. A better example would be an MV with 300 million rows, but disk space is tight for this chapter.

The following DESCRIBE command shows there are just two columns in the *stats* table.

```
SQL>  DESC  STATS

Name        Null?  Type
-------  --------  -------
STAT_NO            NUMBER
RESULT             CHAR(1)
```

There are 880,000 rows in the STATS table, and the average for the STAT_NO column is 440,001. The STAT_NO column contains values from 1 to 880,000. Notice it requires nearly 5 seconds to return this average.

```
SQL>  SELECT AVG(STAT_NO) -- 880,000 Rows
  2    FROM   STATS;

AVG(STAT_NO)
============
     440001

real: 4953(Requires 4.953 Seconds)
```

To avoid possible Oracle errors, from SYS grant the system privilege query rewrite to SYSTEM.

```
SQL> GRANT QUERY REWRITE TO SYSTEM;
Grant succeeded.
SQL> CONNECT SYSTEM/MANAGER
```

The query rewrite feature can only be used by the cost-based optimizer. Set your session to either *all_rows* or *first_rows* to use the cost-based optimizer.

```
SQL> ALTER SESSION SET OPTIMIZER_GOAL =
       ALL_ROWS;
Session altered.
```

Just to be safe, before creating the MV, enable the query rewrite feature for your session.

```
SQL> ALTER SESSION SET QUERY_REWRITE_ENABLED = TRUE;
Session altered.
```

So that you can see how long the following commands require executing, set timing ON for your session:

```
SQL> SET TIMING ON
```

Now you are ready to create the MV named *mv_stats* on your 880,000-row table *stats*.

```
SQL> CREATE   MATERIALIZED VIEW mv_stats
  2            BUILD        IMMEDIATE
  3            REFRESH      COMPLETE
-Truncates And Inserts. Also FAST, FORCE, or NEVER
  4            ENABLE       QUERY REWRITE
  5    AS
  6    SELECT  avg(stat_no) avg_statno,
  7            min(stat_no) min_statno,
  8            max( stat_no) max_statno
  9*   FROM    stats;
Materialized view created.
real: 9688 (Requires 9.688 Seconds)
```

The materialized view, *mv_stats*, might be used when writing the query shown in Exhibit 3. Use EXPLAIN PLAN to determine if the Oracle optimizer would rewrite your query and use your materialized view *mv_stats*. The "Name" column in the table *plan_table* indicates that Oracle would rewrite the statement using your MV instead of performing a full table scan of the 880,000-row *stats* table.

```
SQL> EXPLAIN PLAN FOR
  2 SELECT avg(stat_no) avg_statno,
  3   min(stat_no) min_statno,
  4   max(stat_no) max_statno
  5*FROM stats;
```

```
Explained.
SQL> @F:\V8I\RDBMS\ADMIN\UTLXPLS

Plan Table
=================================================================
|Operation          | Name    | Rows| Bytes|
Cost|Pstart|Pstop|
-----------------------------------------------------------------
|SELECT STATEMENT   |         |  21|  819|   1|        |
|
| TABLE ACCESS FULL |MV_STATS |  21|  819|   1|        |
|
-----------------------------------------------------------------
```

Exhibit 3. *Query Using mv_stats*

The following query uses your MV and returns the information
you need from an 880,000-row table in less than 0.4 seconds.
Well, actually, your query is rewritten to use the MV containing
one row.

```
SQL> SELECT avg(stat_no) avg_statno,
  2          min(stat_no) min_statno,
  3          max(stat_no) max_statno
  4*  FROM    stats;

AVG_STATNO  MIN_STATNO  MAX_STATNO
==========  ==========  ==========
    440001           1      880000
real: 391 (Only Requires .391 Of A Second Using Your MV!)
```

Now try executing the same query not using your MV by setting
the optimizer goal to RULE. Wow! It requires Oracle a
whopping 6.657 seconds to return the information you need
when not using your materialized view. Using your MV only
requires less than 0.4 seconds! What a great enhancement, Oracle
Corporation!

```
SQL> SELECT avg(stat_no) avg_statno,
  2          min(stat_no) min_statno,
  3          max(stat_no) max_statno
  4*  FROM    stats;
```

```
AVG_STATNO   MIN_STATNO   MAX_STATNO
==========   ==========   ==========
    440001            1       880000
real: 6657
```

Stored Outlines

Another 8i feature requiring the cost-based optimizer is stored
outlines. To force Oracle to execute SQL statements the same
way no matter what occurs at the operating system level, database
level, etc., create a stored outline and invoke its category. The
system privilege, QUERY REWRITE, must be granted to the
schema that plans to use stored outlines and materialized views.
The following command is entered from the SYS schema.

```
SQL> GRANT QUERY REWRITE TO SYSTEM;
Grant succeeded.
SQL> CONNECT SYSTEM/MANAGER
```

The following command creates a stored outline named
EMPLOYEES with a category of SALARY.

```
SQL> CREATE OR REPLACE OUTLINE EMPLOYEES
  2    FOR CATEGORY SALARY ON
  3    SELECT  ENAME, SAL, LOC
  4    FROM    EMP, DEPT
  5    WHERE   EMP.DEPTNO = DEPT.DEPTNO;
Outline created.
```

Several data dictionary views get updated when you create stored
outlines. The view *user_outline_hints* is actually looking at
outln.ol$_hints. The following query shows that Oracle stores ten
hints for the SQL statement joining the EMP and DEPT tables
in category SALARY.

```
SQL> SELECT  HINT
  2    FROM    USER_OUTLINE_HINTS
  3    WHERE   NAME = 'EMPLOYEES'
  4*   ORDER   BY HINT;
```

```
HINT
------------------------------
FULL(DEPT)
FULL(EMP)
NOREWRITE
NOREWRITE
NO_EXPAND
NO_FACT(DEPT)
NO_FACT(EMP)
ORDERED
PQ_DISTRIBUTE(EMP NONE NONE)
USE_HASH(EMP)
10 rows selected.
```

Another data dictionary view, *user_outlines*, is actually looking at *outln.ol$*. This view is updated when you create a stored outline. Notice that the outline has not been used.

```
SQL> SELECT NAME,
  2         CATEGORY,
  3         USED
  4* FROM   USER_OUTLINES;

NAME          CATEGORY      USED
-----------   ------------  ---------
EMPLOYEES     SALARY        UNUSED
```

One method of insuring that Oracle uses the cost-based optimizer is to analyze one or more tables used in a query. The following two statements analyze the EMP and DEPT tables.

```
SQL> ANALYZE TABLE EMP COMPUTE STATISTICS;
Table analyzed.

SQL> ANALYZE TABLE DEPT COMPUTE STATISTICS;
Table analyzed.
```

If *query_rewrite_enabled* is not set to true, Oracle will not use a stored outline or materialized view.

```
SQL> ALTER SESSION SET QUERY_REWRITE_ENABLED = TRUE;
Session altered.
```

To cause the cost-based optimizer to rewrite your query and use the stored outline for CATEGORY SALARY, enter the following command.

```
SQL> ALTER SESSION SET
     USE_STORED_OUT LINES = SALARY;
Session altered.
```

Now, the moment of truth we have all been waiting for. Write the query stored in the outline EMPLOYEES category SALARY, and query the data dictionary to see if Oracle used your outline to execute the query. Because the used column shows "USED," Oracle did use your stored outline.

```
SQL> SELECT ENAME, SAL, LOC
 2    FROM    EMP,    DEPT
 3*   WHERE   EMP.DEPTNO = DEPT.DEPTNO;
...... Output Omitted Here ...
SQL> SELECT NAME,
 2    CATEGORY,
 3    USED
 4*   FROM USER_OUTLINES;
```

NAME	CATEGORY	USED
EMPLOYEES	SALARY	USED

To see the EXPLAIN PLAN output for this query, use AUTOTRACE. Notice that Oracle uses a HASH JOIN and a full table scan on each of the two tables, which are hints in *user_outline_hints*.

```
SQL> SET AUTOTRACE TRACEONLY EXPLAIN
SQL> SELECT ENAME, SAL, LOC
 2    FROM    EMP,    DEPT
 3*   WHERE   EMP.DEPTNO = DEPT.DEPTNO;
Execution Plan
----------------------------------------
0   SELECT STATEMENT Optimizer=CHOOSE
        (Cost=3 Card=14 Bytes=266)
1 0 HASH JOIN (Cost=3 Card=14 Bytes=266)
2 1   TABLE ACCESS (FULL) OF 'DEPT'
        (Cost=1 Card=4 Bytes=36)
```

```
3 1 TABLE ACCESS (FULL) OF 'EMP'
      (Cost=1 Card=14 Bytes=140)
```

Bitmap Indexes

Another Oracle 8i feature requiring the cost-based optimizer is bitmap indexes. This is primarily a data-warehousing feature for very large tables. If a column contains only a few values, the table contains millions of rows, and the column is referenced frequently in WHERE clauses, then consider creating a bitmap index. The following command indicates that the SEX column contains only two distinct values: F for female and M for male. The table has one million rows. The SELECTIVITY of the SEX column is very, very low and is an ideal candidate for a bitmap index. The selectivity of the SEX column is 2/1,000,000 or 0.000002. You would never create a btree index on the SEX column. Btree indexes are best suited for columns with high selectivity. Primary key columns, for example, have a selectivity of one, and that is as good as it gets.

```
SQL> COL SEX FORMAT A3
SQL> SELECT  SEX,
  2          COUNT(*)
  3   FROM    STATS
  4*  GROUP   BY SEX;

SEX    COUNT(*)
---  ----------
  F      500000
  M      500000
```

Create a non-unique btree index on the SNAME column of the STATS table.

```
SQL> CREATE INDEX I_STATS_SNAME
  2*         ON STATS(SNAME);
Index created.
```

The following query always results in a full table scan because the SEX column has no indexes.

```
SQL> SET AUTOTRACE TRACEONLY EXPLAIN
SQL> SELECT *
  2    FROM    STATS
  3    WHERE   SNAME = 'NAME IS 222' OR SEX = 'F';

Execution Plan
-------------------------------------------
0 SELECT STATEMENT Optimizer=CHOOSE
    (Cost=520 Card=500001 Bytes=9500019)
1 0 TABLE ACCESS (FULL) OF 'STATS'
    (Cost=520 Card=500001 Bytes=9500019)
```

Now create a bitmap index on the SEX column of the STATS table. Activate TIMING to observe the actual amount of elapsed time to create the bitmap index; 12 seconds is very, very fast.

```
SQL> SET TIMING ON
SQL> CREATE BITMAP INDEX BMI_STATS_SEX
  2          ON STATS(SEX);
Index created.
Elapsed: 00:00:12.08
```

A query against the data dictionary view *user_indexes* displays information about the btree and bitmap indexes on the STATS table.

```
SQL> SELECTINDEX_NAME,
  2    INDEX_TYPE,
  3    UNIQUENESS
  4    FROM USER_INDEXES
  5*   WHERE TABLE_NAME = 'STATS';

INDEX_NAME      INDEX_TYPE   UNIQUENES
------------    -----------  ---------
BMI_STATS_SEX   BITMAP       NONUNIQUE
I_STATS_SNAME   NORMAL       NONUNIQUE
```

Analyze the *stats* table so queries using *stats* will use the cost-based optimizer. You can also use the ALTER SESSION command or a HINT to force Oracle to use the cost-based optimizer. Note the elapsed time of more than eight minutes to analyze the one million row table with two indexes.

```
SQL> ANALYZE TABLE STATS COMPUTE STATISTICS;
Table analyzed.
Elapsed: 00:08:517.04
```

Using AUTOTRACE with the EXPLAIN option, notice that Oracle prefers a full table scan to using both indexes with an estimated cost of 520.

```
SQL> SET AUTOTRACE TRACEONLY EXPLAIN
SQL> SELECT *
 2    FROM    STATS
 3*   WHERE   SNAME = 'NAME IS 222' OR SEX = 'F';

Execution Plan
-----------------------------------------
0 SELECT STATEMENT Optimizer=CHOOSE
     (Cost=520 Card=500001 Bytes=9500019)
1 0 TABLE ACCESS (FULL) OF 'STATS'
     (Cost=520 Card=500001 Bytes=9500019)
```

Using the ALTER SESSION command, tell Oracle to use the cost-based optimizer and select the access path that returns the first row as quickly as possible.

```
SQL> ALTER SESSION SET OPTIMIZER_MODE =
FIRST_ROWS;
Session altered.
```

Executing the command again using the EXPLAIN option of AUTOTRACE indicates that Oracle uses both indexes. The index on the SNAME column is converted to bitmaps, and a BITMAP OR is used for both indexes. The result is converted back to rowids, and the rowids are used to retrieve the rows. The estimated cost to perform this query is 2166.

```
SQL> SELECT *
 2    FROM STATS
 3*   WHERE SNAME = 'NAME IS 222' OR SEX = 'F';
```

```
Execution Plan
------------------------------------------
0    SELECT STATEMENT Optimizer=FIRST_ROWS
        (Cost=2166 Card=500001 Bytes=9500019)
1 0    TABLE ACCESS (BY INDEX ROWID) OF 'STATS'
        (Cost=2166 Card=500001 Bytes=9500019)
2 1      BITMAP CONVERSION (TO ROWIDS)
3 2        BITMAP OR
4 3          BITMAP CONVERSION (FROM ROWIDS)
5 4            INDEX (RANGE SCAN) OF 'I_STATS_SNAME'
(NONUNIQUE)
                (Cost=4)
6 3          BITMAP INDEX (SINGLE VALUE) OF 'BMI_STATS_SEX'
```

Change the optimizer mode for your session back to CHOOSE, which is the default. Execute the query again, using the *index_combine* hint to force the use of the bitmap index on the SEX column. Notice the same results as using the optimizer mode of *first_rows*.

```
SQL> ALTER SESSION SET OPTIMIZER_MODE = CHOOSE;
Session altered.

SQL> SELECT /*+INDEX_COMBINE(STATS) */ *
  2    FROM STATS
  3*   WHERE SNAME = 'NAME IS 222' OR SEX = 'F';

Execution Plan
------------------------------------------
0    SELECT STATEMENT Optimizer=CHOOSE
        (Cost=2166 Card=500001 Bytes=9500019)
1 0 TABLE ACCESS (BY INDEX ROWID) OF 'STATS'
        (Cost=2166 Card=500001 Bytes=9500019)
2 1    BITMAP CONVERSION (TO ROWIDS)
3 2      BITMAP OR
4 3        BITMAP CONVERSION (FROM ROWIDS)
5 4          INDEX (RANGE SCAN) OF 'I_STATS_SNAME'
              (NONUNIQUE)
              (Cost=4)
6 3        BITMAP INDEX (SINGLE VALUE) OF 'BMI_STATS_SEX'
```

Histograms

Another feature requiring the cost-based optimizer is histograms. Histograms are created for indexed columns that are badly skewed, such as the REGION column in the STATS table. The purpose of a histogram is to help the cost-based optimizer make a better decision about whether or not to use an index and to reduce the number of full table scans. The following query shows that one row contains a region code of NW, while the other seven region codes contain either 125,000 or 249,999 entries.

```
SQL> COL    REGION   FORMAT A6
SQL> SELECT REGION, COUNT(*)
  2  FROM    STATS
  3* GROUP   BY REGION;

REGION    COUNT(*)
------  ----------
     E      125000
     N      125000
    NE      125000
    NW           1
     S      125000
    SE      125000
    SW      125000
     W      249999

8 rows selected.
```

Without a histogram on the REGION column, Oracle will not use an index on the REGION column. The following code creates a btree index on the REGION column of the STATS table.

```
SQL> CREATE INDEX I_STATS_REGION ON STATS(REGION);
Index created.
```

Next, analyze the STATS table because you just added a new index.

```
SQL> ANALYZE TABLE STATS COMPUTE STATISTICS;
Table analyzed.
```

Use AUTOTRACE to see the plan.

```
SQL> SET AUTOTRACE TRACEONLY EXPLAIN
```

Notice that without a histogram, the cost-based optimizer would perform a full table scan on a one million-row table to return one row.

```
SQL> SELECT *
  2    FROM    STATS
  3    WHERE   REGION = 'NW';

Execution Plan
-------------------------------------------
0   SELECT STATEMENT Optimizer=CHOOSE
       (Cost=583 Card=125000 Bytes=2625000)
1 0   TABLE ACCESS (FULL) OF 'STATS'
         (Cost=583 Card=125000 Bytes=2625000)
```

Why does Oracle do this? The following two queries reveal why. In *user_indexes*, the DISTINCT_KEYS column shows that Oracle knows there are eight different values. In *user_tables*, the NUM_ROWS column indicates that Oracle knows the number of rows in the *stats* table. You can almost see the light go on in the optimizer. Ah Hah! Because there are one million rows with eight different values, I'll just divide 8 into 1,000,000. The optimizer's incorrect conclusion is that each of the eight values comprise 125,000 rows of the *stats* table. Obviously, the optimizer will not use an index to retrieve 1/8th of the rows from a one million-row table, and will perform a full table scan instead.

```
SQL> SELECT DISTINCT_KEYS
  2    FROM    USER_INDEXES
  3    WHERE   INDEX_NAME = 'I_STATS_REGION';

DISTINCT_KEYS
-------------
            8
SQL> SELECT NUM_ROWS
  2    FROM    USER_TABLES
  3    WHERE   TABLE_NAME = 'STATS';

  NUM_ROWS
----------
   1000000
```

The REGION column is in bad need of a histogram. It is better to ask for too many buckets than to ask for too few. Although you request 250 buckets, Oracle creates 7 buckets (see Exhibit 4).

```
SQL> ANALYZE TABLE STATS -- Default 75 Buckets
  2          COMPUTE STATISTICS -- Maximum Of 254 Buckets
  3          FOR TABLE -- Oracle Uses Only Required Buckets
  4*         FOR COLUMNS REGION SIZE 250;
Table analyzed.

SQL> SELECT NUM_DISTINCT,
  2          LOW_VALUE,
  3          HIGH_VALUE,
  4          DENSITY,
  5          NUM_BUCKETS
  6    FROM   USER_TAB_COL_STATISTICS
  7*   WHERE  TABLE_NAME = 'STATS' AND COLUMN_NAME = 'REGION';

NUM_DISTINCT LOW_VALUE HIGH_VALUE DENSITY    NUM_BUCKETS
------------ --------- ---------- ---------- -----------
           8        45         57 .0000005             7
```

Exhibit 4. *Histogram for REGION Column*

Oracle now has a better feel for how the data is distributed in the REGION column by the values in the ENDPOINT_NUMBER column (see Exhibit 5).

```
SQL> SELECT COLUMN_NAME,
  2          ENDPOINT_NUMBER,
  3          ENDPOINT_VALUE
  4    FROM   USER_HISTOGRAMS
  5    WHERE  TABLE_NAME = 'STATS' AND COLUMN_NAME = 'REGION'
  6*   ORDER  ENDPOINT_NUMBER;
```

```
COLUMN_NAME    ENDPOINT_NUMBER  ENDPOINT_VALUE
-------------  ---------------  --------------
REGION                  125000       3.5827E+35
REGION                  250000       4.0500E+35
REGION                  375000       4.0640E+35
REGION                  375001       4.0676E+35
REGION                  500001       4.3096E+35
REGION                  625001       4.3236E+35
REGION                  750001       4.3273E+35
REGION                 1000000       4.5173E+35
8 rows selected.
```

Exhibit 5. *Data Distribution in the REGION Column*

With this new histogram information, the query executed above
should now cause Oracle to use the index on the REGION
column instead of a full table scan, and it does. Notice the cost is
only 4 compared to a cost of 583. In addition, this query requires
0.1 seconds to execute using the index, whereas a full table scan
requires nearly 10 seconds.

```
SQL> SET AUTOTRACE TRACEONLY EXPLAIN
SQL> SELECT *
  2    FROM    STATS
  3    WHERE   REGION = 'NW';

Execution Plan
-------------------------------------------
0 SELECT STATEMENT Optimizer=CHOOSE
    (Cost=4 Card=1 Bytes=21)
1 0 TABLE ACCESS (BY INDEX ROWID) OF 'STATS'
    (Cost=4 Card=1 Bytes=21)
2 1 INDEX (RANGE SCAN) OF 'I_STATS_REGION' (NON-UNIQUE)
    (Cost=3 Card=1)
```

Hash Joins

Another feature requiring the cost-based optimizer is hash joins.
Generally, hash joins outperform merge joins and nested loop
joins. Because both tables are analyzed and *hash_join_enabled* is set
to true, Oracle would perform a hash join on the following query
joining the two tables EMP and DEPT. Using the ALTER

SESSION command, you can also enable *hash_join_enabled*, as well as using the *use_hash* hint to force a hash join.

```
SQL> SELECT TABLE_NAME,
  2    NUM_ROWS
-- Both Tables Are Analyzed Since NUM_ROWS Is Not Null
  3    FROM   USER_TABLES
  4*   WHERE  TABLE_NAME IN('EMP','DEPT');

TABLE_NAME NUM_ROWS
---------- --------
      DEPT        4
      EMP        14

SQL> SELECT VALUE
-- Hash Joins Are Encouraged At The Instance Level
  2    FROM   V$PARAMETER
  3    WHERE  NAME = 'hash_join_enabled';

VALUE
-----
 TRUE

SQL> SET AUTOTRACE TRACEONLY EXPLAIN
SQL> SELECT ENAME, LOC
  2    FROM   EMP, DEPT
  3    WHERE  EMP.DEPTNO = DEPT.DEPTNO;
Execution Plan
------------------------------------------
0 SELECT STATEMENT Optimizer=CHOOSE
    (Cost=3 Card=14 Bytes=224)
1 0 HASH JOIN (Cost=3 Card=14 Bytes=224)
2 1 TABLE ACCESS (FULL) OF 'DEPT'
    (Cost=1 Card=4 Bytes=36)
3 1 TABLE ACCESS (FULL) OF 'EMP'
    (Cost=1 Card=14 Bytes=98)
```

By changing the *optimizer_mode* to RULE for your session, or using the RULE hint, or having your Oracle DBA change the parameter *optimizer_mode* = RULE, hash joins are not executed, as the following example illustrates.

```
SQL> ALTER SESSION SET OPTIMIZER_MODE = RULE;
Session altered.
```

```
SQL> SET AUTOTRACE TRACEONLY EXPLAIN
SQL> SELECT ENAME, LOC
  2    FROM EMP, DEPT
  3*  WHERE EMP.DEPTNO = DEPT.DEPTNO;

Execution Plan
----------------------------------------------
0    SELECT STATEMENT Optimizer=RULE
1 0    MERGE JOIN
2 1      SORT (JOIN)
3 2        TABLE ACCESS (FULL) OF 'DEPT'
4 1      SORT (JOIN)
5 4        TABLE ACCESS (FULL) OF 'EMP'
```

Hints

Another feature requiring the cost-based optimizer is hints. There are many hints. A hint overrides any session setting and instance setting in the parameter file. All hints but one, RULE, utilize the cost-based optimizer. Hints are treated as special comments. If you make a syntax error in a hint, Oracle does not return an error message. Instead, your hint is ignored. The hint must be the first part of a SELECT, UPDATE, or DELETE statement. You can combine more than one hint per SQL statement as long as they do not conflict. The following example uses the ORDERED hint. The ORDERED hint tells the cost-based optimizer the join chain. The join chain consists of the tables in the FROM clause from the left to right as you read the FROM clause. The table to the far left in the FROM clause is the first table in the join chain. The first table in the join chain is called the DRIVING table or the OUTER table. The following example uses the ORDERED hint. By reading the output of AUTOTRACE top down, the FIRST table you see is the EMP table. The first table down from the top is the DRIVING table.

```
SQL> SET AUTOTRACE TRACEONLY EXPLAIN
SQL> SELECT /*+ORDERED */ ENAME, LOC
  2    FROM EMP, DEPT  -- EMP DRIVES
  3    WHERE EMP.DEPTNO = DEPT.DEPTNO;
```

```
Execution Plan
----------------------------------------
0   SELECT STATEMENT Optimizer=CHOOSE
        (Cost=3 Card=14 Bytes=224)
1 0   HASH JOIN
        (Cost=3 Card=14 Bytes=224)
2 1     TABLE ACCESS (FULL) OF 'EMP'
        (Cost=1 Card=14 Bytes=98)
3 1     TABLE ACCESS (FULL) OF 'DEPT'
        (Cost=1 Card=4 Bytes=36)
```

You can write your hints using one of two formats. The example above uses the C language construct of a comment;" /* comment */". You can also use double dashes "– –." However, using double dashes does not permit you to place any column names on the same line as your hint, as the following code indicates. Notice that the driving table is DEPT because it is to the far left in the FROM clause.

```
SQL> SELECT  --+ORDERED
  2            ENAME, LOC
  3   FROM     DEPT, EMP -- DEPT Drives
  4*  WHERE    EMP.DEPTNO = DEPT.DEPTNO;

Execution Plan
----------------------------------------
0   SELECT STATEMENT Optimizer=CHOOSE
        (Cost=3 Card=14 Bytes=224)
1 0   HASH JOIN
        (Cost=3 Card=14 Bytes=224)
2 1     TABLE ACCESS (FULL) OF 'DEPT'
        (Cost=1 Card=4 Bytes=36)
3 1     TABLE ACCESS (FULL) OF 'EMP'
        (Cost=1 Card=14 Bytes=98)
```

There are hints to invoke each optimizer: use indexes, use full table scans, invoke a join method for joining tables, the join chain, working with views, working with subqueries, parallel queries, and star queries. Oracle continues to add new hints with each release of Oracle. There are some undocumented hints as well. You can view hints that Oracle writes to itself, recursive calls, in the dynamic performance view *v$sqlarea* or *v$sql*.

```
SQL> SELECT    SUBSTR(SQL_TEXT,1,40) CODE
  2  FROM      V$SQLAREA
  3  WHERE     SQL_TEXT LIKE '%--+%' OR
  4            SQL_TEXT LIKE '%/*+%'
  5* ORDER BY SQL_TEXT;

CODE
----------------------------------------
SELECT --+ORDERED      ENAME,  LOC  FROM
SELECT /*+ORDERED */   ENAME,  LOC  FROM
SELECT SUBSTR(SQL_TEXT,1,40) CODE FROM
select /*+ index(idl_char$ i_idl_char1)
select /*+ index(idl_sb4$ i_idl_sb41) +*
select /*+ index(idl_sb4$ i_idl_sb41) +*
select /*+ index(idl_ub1$ i_idl_ub11) +*
select /*+ index(idl_ub2$ i_idl_ub21) +*
select /*+ rule */ bucket_cnt, row_cnt,
```

This list is not exhaustive, but it does include most of the hints available.

```
ALL_ROWS
AND_EQUAL(STATS I1 I2 I3 I4 I5)
APPEND
CACHE(STATS)
CHOOSE
CLUSTER(STATS)
DRIVING_SITE(STATS)
FIRST_ROWS
FULL(STATS)
HASH(STATS)
HASH_AJ(STATS)
HASH_SJ(STATS)
INDEX(STATS I_STATS_REGION)
INDEX_ASC(STATS I_STATS_REGION)
INDEX_COMBINE(STATS IBM_STATS_SEX)
INDEX_COMBINE(STATS)
INDEX_DESC(STATS I_STATS_REGION)
INDEX_FFS(STATS I_STATS_REGION)
INDEX_JOIN
LEADING(STATS)
MERGE(VIEW_NAME)
MERGE_AJ
MERGE_SJ
NOAPPEND
NOCACHE(STATS)
NOPARALLEL
NOPARALLEL_INDEX(STATS,I_STATS_REGION)
NOREWRITE
NO_EXPAND
NO_FACT(STATS)
NO_INDEX(STATS I_STATS_REGION)
NO_MERGE(VIEW_NAME)
```

```
NO_PUSH_JOIN_PRED(STATS)
ORDERED
ORDERED_PREDICATES
PARALLEL(STATS,4)
PARALLEL_INDEX(STATS,I_STATS_REGION,4,2)
PQ_DISTRIBUTE(INNER_TABLE,OUT_DIST,
   INNER_ DIST)
PUSH_JOIN_PRED(STATS)
PUSH_SUBQ
REWRITE
ROWID(STATS)
RULE
STAR
STAR_TRANSFORMATION
USE_CONCAT
USE_HASH(INNER_TABLE)
USE_MERGE(INNER_TABLE)
USE_MERGE(INNER_TABLE) ORDERED
FULL(STATS)
USE_NL(INNER_TABLE) ORDERED
USE_NL(STATS STATS_HIST)
USE_NL(STATS)
```

If you use a table alias in the SQL statement, you must use the same alias in your hint. Otherwise, Oracle ignores your hint. The table alias is **not** case sensitive. The following hint is ignored by Oracle because a table alias of "s" is used, but not referenced in the hint.

```
SQL> SELECT --+FULL(STATS)
  2    *
  3    FROM  STATS s
  4*   WHERE REGION = 'NW';

Execution Plan
----------------------------------------
0    SELECT STATEMENT Optimizer=CHOOSE
        (Cost=4 Card=1 Bytes=21)
1 0    TABLE ACCESS (BY INDEX ROWID) OF
        'STATS' (Cost=4 Card=1 Bytes=21)
2 1      INDEX (RANGE SCAN) OF
          'I_STATS_REGION' (NONUNIQUE)
          (Cost=3 Card=1)
```

The next example uses a table alias of uppercase "S" to verify that the table alias is not case sensitive. The EXPLAIN PLAN output from AUTOTRACE indicates that the table alias is not case sensitive.

```
SQL> SELECT /*+FULL(S) */ *
  2  FROM    STATS s
  3  WHERE   REGION = 'NW';

Execution Plan
----------------------------------------
0 SELECT STATEMENT Optimizer=CHOOSE
      (Cost=583 Card=1 Bytes=21)
1 0 TABLE ACCESS (FULL) OF 'STATS'
      (Cost=583 Card=1 Bytes=21)
```

Indexed Organized Tables

Another feature requiring the cost-based optimizer is indexed organized tables (IOTs). If a table is accessed using all primary key columns and the key columns are short, you might consider creating an indexed organized table. You can also specify an overflow tablespace for rows that are long. The rows are stored in a structure resembling a btree index. However, there are not two structures; there is not a data structure and a separate index structure. Instead, there is only one structure. The following code creates an IOT named *stats_iot*.

```
SQL> CREATE TABLE STATS_IOT
  2       ( SNO PRIMARY KEY,
  3           SNAME,
  4           SEX,
  5           REGION )
  6           ORGANIZATION INDEX
  7*AS SELECT * FROM STATS;
Table created.
```

The data dictionary view *user_tables* shows an *iot_type* of IOT.

```
SQL> SELECT TABLE_NAME,
  2         IOT_NAME,
  3         IOT_TYPE
  4  FROM    USER_TABLES
  5* WHERE   TABLE_NAME = 'STATS_IOT';
TABLE_NAME          IOT_NAME IOT_TYPE
----------  ------------------ --------
  STATS_IOT                      IOT
```

The CREATE TABLE statement above causes Oracle to create a primary key on the SNO column of the IOT. The following query shows the information stored in *user_indexes*. Notice that the index SYS_IOT_TOP_24877 is created because of the PRIMARY KEY code in the CREATE TABLE statement.

```
SQL> SELECT INDEX_NAME,
  2         INDEX_TYPE
  3  FROM    USER_INDEXES
  4* WHERE   TABLE_NAME = 'STATS_IOT';

INDEX_NAME          INDEX_TYPE
----------------  ----------
SYS_IOT_TOP_24877  IOT - TOP
```

Oracle places the object number of the IOT in the name of the primary key index. All IOTs must have primary keys. The object number of the IOT STATS_IOT is 24877.

```
SQL> SELECT OBJECT_TYPE,
  2         OBJECT_NAME,
  3         STATUS
  4  FROM    USER_OBJECTS
  5* WHERE   OBJECT_ID = 24877;

OBJECT_TYPE OBJECT_NAME STATUS
----------- ----------- ------
      TABLE   STATS_IOT  VALID
```

The following query uses the cost-based optimizer and the primary key index to retrieve one row although the IOT has not been analyzed.

```
SQL> SET AUTOTRACE TRACEONLY EXPLAIN
SQL> SELECT *
  2    FROM    STATS_IOT
  3    WHERE   SNO = 222;
Execution Plan
----------------------------------------
0    SELECT STATEMENT Optimizer=CHOOSE
        (Cost=1 Card=1 Bytes=33)
1 0    INDEX (UNIQUE SCAN) OF
          'SYS_IOT_TOP_24877' (UNIQUE)
          (Cost=1 Card=1 Bytes=33)
```

After the IOT is analyzed, the EXPLAIN PLAN output in AUTOTRACE shows a cost of 2 instead of 1. Regardless, Oracle uses the cost-based optimizer to retrieve rows from an IOT.

```
SQL> ANALYZE TABLE STATS_IOT COMPUTE
        STATISTICS;
Table analyzed.

SQL> SELECT *
  2    FROM    STATS_IOT
  3*   WHERE   SNO = 222;

Execution Plan
----------------------------------------
0    SELECT STATEMENT Optimizer=RULE
        (Cost=2 Card=1 Bytes=21)
1 0    INDEX (UNIQUE SCAN) OF
          'SYS_IOT_TOP_24877' (UNIQUE)
          (Cost=2 Card=1 Bytes=21)
```

Conclusion

Oracle8i contains many sought-after enhancements. Many of the new features require the use of the cost-based optimizer. This chapter illustrates those enhancements requiring the cost-based optimizer.

Histograms

Histograms are an important way of influencing the optimizer when data is skewed. Sometimes, with skewed data, the optimizer doesn't make the best decision. But, using histograms can give the optimizer the data it needs to make the correct decision. While some basics of histograms were explained above, the big picture is covered by Joe Johnson:

The Importance of Histograms with the Cost Based Optimizer

Histogram. The mere mention of the word probably conjures up memories of the statistics class you took in your sophomore year of college. But, no matter what your final grade was in Statistics 101, you can still make use of histograms in your role as an Oracle DBA.

Statistics and the Cost-Based Optimizer

The Cost-based Optimizer's (CBO) job is to select the least costly execution plan from among the many possible execution plans available. When making this selection the CBO considers several factors, including the availability of indexes, the number of rows in each table, and the join order of the tables used in the query.

One critical factor in effective CBO functioning is the presence of accurate table and index statistics for the segments being queried. In fact, DBAs whose databases make use of the CBO will often gather these statistics on a weekly, nightly, or even hourly basis in order to give the CBO the most accurate statistics possible. Statistics are important to the CBO because the optimizer uses these statistics to determine the query's selectivity. *Selectivity* refers to the relationship between the number of rows returned by a query versus the total number of rows in the tables being queried. If the query will only return a small portion of the total number of rows in the table, then the query is said to be selective. When the CBO considers a query to be selective, it will usually elect to use indexes (if indexes are available) when retrieving the query's result set. This generally happens whenever the query is expected to return only two to three percent of the total rows in the table.

Table and index statistics are gathered using the ANALYZE TABLE or ANALYZE INDEX command with the COMPUTE or ESTIMATE option. Once gathered, these statistics are stored in the data dictionary and can be seen in the data dictionary views *dba_tables*, *dba_tab_columns* and *dba_indexes*.

Cost-Based Optimizer Assumptions

When making this selectivity determination, the CBO assumes that the data within an indexed column is uniformly distributed among the range of values in that column. In other words, if there are 1,000 records in a table, and the indexed column in our query's WHERE clause is made up of 100 distinct values, the CBO will assume that each of these 100 possible values appears in the column 10 times. Based on this assumption, the CBO bases its selection of the least costly execution plan.

This behavior can result in poorly performing execution plans for tables whose column data is not evenly distributed. This is particularly true for large, multi-million row tables where the difference between using or not using an index during query execution results in millions of more I/Os than would otherwise need to be performed. When the data in an indexed column is not uniformly distributed Oracle DBAs can use histograms to help improve poorly performing queries written against these tables. Histograms help the CBO by providing an accurate representation of the true dispersion of the data within the particular column or columns referenced by the query. The CBO can then use these histogram statistics to determine how frequently each of the values within the range of values will occur in the result set — and then adjust the execution plan accordingly.

How Histograms Help the CBO

Suppose we have a data warehouse application that stores student information for a statewide university system. This information is used by the state legislature when appropriating funds for each campus in the state's university system. There are twenty-six campuses in the system, and the data is retained for ten years. Users of the data warehouse frequently query one of the application tables, *student_summary,* which contains one million rows. Exhibit 1 describes the contents of the *student_summary* table. In the past, the DBAs found that users were frequently constructing queries which WHERE clauses included the DEGREE_AWARDED column from the *student_summary* table. Therefore, the DBAs built an index called *student_summary_deg_award_idx* on this column in an attempt to enhance query performance. However, the DBAs are finding that the addition of the index has had little positive effect on the execution of queries against this table. In order to illustrate how the use of histogram statistics might help solve this performance issue, let's compare the CBO's use of this index without statistics, with statistics, and then with histogram statistics.

COLUMN NAME	CONTENTS	SAMPLE DATA
STUDENT_ID	Nine digit student identification number	123456789
GRADUATION_DATE	Date the student received their degree	02-JUN-98
DEGREE_AWARDED	Type of degree the student received	AS, AA, BA, BBA, BFA, BS, MBA, MFA, MS, EDS, PHD

COLUMN NAME	CONTENTS	SAMPLE DATA
FIN_AID_SOURCE	The type of financial aid the student received, if any	G(rant), L(oan), S(cholarship)
ACADEMIC_HONORS	The academic honors the student received at graduation, if any	C(um Laude) D(ean's List) M(agna Cum Laude) S(umma Cum Laude)

Exhibit 1. *Contents of the student_summary Table*

CBO Behavior without Statistics

When statistics are not available to the CBO, the query is essentially executed in Rule-Based Optimizer (RBO) mode. The RBO uses "rules of thumb" instead of statistics to determine its execution plans. One of the RBO rules of thumb is "if they exist, always use indexes on columns referenced in a WHERE clause". This behavior can be demonstrated with the following query on the *student_summary* table:

```
SQL>       select student_id
2          from student_summary
3          where degree_awarded = 'BBA';
```

Without the benefit of any statistics at all, the RBO uses the following execution plan to satisfy this query:

```
COST  CARDINALITY EXECUTION PLAN
----- ----------- --------------------
                  SELECT STATEMENT
                  TABLE ACCESS BY
                   INDEX ROWID
                   STUDENT_SUMMARY
                  INDEX RANGE SCAN
                   STUDENT_SUMMARY_
                   DEG_AWARD_IDX
```

Interpreting this execution plan we see that the CBO starts the query execution by accessing the index, *student_summary_deg_award_idx*, on the DEGREE_AWARDED column. Then, the index's rowed information is used to locate and return the requested data from the *student_summary* table. The two columns that indicate the relative cost of each step in the execution plan (COST) and the estimated number of rows expected to be accessed by the each step in the execution plan (CARDINALITY) are null because there are no statistics available to the RBO to populate these columns in the explain plan output.

CBO Behavior with Statistics

Next, we will analyze the *student_summary* table to gather current statistic information using the following command:

```
SQL> ANALYZE TABLE student_summary COMPUTE STATISTICS;

Table analyzed.
```

Unlike the RBO, the CBO will use these statistics, and not rules of thumb, when deciding whether to use the index on the DEGREE_AWARDED column. With the addition of these statistics, the CBO formulates the following execution plan for the same query we used in the previous section:

```
COST CARDINALITY EXECUTION PLAN
---- ----------- ---------------------
535  90910       SELECT STATEMENT
535  90910       TABLE ACCESS BY
                  INDEX ROWID
                  STUDENT_SUMMARY
187  90910       INDEX RANGE SCAN
                  STUDENT_SUMMARY_
                  DEG_AWARD_IDX
```

Note that the execution plan itself has not changed, but the presence of statistics has allowed the CBO to assign costs and cardinality estimates to each step in the execution plan.

When deciding to utilize the index on the DEGREE_AWARDED column the CBO has assumed that the types of degrees awarded are uniformly distributed across all one million students in the table. Because there are one million rows in the table and 11 possible values for the type of degree awarded, the CBO has estimated that 1/11 of the rows (i.e., 90,910) have the value of BBA for DEGREE_AWARDED. This can be seen in each step of the execution plan because the cardinality estimate is 90,910 rows. However, as we can see in Exhibit 2, which summarizes the contents of the DEGREE_AWARDED column, this assumption is not true. There are actually 502,216 students who have a value of BBA in the DEGREE_AWARDED, not 90,910 as the optimizer has estimated. In this case it would be much more efficient to simply do a Full Table Scan (FTS) to return the query results than it would be to read the index blocks and then the table blocks for the 502,216 rows that will eventually be returned.

DEGREE CODE	DEGREE TYPE	NUMBER OF RECORDS
AA	Associate of Arts	21,529
AS	Associate of Science	33,446
BA	Bachelor of Arts	156,382
BBA	Bachelor of Bus. Admin.	502,216
BFA	Bachelor of Fine Arts	26,196
BS	Bachelor of Science	217,891
EDS	Educational Specialist	526
MBA	Master of Bus. Admin.	11,231
MFA	Master of Fine Arts	9,520

DEGREE CODE	DEGREE TYPE	NUMBER OF RECORDS
MS	Master of Science	12,331
PHD	Doctor of Philosophy	8,732

Exhibit 2. *The Contents of the DEGREE_AWARDED Column*

It is exactly this kind of situation that can cause the CBO to choose poorly performing execution plans for queries on large tables whose indexed columns contain data that is not uniformly distributed. In order for the CBO to formulate the best possible execution plan we will need to gather histogram statistics for the *student_summary* table.

CBO Behavior with Statistics and Histograms

If the CBO has histogram statistics to draw upon when formulating the execution plan for our example query it is likely that the CBO will favor the FTS over the index-based row retrieval chosen in the previous section. In order to gather histogram statistics, the DBA must ask for them explicitly using one of the ANALYZE options shown in Exhibit 3. For the purposes of our example, we will use the following ANALYZE command:

```
SQL>     ANALYZE TABLE student_summary
          COMPUTE STATISTICS
          FOR COLUMNS degree_
          awarded SIZE 10;
Table analyzed.
```

ANALYZE OPTION	DESCRIPTION
FOR TABLE;	Analyzes table only.
FOR ALL COLUMNS;	Analyzes all columns of the table.

ANALYZE OPTION	DESCRIPTION
FOR ALL COLUMNS SIZE n;	Analyzes all columns of the table, with n buckets to store the resulting values.
FOR ALL INDEXED COLUMNS;	Analyzes only the table's indexed columns.
FOR ALL INDEXED COLUMNS SIZE n;	Analyze all columns that are indexes, with n buckets to store the resulting values.
FOR COLUMNS column_name;	Analyze only the specified column.
FOR COLUMNS column_name SIZE n;	Analyze only the specified column, with n buckets to store the resulting values.
FOR ALL INDEXES;	Analyze the indexes associated with this table.
FOR ALL LOCAL INDEXES;	Analyze all local indexes associated with this table.

Exhibit 3. *ANALYZE Options*

The histogram statistics gathered by the ANALYZE command can be viewed in the data dictionary views listed in Exhibit 4. Given these new histogram statistics to draw upon, the CBO formulates the following execution plan for the same query we used in the previous sections:

```
COST CARDINALITY EXECUTION PLAN
---- ----------- --------------------
545  502216      SELECT STATEMENT
545  502216      TABLE ACCESS FULL
                 STUDENT_SUMMARY
```

DICTIONARY VIEW	VIEW DESCRIPTION
DBA_TAB_HISTOGRAMS	Contains table and view histogram statistics.
INDEX_HISTOGRAMS	Contains statistics on the number of times index key values are repeated in a table column.
DBA_PART_HISTOGRAMS	Contains table partition histogram statistics.
DBA_SUBPART_HISTOGRAMS	Contains table sub-partitions histogram statistics

Exhibit 4. *Data Dictionary Views*

In this execution plan the CBO elects to perform a FTS instead of using the index on the DEGREE_AWARDED column as we saw in the previous two examples. Additionally, the CBO has correctly assigned a cardinality estimate of 502,216 rows to the query's result set — not the 90,910 rows that the CBO estimated without the benefit of histogram statistics. This is a simple, yet powerful, example of how histograms can help the CBO get a clearer picture of the true data composition when the assumption of evenly distributed data is false.

Note: Histogram statistics should be gathered using the FOR COLUMNS clause only *after* regular statistics have been gathered using the standard ANALYZE TABLE…COMPUTE [or ESTIMATE] STATISTICS command.

How Histogram Statistics Are Stored

When histogram statistics are gathered using the ANALYZE command, Oracle creates a height-based histogram of the values contained in the indexed column. The histogram uses containers, referred to as buckets, to store the row statistics. The number of buckets created to store the statistics is determined by the SIZE parameter specified in the ANALYZE command. For example, if a SIZE of 100 is specified, 100 buckets will be created to store the histogram statistics. If no SIZE parameter is specified, it will default to a value of 75. Valid values for SIZE are any integer value between 1 and 254. The default SIZE of 75 is adequate in many cases but, when specified, the value of SIZE should be at least as large as the number of unique values in the indexed column. In any case, the greater the number of buckets, the more granular the histogram definition becomes.

The height of each bucket is given by the dividing the number of rows in the table being analyzed by the SIZE value specified in the ANALYZE command. In our ANALYZE command example above, ten buckets would be created and each bucket would be 100,000 rows "high" (i.e., 1 million rows |SIZE 10 = 100,000 rows per bucket). Oracle then labels each bucket with the beginning and ending values stored within it. Exhibit 5 demonstrates this concept for the DEGREE_AWARDED column of the *student_summary* table. Armed with this histogram information, the CBO can quickly determine that the value BBA appears in six of the ten (i.e., 60 percent) buckets and thus would be most efficiently retrieved using a FTS, not by using the *student_summary_deg_award_*idx index.

BUCKET NUMBER	STARTING VALUE	ENDING VALUE	HISTOGRAM DATA DETAILS (NUMBER ROWS)
1	AA	BA	AA (21,529), AS (33,446), BA (45,025)
2	BA	BA	BA (100,000)

BUCKET NUMBER	STARTING VALUE	ENDING VALUE	HISTOGRAM DATA DETAILS (NUMBER ROWS)
3	BA	BBA	BA (11,357), BBA (88,643)
4	BBA	BBA	BBA (100,000)
5	BBA	BBA	BBA (100,000)
6	BBA	BBA	BBA (100,000)
7	BBA	BBA	BBA (100,000)
8	BBA	BS	BBA (13,573), BFA (26,196) BS (60,231)
9	BS	BS	BS (100,000)
10	BS	PHD	BS (57,660), EDS (526), MBA (11,231), MFA, (9,520), MS (12,331), PHD (8,732)

Exhibit 5. *Beginning and Ending Values for the DEGREE_AWARDED Column*

In reality Oracle will only use five rows to store histogram information in *dba_tab_histograms* for the DEGREE_AWARDED column of the *student_summary* table:

```
SQL>  select    table_name, column_name,
   2            endpoint_number,
               endpoint_value,
   3            endpoint_actual_value
   4   from dba_tab_histograms
   5   where table_name = 'STUDENT_SUMMARY'
   6   and column_name = 'DEGREE_AWARDED'
   7   order by 1;
```

```
TABLE_NAME         COLUMN_NAME
--------------     --------------
STUDENT_SUMMARY    DEGREE_AWARDED
STUDENT_SUMMARY    DEGREE_AWARDED
STUDENT_SUMMARY    DEGREE_AWARDED
STUDENT_SUMMARY    DEGREE_AWARDED
STUDENT_SUMMARY    DEGREE_AWARDED


ENDPOINT     ENDPOINT       ENDPOINT
_NUMBER      _VALUE         _ACTUAL
----------   ------------   ----------
        0    3.3882E+35
        2    3.4401E+35
        7    3.4404E+35
        9    3.4438E+35
       10    4.1685E+35
```

This occurs because, unlike the conceptual example of ten buckets being used to store the histogram data, Oracle stores buckets with repeating endpoints only once in order to conserve space in the data dictionary.

Identifying Histogram Candidates

As we have seen, the use of histograms can greatly enhance the performance of execution plans developed by the CBO. However, histograms are not always appropriate in all situations. Histograms are only effective when used on indexed columns whose data is not uniformly distributed. They do not positively impact queries involving columns whose data is evenly distributed. When identifying columns that may make good candidates for histograms it is useful to look for indexed columns where the number of distinct values represents only a small percentage of the total number of rows in the column. The query shown in Exhibit 6 can be used to identify indexed columns that have these attributes. This query identifies indexed columns whose selectivity is more than 95 percent.

```
SQL>    select   i.table_name,
2                i.index_name,
3                ic.column_name,
4                TO_CHAR(ROUND((i.distinct_keys/i.num_rows),4)
                   *100,'fm00.00') "SELECTIVITY"
5       from     dba_indexes i, dba_ind_columns ic
6       where    i.index_name = ic.index_name
7       and      i.table_name = ic.table_name
8       and      i.table_owner = ic.table_owner
9       and      TO_CHAR(ROUND((i.distinct_keys/i.num_rows),4)
                   *100,'fm00.00') < .05
10      and      (owner != 'SYS' or owner != 'SYSTEM');

TABLE_NAME       INDEX_NAME                     COLUMN_NAME      SELECTIVITY
---------------  -----------------------------  ---------------  -----------
STUDENT_SUMMARY  STUDENT_SUMMARY_DEG_AWARD_IDX  DEGREE_AWARDED   00.00
STUDENT_SUMMARY  STUDENT_SUMMARY_FIN_AID_IDX    FIN_AID_SOURCE   00.00
STUDENT_SUMMARY  STUDENT_SUMMARY_ACD_HONORS_IDX ACADEMIC_HONORS  00.00
STUDENT_SUMMARY  STUDENT_SUMMARY_GRAD_DATE_IDX  GRADUATION_DATE  00.00
```

Exhibit 6. *Identifying Good Candidates for Histograms*

Once you have identified the indexed columns with high selectivity, you must then determine which of those columns have uneven data distributions. The anonymous PL/SQL block shown in Exhibit 7 can be used for this purpose. This PL/SQL block examines the table and column names you specify at runtime and checks to see if the values in that column match the CBO's assumption of being evenly distributed. The findings are then reported back as a recommendation to gather, or not gather, histogram statistics for that particular column.

```
-- ************************************************
-- Copyright © 2003 by Rampant TechPress
-- This script is free for non-commercial purposes
-- with no warranties.  Use at your own risk.
--
-- To license this script for a commercial purpose,
-- contact info@rampant.cc
************************************************

set serveroutput on echo off feedback off verify off
clear screen
ACCEPT tabname PROMPT "Enter the name of the table you wish
to examine: "
ACCEPT colname PROMPT "Enter the name of the column you wish
to examine: "

DECLARE
```

```
v_total_nn_values                NUMBER;
v_distinct_keys                  NUMBER;
v_assumed_selectivity            NUMBER;
v_high_selectivity_range         NUMBER;
v_low_selectivity_range          NUMBER;
v_actual_selectivity             NUMBER;
v_values_matching_selectivity    NUMBER :=0;


CURSOR c_data_distribution IS
  SELECT    &colname, num_records
  FROM
  (SELECT   &colname, COUNT(rowid) "NUM_RECORDS"
  FROM      &tabname
  WHERE     &colname IS NOT NULL
  GROUP BY &colname);

BEGIN
SELECT i.num_rows, i.distinct_keys
  INTO v_total_nn_values, v_distinct_keys
FROM    user_indexes i, user_ind_columns ic
WHERE   i.table_name = UPPER('&tabname')
AND     ic.column_name = UPPER('&colname')
AND     ic.index_name = i.index_name;
v_assumed_selectivity := ROUND (1 / v_distinct_keys,4);
-- set a range of acceptable selectivity values (± 20%)
around
-- the assumed value
v_low_selectivity_range := ROUND (v_assumed_selectivity *
.80,4);
v_high_selectivity_range := ROUND (v_assumed_selectivity *
1.20,4);
FOR r_data_distribution IN c_data_distribution LOOP
-- find actual selectivity using formula from Oracle
-- documentation
-- "Oracle8i Designing and Tuning for Performance", pg.8-20
  v_actual_selectivity := ROUND
   (r_data_distribution.num_records/v_total_nn_values,4);
  IF v_actual_selectivity BETWEEN v_low_selectivity_range AND
    v_high_selectivity_range
    THEN v_values_matching_selectivity :=
      v_values_matching_selectivity + 1;
  END IF;
END LOOP;
IF v_values_matching_selectivity >= ROUND
(v_distinct_keys/2,0)
-- if more than half the values meet the selectivity
assumption,
-- then skip the histogram
  THEN
```

```
    dbms_output.put_line ('&colname will probably NOT benefit
    from histogram statistics');
  ELSE
    dbms_output.put_line ('&colname WILL probably benefit
from
    histogram statistics');
END IF;
EXCEPTION
  WHEN OTHERS THEN
    dbms_output.put_line ('ERROR: Make sure you supplied a
valid
      table and column name.');
END;
/
```

Exhibit 7. *PL/SQL Block Used to Determine which of those Columns Have Uneven Data Distributions*

Gathering histogram statistics for columns that do not meet these guidelines should be avoided. The presence of excessive histogram statistics may cause the CBO to waste parse time by considering too many additional execution plans before choosing the best one. One way to minimize this problem is to experiment with the *optimizer_max_permutations init.ora* parameter. This parameter allows you to set the maximum number of possible execution plans the CBO will consider before selecting the plan it feels is most efficient. This parameter can be set to any value between 4 through 2_{23}. The default value is 80,000, which has the effect of allowing an unlimited number of execution plans to be considered. Care should be taken when using this parameter. While setting *optimizer_max_permutations* to a low value will cause the CBO parse times to be reduced, it may also cause the CBO to overlook more efficient execution plans.

Summary

The CBO relies heavily on accurate table and index statistics when formulating its execution plans. Histograms further help the CBO by providing a more accurate picture of indexed columns that contain non-uniformly distributed data. You can use the techniques discussed in this chapter to identify the columns that will benefit most from histogram statistic collection. Histogram statistics should only be collected for these columns so that the CBO is not negatively impacted by having too many execution plan choices to consider at parse time.

NOTE: Oracle 9i release 2 has some enhancements that make the process of creating index histograms for the optimizer much easier.

Donald K. Burleson provided some examples of these new processes in a recent article. Basically, you can now tell Oracle to look for columns that should have histograms, and go ahead and create them. To do this, there is a new parameter included in the *dbms_stats* package – *method_opt*:

These automate the detection of columns that require histograms, and automatically create them:

```
method_opt=>'for all columns size skewonly'
method_opt=>'for all columns size repeat'
method_opt=>'for all columns size auto'
```

Remember, analyzing for histograms is time-consuming, and histograms are used under two conditions:

Table join order – The CBO must know the size of the intermediate result sets (cardinality) to properly determine the correct join order the multi-table joins. This is normally performed for foreign key constraints, and non-constraint, non-unique columns that are used in table joins. This is a critical task for the CBO to determine the optimal sequence for joining many tables together as efficiently as possible.

Table access method – The CBO needs to know about columns in SQL where clauses, where the column value is skewed such that a full-table scan might be faster than an index range scan. Oracle uses this skew information in conjunction with the *clustering_factor* columns of the *dba_indexes* view.

Hence, this is the proper order for using the *dbms_stats* package to locate proper columns for histograms:

- **Skewonly option** - You want to use *skewonly* to do histograms for skewed columns, for cases where the value will make a difference between a full-table scan and an index scan.

- **Monitor** - Next, turn-on monitoring. Issue an *alter table xx monitoring* and *alter index yyy monitoring* command for all segments in your schema. This will monitor workload against the table and index.

- **Auto option** - Once monitoring is in-place, you need to re-analyze with the "auto" option to create histograms for join columns within tables. This is critical for the CBO to determine the proper join order for finding the driving table in multi-table joins.

- **Repeat option** - Finally, use the "repeat" option to re-analyze only the existing histograms.

Periodically you will want to re-run the *skewonly* and *auto* option to identify any new columns that require histograms. Once located, the repeat option will ensure that they are refreshed with current values.

Now that we've covered how the optimizer works, let's look at what YOU can control – what your SQL looks like. Donald K. Burleson, noted SQL Tuning expert has provided in-depth insight into tips on tuning SQL:

SQL Tuning Tips – Donald K. Burleson

Oracle SQL tuning is a phenomenally complex subject, and entire books have been devoted to the nuances of Oracle SQL tuning. However there are some general guidelines that every Oracle DBA follows in order to improve the performance of their systems. The goals of SQL tuning are simple:

- Remove unnecessary large-table full table scans Unnecessary full table scans cause a huge amount of unnecessary I/O, and can drag down an entire database. The tuning expert first evaluates the SQL based on the number of rows returned by the query. If the query returns less and 40 percent of the table rows in an ordered table, or 7 percent of the rows in an unordered table), the query can be tuned to use an index in lieu of the full table scan. The most common tuning for unnecessary full table scans is adding indexes. Standard B-tree indexes can be added to tables, and bitmapped and function-based indexes can also eliminate full table scans. The decision about removing a full table scan should be based on a careful examination of the I/O costs of the index scan vs. the costs of the full table scan, factoring in the multiblock reads and possible parallel execution. In some cases an unnecessary full table scan can be forced to use an index by adding an index hint to the SQL statement.

- Cache small-table full table scans In cases where a full table scan is the fastest access method, the tuning professional should ensure that a dedicated data buffer is available for the rows. In Oracle7 you can issue alter table xxx cache. In Oracle8 and beyond, the small table can be cached by forcing to into the KEEP pool.

- Verify optimal index usage This is especially important for improving the speed of queries. Oracle sometimes has a choice of indexes, and the tuning professional must examine each index and ensure that Oracle is using the proper index. This also includes the use of bitmapped and function-based indexes.

- Verify optimal JOIN techniques Some queries will perform faster with NESTED LOOP joins, others with HASH joins, while other favor sort-merge joins.

These goals may seem deceptively simple, but these tasks comprise 90 percent of SQL tuning, and they don't require a through understanding of the internals of Oracle SQL. Let's begin with an overview of the Oracle SQL optimizers.

Of course, you can tune the SQL all you want, but if you don't feed the optimizer with the correct statistics, the optimizer still may not make the correct decisions. It is important to ensure that you have statistics present, and that they are current. Some believe in the practice of running stats weekly, or on some other schedule. Others believe in just calculating statistics when the data changes. Still a 3rd group of folks say that you only run statistics to fix a poor access path, and once things are good – don't touch them. It is difficult to say who is correct. Therefore, the new features in Oracle 10g that will tell you when statistics are old and need to be recalculated are extremely helpful – gone are the days when we calculated statistics weekly (or on whatever schedule), just in case the data changed. Now we know for sure one way or the other. Of course, some will still say – only calculate new statistics if you are having a problem – once you have decent access paths – leave it alone.

Regardless of how often you choose to calculate your stats, there is a new package, *dbms_stats,* that Oracle recommends be used instead of the old *analyze table* command.

Compute vs. Estimate

There is still the age-old argument about computing statistics vs. estimating. If the world were perfect, both would yield the same result. But, alas, that is not the case. Some have actually experienced the scenario where different access paths were produced by using different values of estimate (20%, 25%, 30%) or by using compute. However, the good news is that the optimizer gets better and better with each new version.

So, what is the recommendation? For large tables (over 1 million rows), try using estimate stats. You can start with 30%, and work up or down as needed. Then, test things out. You can make adjustments and rerun accordingly. You should not have to drop the statistics before recalculating them, but there are odd instances where this seems to matter, so that is always another option.

The following are some examples of calculating statistics (without histograms), and the differences between compute and estimate:

Compute Statistics on scott.emp and its indexes without histograms:

```
exec dbms_stats.gather_table_stats(ownname=>scott,
tabname=>emp, cascade=> true);
```

Estimate Statistics on scott.emp and its indexes at 30% without histograms:

```
exec dbms_stats.gather_table_stats(ownname=>scott,
tabname=>emp, cascade=> true, estimate_percent => 15);
```

Calculate Statistics on scott.emp but not for columns or indexes:

```
exec dbms_stats.gather_table_stats(ownname=>scott,
tabname=>emp, cascade=> true, method_opt => 'for columns');
```

Conclusion

This chapter provided an overview of the cost-based optimizer, including the importance of having the correct statistics, and some tips for tuning SQL.

In general, the optimizer makes decisions on the access path that it will use to access data. It analyzes all access path options (or many, at least, depending on how many there are), and takes its best guess as to the best way to get the data. Sometimes the optimizer makes a bad choice, and needs to be given hints or directives on using a different path. Unfortunately, the optimizer doesn't always listen when given hints, so it is always best to double check the access path with an EXPLAIN PLAN.

SQL Execution Internals

Oracle Hints

Now that you know how the cost-based optimizer works, what if you don't like the decision it has made? One option is to try to force the optimizer to do something differently using a hint. The problem here is that a hint is more like a suggestion than issuing a directive. The optimizer doesn't have to follow your hint if it doesn't want to, and it doesn't have to tell you so. The only way to know for sure is to look at Explain Plan output. The basics of the Oracle hints can be most easily understood using a series of examples, provided by Oracle-SQL Expert, Jonathan Lewis:

Internals of Oracle Hints

One of the long-running questions about cost-based optimization (CBO) is the meaning of the word *hint*. As far as CBO is concerned, is a hint a hint, or is it a directive? Personally, I am convinced that the answer is that it is a directive; this chapter argues my case and examines why there is so much room for doubt. This chapter is based on information previously published on the Web at www.jlcomp.demon.co.uk.

My Hint Is Not Working

Hints exist to allow programmers to tell Oracle that they already know the best execution path for a query and give Oracle details of that path so that Oracle will take it. However, there remains a lot of discussion about the word *hint*, and whether it has its normal English meaning of "a polite but perhaps over-subtle suggestion which may not be noticed and could be ignored" or does it actually mean "a direct command and you had better have a good reason for not doing what you are told"?

The most common argument for regarding hints as a "suggestion" that Oracle may ignore comes from the often-heard complaint: "I put this hint in and Oracle still doesn't do …". Does this mean that the hint has been ignored? Not necessarily.

There are four main reasons why Oracle appears to treat hints with disdain.

- There are (or have been) bugs in various pieces of Oracle code.

- Illegal or incorrect hints are not hints; they are comments.

- Oracle ignores hints that cannot be applied.

- Most importantly, the optimizer is sufficiently complex that it is possible for Oracle to find ways of making hints inapplicable.

Let's examine an example of each issue. Consider the hint:

```
/*+index(t1,t1_pk)*/
```

This appears to be a perfectly valid hint that appears (based on names) to be instructing Oracle to use the index representing the primary key when accessing table T1. Due to a bug in various versions of PL/SQL, this hint will *not* be effective if it appears as part of a SQL statement embedded in a PL/SQL block unless you make sure you have left a space after the plus sign.

As an example of an incorrect hint, take a look at the most commonly occurring error in the book:

```
select
  /*+ index(big1, big1_pk) */
  {list of columns}
from
  big1 t
where
  {list of conditions}
;
```

Again, we appear to be telling Oracle to use an index representing the primary key to access a table *big1*. The problem here is that we have given the table an *alias*, and hints have to use the table alias, not the table name. In this case, the hint should be:

```
/*+ index(t, big1_pk) */
```

As an example of a hint that appears valid but cannot be applied, we can highlight another common error. The example is a very simple one that would be very easy to spot, but the nature of the error does cause some surprises in more complex situations.

```
select
  /*+ index(t, big1_uk) */
  count(*)
from
  big1 t
where
  {list of conditions}
  {but none on the Unique Key}
;
```

Note in this example that we have changed to a hint that appears to be asking Oracle to use an index *big1_uk* that represents a *unique* constraint to access the table *big1*.

The problem here is that *unique* constraints do not imply *not null* constraints (unlike *primary* key constraints, which imply *unique* and *not null*). In this example, and assuming that we had not introduced a *not null* constraint on at least one of the columns in the unique key, Oracle cannot use the index because there may be rows in the table that do not appear in the index. That is, using the index could produce the wrong answer.

Finally, we come to the situations that leave most of us thinking that Oracle is simply ignoring our hints because it wants to. Before looking at, and explaining, an example of Oracle "manufacturing" a reason for rejecting a hint, I would like to offer three logical arguments why hints must really be directives.

- Oracle Corporation uses hints internally to make code work (we hope) in the most efficient manner. Examine recursive SQL or the SQL generated for parallel query slaves, for example. If hints were simply there to be ignored, entire swathes of the Oracle product base would become unstable.

- Oracle Corporation has introduced *plan stability*, also known as *stored outlines*, in Oracle 8.1 to guarantee (so the documents say) that execution paths will not change, even across product upgrades. How is plan stability implemented? As a set of hints stored in the database. So if hints are not directives, plan stability is not stable.

- If Oracle has the option to ignore hints, how could it decide to ignore them? Presumably, it would have to run through the normal optimization code to find the cost of the path and then decide to take it or not. But one reason for hinting the SQL is to reduce the parse (or, more specifically, optimization) time, so Oracle must be skipping at least some optimization because of the hints. Moreover, if Oracle calculates the cost of your hinted path and then decides whether or not to take it, what criteria does it use in its decision? Does it run the calculations without the hint and compare costs? Presumably not, because that would be just the standard cost-based optimization mechanism.

Clearly, hints make something (not) happen, and there must always be a good reason why Oracle has decided that a hint cannot be applied.

It is time for an example. Exhibit 1 is a simple script to build a pair of tables. This script was run on an Oracle 8.1.7 system using a 4K blocksize.

```
-- ************************************************
-- Copyright © 2003 by Rampant TechPress
-- This script is free for non-commercial purposes
-- with no warranties.  Use at your own risk.
--
-- To license this script for a commercial purpose,
-- contact info@rampant.cc
-- ************************************************

create table ignore_1
nologging
as
select
  rownum id, rownum val,
  rpad('x',250) padding
from all_objects
where rownum <= 3000;

create table ignore_2
nologging
as
select
  rownum id, rownum val,
  rpad('x',250) padding
from all_objects
where rownum <= 500;

alter table ignore_2
add constraint ig2_pk primary key (id);

analyze table ignore_1
  compute statistics;
analyze table ignore_2
  compute statistics;
```

Exhibit 1. *Creating the Sample Data Set*

Now we run a simple query against these two tables, joining them on the `id` column. Our query will pick a small number of rows from the larger table and join them to the matching rows in the smaller table. To encourage Oracle to use the conveniently created primary key index, we will include a hint to tell Oracle to use a nested loop join between the tables (see Exhibit 2).

```
--   **************************************************
-- Copyright © 2003 by Rampant TechPress
-- This script is free for non-commercial purposes
-- with no warranties.  Use at your own risk.
--
-- To license this script for a commercial purpose,
-- contact info@rampant.cc
--   **************************************************

set autotrace traceonly explain

select /*+ use_nl(i2) */
       i1.val val1,
       i2.val val2
from
       ignore_1 i1,
       ignore_2 i2
where
       i2.id = i1.id
and    i1.val <= 10
;

SELECT STATEMENT Optimizer=ALL_ROWS
  HASH JOIN (Cost=44 Card=11 Bytes=132)
    TABLE ACCESS (FULL) OF 'IGNORE_1' ( (Cost=36 Card=11)
    TABLE ACCESS (FULL) OF 'IGNORE_2' ( (Cost=7 Card=500)
```

Exhibit 2. *A Query that Will Not Take the Hint*

Our query, with the hint, visits the tables in the order we expect but appears to ignore our hint to use_nl(i2). The definition of this hint means:

When examining paths entering table (aliased by) i2, you should consider only a nested loop join to get into table i2.

At this point, some developers will change the hint to read:

```
/*+ use_nl(i1 i2) */
```

and find that the query suddenly changes to the nested loop that they expect. This is sometimes taken as an indication that you need to specify both ends of the nested loop join in this hint. This is not true; the altered path would actually be a side effect of, not a direct result of, this change. In its modified form, the hint now reads:

> When examining paths entering the table (aliased by) i2, you should consider only a nested loop join to get into table i2; and when examining paths entering the table (aliased by) i1, you should consider only a nested loop join to get into table i1.

Other developers may come up with the "more correct" solution of changing the hint to read:

```
/*+ ordered use_nl(i2) */
```

This tells Oracle to visit the tables i1 and i2 in the correct order (as listed in the `from` clause) and to use a nested loop to get into i2.

Why is there a problem, and why is this the solution?

The answer comes from examining the 10053 trace file. If we have no hints, the trace file will show the stages (edited for extreme compaction) shown in Exhibit 3. The interesting quirk appears when we use only the use_nl(i2) hint. We have *not* told Oracle to avoid examining join orders from i2 to i1, so the trace looks like Exhibit 4.

```
Try the order i1 to i2 using NL.
Try the order i1 to i2 using sort/merge
Try the order i1 to i2 using hash
  Hash is the cheapest

Try the order i2 to i1 using NL.
Try the order i2 to i1 using sort/merge
Try the order i2 to i1 using hash
  Hash is the cheapest

Hash i1 -> i2 is the cheapest overall
```

Exhibit 3. *A Shortened 10053 Trace*

Thus, given the restrictions imposed by the hints, the best available execution path from Oracle's perspective is to hash the two tables going in the order i2 to i1 — but swapping the join inputs. That is, Oracle has legally found a way of bypassing our demand that it should only consider a nested loop when entering table i2. As we can see from Exhibit 4, when deliberately considering methods of getting into i2, the only option examined was the nested loop. The unexpected hash join appears only as an "accidental" by-product of considering paths into i1. This, of course, is why the addition of the ordered hint is the correct solution to the problem; it stops Oracle from considering any paths into i1 and therefore blocks the emergence of the swapped hash join.

```
Try the order i1 to i2 using NL.
  Use_nl is the cheapest

Try the order i2 to i1 using NL.
Try the order i2 to i1 using sort/merge
Try the order i2 to i1 using hash,
Try the hash again with "(sides swapped)"
  Swapped Hash is the cheapest

Hash i2 -> i1 is the cheapest overall
```

Exhibit 4. *The Trace after the Use_Nl() Hint*

Just for the sake of completeness, Exhibit 5 shows an extract of the trace information you would get from the two hint modifications given above.

```
/*+ ordered use_nl(i2) */

Try the order i1 to i2 using NL.
  Nested loop is the cheapest

NL i1 -> i2 is the cheapest overall

/*+ use_nl(i1,i2) */

Try the order i1 to i2 using NL.
  Nested loop is the cheapest

Try the order i2 to i1 using NL.
  Nested loop is the cheapest

NL i1 -> i2 is the cheapest overall
```

Exhibit 5. *Alternative Traces*

Conclusion

Hints are not mildly worded suggestions; they are directives to the optimizer to reduce the number of different options it is allowed to examine.

Unfortunately, it is easy to be convinced for several reasons that your hints are being ignored; and this may simply mean that there is something trivially wrong with your hinting.

There are cases, however, where the increasing sophistication of the optimizer allows it to use alternative mechanisms to reach a path that you thought you had blocked by the use of hints.

If you are going to use hints, be very thorough with the hints you apply. If there is a valid path that you want Oracle to take, the correct and complete set of hints will ensure that Oracle does take it.

Using STATSPACK Utility

Now, how do you know if need to use a hint, or if Oracle is in fact using the best access path it can? One of the easiest ways to figure out what is going on is to use the STATSPACK utility that Oracle comes with, to see what is going on in your system. The setup of STATSPACK is quite easy:

The installation script for STATSPACK is located in: $ORACLE_HOME/rdbms/admin/spcreate.sql:

cd $ORACLE_HOME/rdbms/admin
```
sqlplus / as sysdba
@spcreate
```

You will be prompted for a default tablespace and a temporary tablespace for the id that this creates – perfstat. Note that the default password for the perfstat is perfstat (same id and password), and obviously should be changed. But, for purposes of the examples below, we'll keep it the same.

There is an instruction document typically located in this same directory, and it is called either spdoc.txt or statspack.doc

Once you have created the STATSPACK structures, grabbing a snapshot is relatively simple:

```
sqlplus perfstat/perfstat
exec statspack.snap
```

The code above will grab a snapshot right now. Then, wait 5 or 10 or 15 minutes, and run the same thing again. Now you have two snapshots, with which to compare.

Now, you need to get a report of what was happening during your timeslot:

```
sqlplus perfstat/perfstat
@report
```

You will be prompted for the ids of the beginning time and end time, and the output file name. Then your report will be generated.

For example:

```
sqlplus perfstat/perfstat
@report
```

Sample output:

```
   DB Id DB      Name     Instance#    Instance
----------- ---------- ---------- ----------
   123456789   ORCL          1       ORCL
Completed Snapshots

Instance    DB Name    SnapId    Snap Started         Snap Level
---------- ---------- ------ --------------------- ----------
ORCL        ORCL          1    1 Jan 2004 13:00:02       5
                          2    1 Jan 2004 13:05:54       5

    Enter beginning Snap Id: 1
    Enter ending    Snap Id: 2
Enter name of output file [sp_1_2] : <press return or enter a new name>
```

Then your report is generated, into whatever output file you designated (note – be sure that your *init.ora* or *spfile* parameter *timed_statistics* is set to true or you won't get all the information that you need).

There are lots of options that you can tweak in STATSPACK, but what is covered above is just the basic, default installation and report.

It is possible to change the options that STATSPACK is using in which to generate the report. I typically go with the defaults, to start with, but for the sake of completeness, they are listed below:

- Snapshot level – values 0 – 10, defaults to 5, which is gather general performance statistics on things like waits, system and session events, SGA, background events, locks, latches, buffer pool statistics, rollback segment information, row cache statistics, and high resource SQL statements. Using a level of 0 would do all of the above except the high resource SQL statements.

- Using a Level 6 plan usage data to the report (assuming the statement is in the shared pool when the snapshot is taken, and it exceeds one of the thresholds defined below).

- Using a Level 10 would add child latch statistics to the report. This can have a performance impact on your system, and isn't recommended unless Oracle Technical Support tells you to turn it on.

High resource SQL statements – what is high? The answer is, it is all relative. So, there are thresholds that you can set, so you can use the definition of high that is appropriate for your system.

There are 4 main thresholds that you can change:

- Number of executions of the SQL statement (default value = 100)

- Number of parse calls executed by a given SQL statement (default value = 1000)

- Number of disk reads executed by a given SQL statement (default value = 1000)

- Number of buffer gets executed by a statement (default value = 1000)

So, for example, if you run with the defaults, and an SQL statement gets more than 1000 buffers, that SQL statement will appear on the report.

- If a given SQL statement performs more than 1000 disk reads, it will appear on the report.

- If a SQL statement is executed more than 100 times, it will appear on the report.

When following a tuning methodology, this reports makes it easy to zero in on the statements that are using all the resources of your system. If you see a handful of SQL statements running over and over again, and doing lots of I/O, you know just where to start!

You can either change these defaults permanently, or just for the current execution of a snap.

To change the default permanently:

```
execute statspack.snap (i_snap_level => 6,
i_modify_parameter=>'true');

execute statspack.snap (i_buffer_gets_th => 5000,
i_modify_parameter=>'true');
```

To change the default just for the current run:

```
execute statspack.snap (i_snap_level => 6);

execute statspack.snap (i_buffer_gets_th => 5000,
i_modify_parameter=>'false');
```

(either setting the *i_modify_parameter* to false, or not specifying it at all, will just change defaults for the current run).

Or, you can change defaults permanently, in preparation for your next snapshot, without actually getting a snapshot, using the following:

```
execute statspack.modify_statspack_parameter
(i_snap_level=>6, i_executions_th => 200,
i_buffer_gets_th=>5000, i_disk_reads_th=>5000,
i_parse_calls_th =>5000);
```

A partial sample output from STATSPACK:

```
STATSPACK report for

DB Name        DB Id       Instance     Inst Num Release     Cluster Host
------------ ----------- ------------ -------- ----------- ------- -----------
TOY          2410677970 TOY                 1 9.2.0.3.0   NO      matthew

               Snap Id    Snap Time       Sessions Curs/Sess Comment
               -------  ------------------ -------- --------- --------------------
Begin Snap:      835 19-Jan-04 22:16:20      13       2.6
  End Snap:      836 19-Jan-04 22:30:13      12       4.1
  Elapsed:                13.88 (mins)

Cache Sizes (end)
~~~~~~~~~~~~~~~~~
              Buffer Cache:       8M    Std Block Size:      16K
          Shared Pool Size:       8M        Log Buffer:      32K

Load Profile
~~~~~~~~~~~~                    Per Second      Per Transaction
                              ---------------    ---------------
               Redo size:          397.05            330,740.00
           Logical reads:           68.15             56,769.00
           Block changes:            0.52                431.00
          Physical reads:            0.33                272.00
         Physical writes:            0.15                123.00
              User calls:           14.66             12,212.00
                  Parses:            0.68                569.00
             Hard parses:            0.00                  0.00
                   Sorts:            0.27                221.00
                  Logons:            0.00                  0.00
                Executes:            1.10                913.00
            Transactions:            0.00

    % Blocks changed per Read:   0.76   Recursive Call %:    14.04
    Rollback per transaction %:  0.00      Rows per Sort:    24.33

Instance Efficiency Percentages (Target 100%)
~~~~~~~~~~~~~~~~~~~~~~~~~~~~~~~~~~~~~~~~~~~~~~~~~
              Buffer Nowait %:  100.00       Redo NoWait %:  100.00
              Buffer  Hit   %:   99.58    In-memory Sort %:   98.64
              Library Hit   %:  100.00        Soft Parse %:  100.00
              Execute to Parse %:  37.68        Latch Hit %:  100.00
    Parse CPU to Parse Elapsd %:  119.05    % Non-Parse CPU:   98.32

    Shared Pool Statistics        Begin    End
                                  ------   ------
               Memory Usage %:    86.17    86.09
        % SQL with executions>1:  78.14    78.14
        % Memory for SQL w/exec>1: 79.65   79.65
```

```
Top 5 Timed Events
~~~~~~~~~~~~~~~~~~~                                                % Total
Event                                      Waits    Time (s) Ela Time
------------------------------------ ------------ ----------- --------
CPU time                                                  15    79.57
control file parallel write                   270          3    15.11
db file sequential read                       174          1     4.12
db file scattered read                         15          0      .86
control file sequential read                  137          0      .27
                                     ------------------------------------------


Wait Events for DB: TOY  Instance: TOY  Snaps: 835 -836
-> s  - second
-> cs - centisecond -      100th of a second
-> ms - millisecond -     1000th of a second
-> us - microsecond - 1000000th of a second
-> ordered by wait time desc, waits desc (idle events last)

                                                         Avg
                                           Total Wait   wait     Waits
Event                Waits    Timeouts     Time (s)     (ms)     /txn
------------------- ------------ ---------- ---------- ------ --------
control file parallel write      270          0          3     10    270.0
db file sequential read          174          0          1      4    174.0
db file scattered read            15          0          0     11     15.0
control file sequential read     137          0          0      0    137.0
log file sync                      1          0          0     13      1.0
log file parallel write           24         24          0      0     24.0
direct path read                  15          0          0      0     15.0
db file parallel write             8          0          0      0      8.0
direct path write                  6          0          0      0      6.0
SQL*Net message from client    11,769        0      4,199    357 ########
SQL*Net message to client      11,768        0          0      0 ########
                                     ------------------------------------------


Background Wait Events for DB: TOY  Instance: TOY  Snaps: 835 -836
-> ordered by wait time desc, waits desc (idle events last)

                                                         Avg
                                           Total Wait   wait     Waits
Event                Waits    Timeouts     Time (s)     (ms)     /txn
------------------- ------------ ---------- ---------- ------ --------
control file parallel write      270          0          3     10    270.0
db file scattered read            11          0          0     14     11.0
db file sequential read           15          0          0      6     15.0
control file sequential read     108          0          0      0    108.0
log file parallel write           24         24          0      0     24.0
db file parallel write             8          0          0      0      8.0
rdbms ipc message                850        833      3,922   4614    850.0
smon timer                         3          3        900 ######      3.0
pmon timer                       280        280        814   2907    280.0
                                     ------------------------------------------
```

Now that we've looked at STATSPACK, and we've looked at our top 5 waits, the next step is to take a look at our highest resource-utilizing SQL and see if we can tweak it.

Some of the things to zero in on are correlated subqueries, which can sometimes be poor performers, as well as the join type that Oracle is using. Richard Earp and Sikha Bagui have both done detailed analysis this area, and it is shared below:

An In-Depth Look at Oracle's Correlated Subqueries

A correlated subquery is one where there is (1) a subquery (and hence a main outer query) and (2) the information in the subquery is referenced by the outer main query such that the inner query may be thought of as being executed repeatedly. Correlated queries present a different execution scenario to the database manipulation language (DML) — different from ordinary subqueries. The efficiency of the correlated subquery varies; in Oracle, it may be worthwhile to test the efficiency of correlated versus uncorrelated subqueries. A situation in which one cannot avoid correlation is the "for all" query, which is discussed later in this chapter. We start with a discussion of non-correlated queries and then go on to discuss correlated queries.

What Are *Non-Correlated* Subqueries?

Suppose we have two tables, *student* (with fields stno, sname, major, class, and bdate) and *grade_report* (with fields student_number, section_id, and grade). We are trying to find the names of the students who have a grade of "A." The *student* table does not have a grade field. All grades are kept in *grade_report*. Thus, we can write the following non-correlated query:

```
SELECT  s.sname
FROM    student s
WHERE   s.stno IN
  (SELECT gr.student_number
   FROM   grade_report gr
   WHERE  gr.grade = 'A');
```

The part of the query in parentheses is called a "subquery" — a.k.a., "nested query" or "embedded query." Note that the subquery is an independent entity and would work by itself.

In this example, the subquery

```
(SELECT gr.student_number
 FROM   grade_report gr
 WHERE  gr.grade = 'A')
```

can be thought of as being evaluated first. Then, the resulting set is used to determine which tuples (rows) in the main query will be SELECTed. The first part is called the "outer" or "main" query, and the second is called the "inner query" or the "subquery."

```
SELECT s.sname -- outer
FROM    student s -- outer
WHERE   s.stno IN -- outer
  (SELECT gr.student_number -- inner
   FROM grade_report gr -- inner
   WHERE gr.grade = 'A') -- inner
;
```

Correlated Subqueries

Here is an example of a correlated query:

```
SELECT  s.sname
FROM    student s
WHERE   s.stno IN
  (SELECT gr.student_number
   FROM    grade_report gr
   WHERE   gr.student_number = s.stno
   AND gr.grade = 'B');
```

The inner query references the outer one; observe the use of s.stno in the WHERE clause of the inner query. Rather than thinking of this query as creating a set of student-numbers that have Bs, each tuple (row) from the outer query can be considered to be SELECTed individually and tested against all rows of the inner query one at a time until it is determined whether or not a given student number is in the inner set.

This situation is like a nested DO-loop in a programming language, where the first student tuple is SELECTed, then tested against all *grade_report* tuples, and then the second student tuple is SELECTed and tested against all *grade_report* tuples. Here is the DO-loop in pseudo-code:

```
LOOP1: For each tuple in student s DO
  LOOP2: For each tuple in grade_report
    gr DO
      IF (gr.student_number = s.stno)
        then
          IF (gr.grade = 'B') THEN TRUE
      END LOOP2;
        if TRUE, then student tuple is
          SELECTed
END LOOP1;
```

This query could have been done without correlation. You might think that correlated queries may be less efficient than doing a simple subquery because the simple subquery is done once and the correlated subquery is done once for each outer tuple (row). The internal handling of how the query executes depends on the SQL and the optimizer (compiler) for that database engine. In Oracle, the database engine is designed so that correlated queries are quite efficient.

Existence Queries and Correlation

Correlated queries are often written so that the question in the inner query is one of existence. We illustrate this by introducing a third table called *section*, with the attributes *section_id*, *course_number*, *semester*, *year*, *instructor*, *bldg*, and *room*. Now let us study the query, "Find the names of students who have taken a computer science class and made a grade of 'B.'" This query can be done several ways, as discussed below.

As a non-correlated subquery:

```
SELECT s.sname
FROM    student s
WHERE   s.stno IN
  (SELECT gr.student_number FROM
    grade_report, section
  WHERE section.section_id = gr.section_id
/* join condx grade_reportsection */
  AND section.course_num LIKE
    'COSC____'
  AND gr.grade = 'B');
```

You can think of this query as forming the set of student numbers of students who have made Bs in COSC courses — the inner query. In the inner query, we need to have both the *grade_report* and the *section* tables because the grades are in *grade_report* and the course numbers are in *section*. Once we form this set of student numbers (i.e., we complete the inner query), the outer query looks through the student table and SELECTs only those students who are members of the inner query set. Note that this query could also be done by creating a double-nested subquery containing two INs or could be found using a three table join.

Had we chosen to write the query with an unnecessary correlation, it might look like this:

```
SELECT s.sname
FROM    student s
WHERE   s.stno IN
  (SELECT gr.student_number
    FROM grade_report gr, section
  WHERE section.section_id = gr.section_id
/* join condx grade_report-section */
  AND section.course_num LIKE
    'COSC____'
  AND gr.student_number = s.stno
  AND gr.grade = 'B');
```

In this case, the use of the student table in the subquery is totally unnecessary. Although correlation is unnecessary, we provide this example for several reasons:

- To show when correlation is necessary

- To show how to untangle unnecessarily correlated queries

- To show how you might migrate your thought process toward correlation — another query option

We can perform the query a different way using the keyword EXISTS. There will be situations in which the correlation of a subquery is necessary. Because this is true, we show another way to do the correlated query with EXISTS; it looks like this:

```
SELECT  s.sname
FROM    student s
WHERE EXISTS
  (SELECT 1 FROM grade_report gr, section
  WHERE section.section_id = gr.section_id
  /* join condx grade_report-section */
  AND section.course_num like
  'COSC____'
  AND gr.student_number = s.stno
  AND gr.grade = 'B');
```

The EXISTS predicate says, "Choose the row from student in the outer query if the subquery is TRUE (i.e., if it finds anything)." In the non-correlated case, we tied the student number in the student table to the inner query by the IN predicate:

```
SELECT  s.stno
FROM    student s
WHERE   s.stno IN
  (SELECT "student number ...)
```

With EXISTS, we do not use any attribute of the *student* table, and we have indicated using EXISTS with (SELECT 1 ...).

The use of SELECT * in the inner query is common among SQL programmers. However, from an "internal" standpoint, SELECT * causes the SQL engine to check the data dictionary unnecessarily. Because the actual result of the inner query is not important, it is strongly suggested that you use SELECT 'X' (or SELECT 1) ... instead of SELECT * ... so that a constant is SELECTed instead of some "sensible" entry. The SELECT 'X' ... or SELECT 1 ... is simply more efficient.

In the EXISTS case, we do not specify what attributes need to be SELECTed in the inner query's result set; rather, we use a connection in the WHERE clause of the inner query. EXISTS forces us to correlate the query. This query:

```
SELECT s.sname /* exists-uncorrelated */
FROM    student s
WHERE EXISTS
   (SELECT 'X' FROM grade_report gr,section t
   WHERE t.section_id = gr.section_id
   /* join condx grade_report-section */
   AND t.ccourse_num like 'COSC____'
   AND gr.grade = 'B');
```

(without the correlation, but with EXISTS) means that for each student tuple, you test the joined *grade_report* and *section* to see whether there is a course number like 'COSC' and a grade of 'B' (which, of course, there is) — you unnecessarily ask the subquery question over and over again. The result from this latter uncorrelated EXISTS query is the same as:

```
SELECT s.sname FROM student s
```

The point is that the correlation is necessary when we use EXISTS.

Consider another example in which a correlation can be used. Suppose we want to "Find the names of all students who have three Bs." A first pass at a query might be something like this:

```
SELECT s.sname
FROM    student s WHERE "something" IN
  (SELECT "something"
  FROM grade_report
  WHERE "count of grade = 'B'" > 2);
```

This query can be done with an uncorrelated HAVING clause, but we want to show how to do this with a correlated query. Suppose we arrange the subquery to use the student number from *student* table as a filter, and count in the subquery only when a row in *grade_report* correlates to that student. The query (this time with an implied EXISTS) looks like this:

```
SELECT s.sname
FROM    student s
  WHERE 2 < (SELECT count(*)
    FROM grade_report gr
    WHERE gr.student_number = s.stno
    AND gr.grade = 'B');
```

Although there is no EXISTS in the query, it is implied. The syntax of the query does not allow an EXIST, but the sense of the query is "WHERE EXISTS a COUNT OF 2 WHICH IS LESS THAN … ". In this correlated query, we have to examine the *grade_report* table for each member of the *student* table to see whether or not the student has two Bs. We test the entire *grade_report* table for each student tuple in the other query.

If it were possible, a subquery without the correlation could be more desirable. The overall query might be:

```
SELECT s.sname
FROM    student s
WHERE   s.stno in
(subquery that defines a set of students who have made 3 B's)
```

And we might attempt to do this:

```
SELECT  s.sname
FROM    student s
WHERE   s.stno IN
  (SELECT gr.student_number FROM grade_report gr WHERE
gr.grade
  = 'B');
```

However, that would give us only students who had made at least one B. To get to the 3 B's we could try this:

```
SELECT  s.sname
FROM    student s
WHERE   s.stno IN
  (SELECT gr.student_number, count(*)
   FROM grade_report gr
   WHERE gr.grade = 'B'
   GROUP BY gr.student_number
   HAVING count(*) > 2);
```

This won't work because the subquery cannot have two attributes unless the main query has two attributes — it has to have only *gr.student_number* to match *s.stno*. So, we might settle on this cumbersome query:

```
SELECT  s.sname
FROM    student s
WHERE   s.stno IN
  (SELECT student_number
   FROM (SELECT student_number,
     count(*)
   FROM grade_report gr
   WHERE gr.grade = 'B'
   GROUP BY student_number
     having count(*) > 2));
```

There are several ways to query the database with SQL. In this case, the correlated query may be the easiest to see and perhaps the most efficient.

From IN to EXISTS

A simple example of converting from IN to EXISTS, uncorrelated to correlated (or vice versa), would be to move the set test to the WHERE … IN of the uncorrelated query of the WHERE of the EXISTS.

Example:

- Uncorrelated:

```
SELECT *
FROM    student s
WHERE   s.stno IN
  (SELECT g.student_number
   FROM grade_report g
   WHERE grade = 'B');
```

- Correlated:

```
SELECT *
FROM    student s
WHERE EXISTS
  (SELECT g.student_number
   FROM grade_report g
   WHERE grade = 'B'
   AND s.stno = g.student_number);
```

This example may not always work, but often it will give you a pattern to move from one kind of query to the other and to test the efficiency of both kinds of queries.

NOT EXISTS

There are some situations in which the predicates EXISTS and NOT EXISTS are vital. The situation in which we ask a "for all" question has to be answered by "existence" (actually, the lack of it ["not existence"]). In logic, the statement, "find x for all y" is logically equivalent to "do not find x where there does not exists a y." In SQL, there is no "for all" predicate. Instead, SQL uses the idea of "for all" logic with NOT EXISTS. How do EXIST and NOT EXISTS work in SQL? Consider this query:

```
SELECT s.sname
FROM student s
WHERE EXISTS
  (SELECT 'X'
   FROM grade_report gr
   WHERE s.stno = gr.student_number
   AND gr.grade = 'C');
```

For this correlated query, "student names" are SELECTed when (1) the student is enrolled in a section (WHERE *s.stno* = *gr.student_number*), and (2) the same student has a C.

Both (1) and (2) must be TRUE for the student tuple to be SELECTed; SELECT ... EXISTS "says" SELECT ... WHERE TRUE, and the inner query is TRUE if any tuple is SELECTed. Now consider the following query with a NOT EXISTS in it:

```
SELECT s.sname
FROM student s
WHERE NOT EXISTS
  (SELECT 'X'
   FROM grade_report gr
   WHERE s.stno = gr.student_number
   AND gr.grade = 'C');
```

In this query, we are still SELECTing with the pattern: SELECT ... WHERE TRUE because all SELECTs work that way. But, the twist is that the subquery has to be FALSE to be SELECTed; if the subquery is FALSE, then NOT EXISTS is TRUE and the tuple is SELECTed.

Now, logic implies that if either (1) *s.stno* < > *gr.student_number*, or (2) *gr.grade* < > 'C', then the subquery "fails"; it is FALSE for that student tuple. Because the subquery is FALSE, the NOT EXISTS would return a TRUE for that tuple. Unfortunately, this logic is not quite what happens. Recall that we characterized the correlated query as:

```
LOOP1: For each tuple in student s DO
  LOOP2: For each tuple in grade_report
    DO
    IF (gr.student_number = s.stno) THEN
      IF (gr.grade = 'C') THEN TRUE
  END LOOP2;
    if TRUE, then student tuple is SELECTed
END LOOP1;
```

Note that LOOP2 is completed before the next student is tested. In other words, just because there exists a student number that is not equal will not cause the subquery to be false. Rather, the entire subquery table is parsed and the logic is more like this:

> For the case ... EXISTS WHERE s.stno = gr.student_number ..., is there a gr.grade = 'C'? *If*, when the student numbers are equal, no C can be found, *then* the subquery *fails*; it is FALSE for that student tuple. So with NOT EXISTS we will SELECT students who don't have Cs — student numbers equal in *grade_report* and *student*, but no C in *grade_report*. The point about "no C in *grade_report*" can only be answered TRUE by looking at all the rows in the inner query.

The Universal and Existential Qualifiers

"For all" or "for each" are the universal qualifiers. "There exists" is the existential qualifier. SQL does not have a "for all" predicate; however, logically, the following relationship exists:

```
For all x, WHERE P(x) is true
```

Is logically the same as:

```
There does not exist an x, WHERE P(x) is not true.
```

A "for all" type SQL query is less straightforward than simple EXISTS types. It involves a double-nested, correlated query using the NOT EXISTS predicate. To show this query, we will use a different database. Suppose we have a single-table database called *cap*. This table has names of students that have multiple foreign-language capabilities. We begin by looking at the table:

```
SELECT *
FROM cap
ORDER BY name;

NAME        LANGU
----------- ----------------
BRENDA      FRENCH
BRENDA      CHINESE
BRENDA      SPANISH
JOE         CHINESE
KENT        CHINESE
LUJACK      FRENCH
LUJACK      GERMAN
LUJACK      CHINESE
LUJACK      SPANISH
MARY JO     GERMAN
MARY JO     CHINESE
MARY JO     FRENCH
MELANIE     FRENCH
MELANIE     CHINESE
RICHARD     GERMAN
RICHARD     SPANISH
RICHARD     CHINESE
RICHARD     FRENCH
** 18 Rows Displayed ***
```

Suppose we would like to find out "What language is spoken by all students?" or "For each language, does it occur with all students?"

To see how to answer a question of this type, we will give the answer to the query and then dissect the result. The query to answer the question of "What language is spoken by all students?" looks like this:

```
SELECT name, langu
FROM cap x
WHERE NOT EXISTS
   (SELECT 'X'
    FROM cap y
    WHERE NOT EXISTS
    (SELECT 'X'
      FROM cap z
      WHERE x.langu =z.langu
      AND y.name=z.name));
```

As you will see, all of the "for all/for each" questions follow this double-nested, correlated NOT EXISTS pattern. We will show that the query works as demonstrated and then discuss how it works.

The Way the Query Works

For every cap row (x), we test the following. For every cap row (y), we find out if the cap (z) exists in all rows for every language. From the innermost query, if there is a result (a "match"), some row is SELECTed and then the innermost query is TRUE. Every time the innermost query is TRUE, the innermost query tells the middle query FALSE (because it contains "WHERE NOT EXISTS"). If the innermost query fails (i.e., it is FALSE), then the middle query sees TRUE, which is passed back to the outermost query as FALSE. To succeed (i.e., to SELECT a "language"), the query has to have this configuration:

- SELECT a row in cap (x) (outer query).

- For that row, begin SELECTing each row again in *cap* (y) (middle query).

- For each of the middle query rows, you want the inner query (cap z) to be TRUE for all cases of the middle query — remember that TRUE is translated to FALSE by the NOT EXISTS. As each inner query is satisfied (it is TRUE), it forces the middle query to continue looking for a match — to look at all cases and eventually conclude FALSE (evaluate to

FALSE overall). If the middle query is FALSE, the outer query sees TRUE because of its NOT EXISTS.

To make the middle query (y) find FALSE, all of the inner query (z) occurrences must be TRUE (i.e., the languages from the outer query must exist with all names from the middle one (y) in the inner one (z)). For an eventual "match," every row in the middle query for an outer query row must be FALSE (i.e., every row in the inner query is TRUE).

Example for the query (What language is spoken by all students?):

```
SELECT name, langu
FROM cap x
WHERE NOT EXISTS
  (SELECT 'X'
   FROM cap y
   WHERE NOT EXISTS
     (SELECT 'X'
      FROM cap z
      WHERE x.langu = z. langu
      AND y.name = z.name))
ORDER BY langu;
```

Suppose we had this table:

```
NAME   LANGUAGE
Joe    Spanish
Mary   Spanish
Mary   French
```

- The tuple <Joe, Spanish> is SELECTed by the outer query (x).

- The tuple <Joe, Spanish> is SELECTed by the middle query (y).

- The tuple <Joe, Spanish> is SELECTed by the inner query (z).

- The inner query is TRUE:

```
X.LANGUAGE = Spanish
Z.LANGUAGE = Spanish
Y.NAME = Joe
Z.NAME = Joe
```

- Because the inner query is TRUE, the NOT EXISTS of the middle query translates this to FALSE and continues with the next row in the middle query. The middle query SELECTs <Mary, Spanish> and the inner query begins again with <Joe, Spanish> seeing:

```
X.LANGUAGE = Spanish
Z.LANGUAGE = Spanish
Y.NAME = Mary
Z.NAME = Joe
```

This is FALSE, so the inner query SELECTs a second row <Mary, Spanish>:

```
X.LANGUAGE = Spanish
Z.LANGUAGE = Spanish
Y.NAME = Mary
Z.NAME = Mary
```

This is TRUE, so the inner query is TRUE. (Notice that the X.LANGUAGE has not changed yet; the outer query (X) is still on the first row.)

- Because the inner query is TRUE, the NOT EXISTS of the middle query translates this to FALSE and continues with the next row in the middle query. The middle query now SELECTs <Mary, French> and the inner query begins again with <Joe, Spanish> seeing:

```
X.LANGUAGE = Spanish
Z.LANGUAGE = Spanish
Y.NAME = Mary
Z.NAME = Joe
```

This is FALSE, so the inner query SELECTs a second row <Mary, Spanish>:

```
X.LANGUAGE = Spanish
Z.LANGUAGE = Spanish
Y.NAME = Mary
Z.NAME = Mary
```

This is TRUE, so the inner query is TRUE.

- Because the inner query is TRUE, the NOT EXISTS of the middle query again converts this TRUE to FALSE and wants to continue, but the middle query is out of tuples. This means that the middle query is FALSE.

- Because the middle query is FALSE, and because we are testing

```
"SELECT distinct name, language
FROM cap x
WHERE NOT EXISTS
   (SELECT 'X' FROM cap y ...",
```

the FALSE from the middle query is translated to TRUE for the outer query and the tuple <Joe,Spanish> is SELECTed for the result set. Note that "Spanish" occurs with both "Joe" and "Mary."

- The second row in the outer query will repeat the steps from above for <Mary, Spanish>. The value "Spanish" will be seen to occur with both "Joe" and "Mary" as <Mary, Spanish> is added to the result set.

- The third tuple in the outer query begins with <Mary, French>. The middle query SELECTs <Joe, Spanish> and the inner query SELECTs <Joe, Spanish>. Inner query sees:

```
X.LANGUAGE = French
Z.LANGUAGE = Spanish
Y.NAME = Joe
Z.NAME = Mary
```

This is FALSE, so the inner query SELECTs a second row, <Mary, Spanish>:

```
X.LANGUAGE = French
Z.LANGUAGE = Spanish
Y.NAME = Joe
Z.NAME = Mary
```

This is FALSE, so the inner query SELECTs a third row, <Mary, French>:

```
X.LANGUAGE = French
Z.LANGUAGE = French
Y.NAME = Joe
Z.NAME = Mary
```

This is also FALSE. The inner query fails. The inner query evaluates to FALSE, which causes the middle query to see TRUE because of the NOT EXISTS. Because the middle query sees TRUE, it is finished, evaluated to TRUE. And because the middle query evaluates to TRUE, the NOT EXISTS in the outer query changes this to FALSE and "X.LANGUAGE = French" fails. It fails because X.LANGUAGE = French did not occur with all values of NAME.

The tip-off of what a query of this kind means can be found in the inner query where the outer query is tested. In the above, you will find a phrase that says, WHERE x.langu = z. langu … . The x.langu is where the query is testing for all names to occur with a given language. The query is asking, "What language is spoken by all students?" Put another way, "What language occurs *for all* names?"

Note that the above query is completely different from the following one, which asks, "Which students speak all languages?":

```
SELECT distinct name, langu
FROM cap x
WHERE NOT EXISTS
  (SELECT 'X'
   FROM cap y
   WHERE NOT EXISTS
     (SELECT 'X'
      FROM cap z
    WHERE y.langu = z.langu
      AND x.name = z.name))
ORDER BY langu;
```

which produces the following response:

```
NAME        LANGU
----------  ----------
MARY        FRENCH
MARY        SPANISH
2 Rows Displayed ***
```

Here, note that the inner query contains x.name, which means the question was "Which names occur *for all* languages?"; or put another way, "Which students speak all languages?". The "all" goes with languages. In general, then, if a table T has attributes (A, B) and you ask the question, "Is there a value of B that occurs for all A?", the query will be:

```
SELECT DISTINCT A,B
FROM T X
WHERE NOT EXISTS
  (SELECT 'X'
   FROM T Y
   WHERE NOT EXISTS
     (SELECT 'X'
      FROM T Z
    WHERE X.B = Z.B
      AND Y.A = Z.A) ;
[ORDER BY is optional]
```

Summary

This chapter has explored the use of correlated queries. Correlated queries are often an alternative to uncorrelated queries or joins. Which query is most efficient depends on many factors, for example, the engine optimizer, table size, indexing. Uncorrelated queries can be thought of as executing first, whereas correlated queries emulate a DO-loop structure. Of particular interest in this chapter is the exploration of the "for all" query. The "for all" query in SQL is implemented with a double-nested, correlated NOT EXISTS structure. While this structure looks foreboding, some examples and guidance are provided to understand how to write and interpret the "for all" question.

Note that correlated subqueries are not always a bad thing. As Donald K. Burleson points out below, there are cases where a correlated subquery will work better than a non-correlated subquery (but an outer join works best of all):

In this example, we select all books that do not have any sales. Note that this is a non-correlated sub-query, but it could be re-written in several ways.

```
select
   book_key
from
   book
where
   book_key NOT IN (select book_key from sales);
```

There are serious problems with subqueries that may return NULL values. It is a good idea to discourage the use of the NOT IN clause (which invokes a sub-query) and to prefer NOT EXISTS (which invokes a correlated sub-query), since the query returns no rows if any rows returned by the sub-query contain null values.

```
select
   book_key
from
   book
where
   NOT EXISTS (select book_key from sales);
```

Subqueries can often be re-written to use a standard outer join, resulting in faster performance. As we may know, an outer join uses the plus sign (+) operator to tell the database to return all non-matching rows with NULL values. Hence we combine the outer join with a NULL test in the WHERE clause to reproduce the result set without using a sub-query.

```
select
   b.book_key
from
   book  b,
   sales s
where
   b.book_key = s.book_key(+)
and
   s.book_key IS NULL;
```

This execution plan will also be faster by eliminating the sub-query.

Joins

Oracle's Joins - Richard Earp and Sikha Bagui

There is often a need to select data from columns from more than one table. A join combines columns and data from two or more tables (and in some cases, of one table with itself). The tables are listed in a from clause of a select statement, and a join condition between the two tables is specified in a where clause.

For example, suppose we create a table called Emp with an employee number (Empno) and a job code (JobCode) as follows:

```
Emp
Empno JobCode
----- -------
  101      cp
  102      ac
  103      de
```

And then we create a second table called Job, which contains the job code (JobC) and a job title (JobTitle):

```
Job
JobC     JobTitle
----     ----------
  de       dentist
  cp     programmer
  ac     accountant
  do        doctor
```

We can use the following join command:

```
SELECT *
FROM job, emp
WHERE job.jobc = emp.jobcode;
```

This will display those resultant tuples that have jobc in Job equal to jobcode in Emp, as follows:

```
Empno | JobCode | JobC |    JobTitle
--------------------------------------
  102 |      ac |   ac | accountant
  101 |      cp |   cp | programmer
  103 |      de |   de |    dentist
```

Tuples from Job without a matching tuple in Emp are eliminated from the JOIN result. Tuples with nulls in the join attributes are also eliminated.

Cartesian Product

Joining two tables together without using a where clause will produce a Cartesian product. A Cartesian product for the above example would be:

```
SELECT *
FROM job, emp;
```

The above command says to combine all of the data in both tables and make a new table. The result would be:

```
Empno   JobCode   JobC    JobTitle
-------------------------------------
  101      cp       de      dentist
  102      ac       de      dentist
  103      de       de      dentist
  101      cp       cp     programmer
  102      ac       cp     programmer
  203      de       cp     programmer
  101      cp       ac     accountant
  102      ac       ac     accountant
  103      de       ac     accountant
  101      cp       do      doctor
  102      ac       do      doctor
  103      de       do      doctor
```

Therefore, the result of a Cartesian join will be a relation say Q, which will have n*m attributes (where n is the number of tuples from the first relation, and m is the number of tuples from the second relation). In our example above, there is a result of 12 tuples (3·4) in the resulting set, with all possible combinations of tuples from Emp and Job. A Cartesian product can be called a JOIN with no join condition.

Oftentimes, the Cartesian product also gives data that has little meaning, and is usually a result of the user having forgotten to use an appropriate where clause in the select statement.

Equi-joins

The most common JOIN involves join conditions with equality comparisons. Such a join, where the comparison operator is '=', is called an equi-join (as in the example shown below):

```
SELECT *
FROM job, emp
WHERE job.jobc = emp.jobcode;
```

Examining the two resulting tables from above, one can see that the equi-join is actually a Cartesian product followed by a relational algebra equality selection and, in fact, the equi-join is defined in relational algebra as a Cartesian product followed by a relational algebra select (not to be confused with an SQL select). Tables can also be joined using other relational operators such as >, >=, <, <=, and <>.

Natural Join

The term "natural join" in relational algebra refers to an equi-join without the duplicate column and with the obvious join condition. If one spoke of the natural join on Emp and Job, it would produce:

```
Empno   JobCode     JobTitle
  102        ac   accountant
  101        cp   programmer
  103        de      dentist
```

The implied join condition is the equality of job code in the two tables.

Unfortunately, some authors also use the term "natural join" to mean a join between a table with a foreign key and the table that contains the referenced primary key. Because of this confusion and ambiguity, we will not refer to the natural join again in this chapter.

Joining More Than One Table

Multiple tables can be joined using join conditions. For example, if we create another table as follows:

```
EmpN
EmpName         Empno
John Smith      103
Sally Cox       101
George Pilcher  102
```

And then join the three tables as follows:

```
SELECT Jobc, JobTitle, Empno, EmpName
FROM job, emp, empn
WHERE job.jobc=emp.jobcode
AND emp.empno=empn.empno;
```

The result of the join will be:

```
Jobc  JobTitle     Empno  EmpName
------------------------------------
  ac  accountant    102   George Pilcher
  cp  programmer    101   Sally Cox
  de  dentist       103   John Smith
```

This join is a pairwise operation. This "triple join" is actually either (EmpN join Emp) join Job, or EmpN join (Emp join Job). The choice of how the join is executed is usually made by the database's optimizer.

Outer Joins

In an equi-join, tuples without matching tuples values are eliminated from the JOIN result. For example, in the following join example, we have lost the information on the 'doctor' from the Job table because no employee is a doctor.

```
SELECT *
FROM job, emp
WHERE job.jobc = emp.jobcode;


Empno   JobCode   JobC   JobTitle
-------------------------------
  102       ac      ac   accountant
  101       cp      cp   programmer
  103       de      de   dentist
```

In some cases, it may be desirable to include rows from one table that have no matching rows in the other table. Outer joins are used when we want to keep all the tuples from the first relation, Emp, or all the tuples from the second relation, Job, whether or not they have matching tuples in the other relation. An outer join where we want to keep all the tuples from the first relation (or left relation) is called a left outer join . An outer join where we want to keep all the tuples from the second relation (or right relation) is called the right outer join. The term full outer join is used to designate the union of the left and right outer joins.

In Oracle, the (+) makes the join an outer join. Also, in Oracle, the standard left and right designations are not used. Instead, Oracle uses the terms "driving table" and "driven table" to designate the outer join. In the expression

```
WHERE Job.Jobc = Emp.Jobcode(+)
```

Job is the driving table, and Emp is the driven table. Hence, in Oracle, what is left or right is irrelevant.

```
A right outer join
SELECT *
FROM Emp, Job
WHERE Emp.JobCode(+) = Job.Jobc;
```

```
Empno   JobCode   JobC   JobTitle
-------------------------------
  102       ac      ac    accountant
  101       cp      cp    programmer
  103       de      de    dentist
                    do    doctor
```

This lists all the job codes available in the table Job, even if there are no employees using those codes in Emp yet. Here, Job is the driving table.

```
A left outer join
SELECT *
FROM Emp, Job
WHERE Emp.JobCode=Job.Jobc(+);
```

```
Empno   JobCode   JobC   JobTitle
-------------------------------
  102       ac      ac    accountant
  101       cp      cp    programmer
  103       de      de    dentist
```

This table shows all the Empno and JobCodes of the employees (from the Emp table), even if there is no corresponding JobCode or JobTitle in the Job table. Here Emp, is the driving table.

We will now look at some examples of "extended outer joins."

Outer Join with an AND

If we add an AND condition in the where clause, we produce this result:

```
SELECT *
FROM Emp, Job
WHERE Emp.JobCode=Job.Jobc(+)
AND Job.Jobc='cp';
```

```
Empno   JobCode   JobC   JobTitle
---------------------------------
  102        ac
  101        cp      cp    programmer
  103        de
```

This table purports to show all the Empno and JobCodes of the employees (from the Emp table), even if there is no corresponding JobCode or Job- Title in the Job table and where the JobCode from the Job table is 'cp'. This result turns out to be the same as an ordinary join. The effect of the outer join in the WHERE clause is not apparent because no outer join has been included in the AND clause. To correct this, when using outer joins, the (+) must also be placed in the *other* conditions, as shown below:

```
Outer join in other conditions
SELECT *
FROM Emp, Job
WHERE Emp.JobCode=Job.Jobc(+)
AND Job.Jobc(+)='cp';
```

```
Empno   JobCode   JobC   JobTitle
---------------------------------
  102        ac
  101        cp      cp    programmer
  103        de
```

This table shows all the Empno and JobCodes of the employees (from the Emp table), even if there is no corresponding JobCode or JobTitle in the Job table, and includes all the Empnos and Job-Codes from the Emp table including the Empno with a JobCode of 'cp'. But why did we get the other two rows with nulls? Because of the outer join in

```
AND Job.Jobc(+)='cp'.
```

This tells Oracle to include in the answer all rows where the outer join produces a 'cp' for Job.Jobc(+). No row matches Emp.JobCode= 'ac', so we get a null for that row because of the outer join. Also, no row matches Emp.JobCode='de', so we get a null row for that. There is however, a match for Emp.JobCode='cp', so that row prints < 101, cp, cp, programmer> .

Outer Joins and Nulls

Suppose we test for nulls in the outer join result table:

```
SELECT *
FROM Emp, Job
WHERE Emp.JobCode=Job.Jobc(+)
AND Job.Jobc(+) is null;
```

```
Empno   JobCode   JobC   JobTitle
------------------------------------
 102       ac
 101       cp
 103       de
```

This result may be explained as follows. First, by putting a (+) on the Job.Jobc condition, we are telling Oracle to create a row for every Emp row, match or not. Then, by including

```
AND Job.Jobc(+) is null;
```

we are telling Oracle to include in the answer the rows where the outer join produces a null for Job.Jobc(+). The thing to remember is that during the process of creating an outer join, some rows match some values of JobCode, but some do not; hence, the "is null" condition is true for those cases.

Outer Join Not Included in the Null Condition

If we do not include a (+) on the null condition:

```
SELECT *
FROM Emp, Job
WHERE Emp.JobCode=Job.Jobc(+)
AND Job.Jobc is null;

no rows selected
```

Here, we are telling Oracle to create the outer join first, and then report only those rows where there is a null for Jobc in Job. Because no rows have been selected, it shows that all employees have a matching job code.

```
SELECT *
FROM Emp, Job
WHERE Emp.JobCode=Job.Jobc(+)
AND (Job.Jobc is null or Job.Jobc = 'ac');

Empno   JobCode   JobC   JobTitle
------------------------------
  102      ac      ac    accountant
```

Again, this becomes a simple equi-join because the (+) was not included in the

```
AND (Job.Jobc is null or Job.Jobc = 'ac');.
```

Outer Join with OR and IN

Changing the previous query to test the outer join condition, we might try:

```
SELECT *
FROM Emp, Job
WHERE Emp.JobCode=Job.Jobc(+)
AND (Job.Jobc(+) is null or Job.Jobc(+) = 'ac');
AND (Job.Jobc(+) is null or Job.Jobc(+) = 'ac');

                       *
ERROR at line 4: outer join operator (+) not
  allowed in operand of OR or IN
```

As shown above, an outer join is not allowed in connection with OR and IN.

Inline Views and Outer Joins

If tables would be appropriate for an outer-join query, creating an inline view as a table (with an alias — we used exp as our table alias) may be the best way to handle outer joins. For example:

```
SELECT * FROM
(SELECT *
FROM Emp, Job
WHERE Emp.Jobcode=Job.jobc(+)) exp
WHERE exp.jobc='cp' or exp.jobc='ac';
```

The output would be:

```
Empno  JobCode  JobC  JobTitle
-------------------------------
  102       ac    ac  accountant
  101       cp    cp  programmer
```

Using the inline view eliminates the problem of guessing the result of added conditions because once the outer join is created, it then behaves like an ordinary table when placed in the view.

Symmetric Outer Joins

An outer join cannot be symmetric. This means that two tables may not be outer joined to each other [the (+) cannot be on both sides of the condition at the same time] in Oracle. For example:

```
SELECT *
FROM job, emp
WHERE job.jobc(+)=emp.jobcode(+);
WHERE job.jobc(+)=emp.jobcode(+);
                   *
ERROR at line 3: a predicate may reference only
  one outer-joined table
```

In this example, there is no driving table and, hence, Oracle disallows the double outer join. A way to work around this problem would be to UNION the left and right outer joins, which would produce the symmetric join.

Chaining Outer Joins

As with ordinary joins, several levels of an outer join are possible. If a table Z is outer joined to a table Y, and then the outer join result is outer joined to a table X, this is known as *chaining* on the outer join.

Below is an example of chaining of an outer join — the table Job is outer joined to Emp, which can then be thought of as being outer joined to EmpN:

```
SELECT *
FROM job, emp, empn
WHERE job.jobc(+)=emp.jobcode
AND emp.empno(+)=empn.empno;
```

And the result would be:

Jobc	JobTitle	Empno	JobCode	EmpName	Empno
ac	accountant	102	ac	George Pilcher	102
cp	programmer	101	cp	Sally Cox	101
De	dentist	103	de	John Smith	103

The important thing to note here is that the outer join has to be carried all the way through.

A table cannot be outer joined to more than one table at the same time as in:

```
SELECT *
FROM job, emp, empn
WHERE job.jobc=emp.jobcode(+)
AND emp.empno(+)=empn.empno;
FROM job, emp, empn


                      *
ERROR at line 2: a table may be outer joined
   to at most one other table
```

Performance of Outer Joins

Outer joins are inherently not any different from inner joins. If only one of the tables being used in an outer join has an index, the optimizer usually chooses the table without the index as the driving table. If the outer join forces the indexed table to be the driving table [by including the (+) on the other table] and if this is the only index, the index cannot be used. If both tables have indexes on the join column, the outer join can be used to force which table should be the driving table [Note: The driving table would be the table without the (+)].

Self Join

A self-join is where a table is joined to itself. In this case, the query "sees" two identical copies of the table and table aliases must be used to distinguish between the two tables. An example of a self-join would be if we included a supervisor's social security number (superssn) and employee's social security number (ssn) in our EmpN table and there exists in our table some employees who supervise other employees. The table would look like:

```
EmpN
EmpName         EmpNo   SuperSSN      SSN
-------------------------------------------
John Smith       103   1234090992
Sally Cox        101   1234090992   1234090991
George Pilcher   102   1234090991   1234090995
```

From this table, we can see that John Smith is Sally Cox's supervisor, Sally Cox is George Pilcher's supervisor, and John Smith has no supervisor. A listing of employees and their supervisors could be shown by using a self-join of this table as follows:

```
SELECT e.empname employee_name, s.empname
supervisor_name
FROM empn e, empn s
WHERE e.superssn=s.ssn;


EMPLOYEE NAME    SUPERVISOR NAME
------------------------------
George Pilcher   Sally Cox
Sally Cox        John Smith
```

An outer join can also be included in a self-join. For example, we could show all employees whether or not they have a supervisor.

```
SELECT e.empname employee_name, s.empname
supervisor_name
FROM empn e, empn s
WHERE e.superssn=s.ssn(+);


EMPLOYEE NAME    SUPERVISOR NAME
------------------------------
John Smith
George Pilcher   Sally Cox
Sally Cox        John Smith
```

Joining Views

Views are joined just as tables are joined. The views to be joined would be listed in the from clause, and the relationships in the where clause.

Joining More than Two Tables

When more than two tables are being joined, the optimizer treats the query as a set of binary joins. This means that if a query has to join three tables, the optimizer will first join two of the three tables, then join this result to the third table.

If the three tables to be joined are of different sizes, the order in which the joins are performed may affect the efficiency of the query. If the size of the resulting set from the first join is large, then many rows will have to be processed by the second join. So, it may be advisable to join the two smallest tables first, and then join this result to the larger table. The *Explain Plan* command shows how to interpret the order of the joins. The *Explain Plan* output is most easily obtained using SET AUTOTRACE ON, but be advised that the *Explain Plan* table has to be created before SET AUTOTRACE ON is executed. The *Explain Plan* table is best created by a utility supplied by Oracle called UTLXPLAN.SQL.

Tuning Issues and Processing of Joins

Oracle has three methods for processing joins: MERGE JOIN, NESTED LOOP, and HASH JOIN. Depending on the nature of the application and queries, one may sometimes want to force the optimizer to use a method different from its first choice by the optimizer of join methods. Below is an explanation of the different join operations available, and a summary of when each may be most useful.

Merge Join

In a MERGE JOIN operation, the tables to be joined are processed separately, sorted, and then merged (joined). MERGE JOIN operations are commonly used when there are no indexes available. Let us use the following join to further understand the MERGE JOIN:

```
SELECT /*+ ORDERED USE_MERGE */ *
FROM emp, job
WHERE emp.jobcode = job.jobc;
```

Output will be:

```
Empno  JobCode  JobC  JobTitle
-------------------------------
  102      ac     ac  accountant
  101      cp     cp  programmer
  103      de     de  dentist


Execution Plan
0   SELECT STATEMENT Optimizer=CHOOSE
1 0 MERGE JOIN
2 1 SORT (JOIN)
3 2 TABLE ACCESS (FULL) OF 'JOB'
4 1 SORT (JOIN)
```

Note: The /*+ ORDERED USE_MERGE */ after the SELECT statement is called a "hint." A hint is used to force a join method to be used by the optimizer. Here the optimizer is being forced to use a SORT MERGE JOIN.

In the above query, Job and Emp were joined, but no indexes were used. Because in a MERGE JOIN operation each table is preprocessed separately before being joined, Job and Emp were first read individually by a TABLE ACCESS FULL operation, and then the set of rows returned from the table scan of the Job table was sorted by a SORT JOIN operation. Then a set of rows was returned from the table scan of Emp, and sorted by a second SORT JOIN operation. Data from the two SORT JOIN operations was then merged by a MERGE JOIN operation. Because the MERGE JOIN operation has to wait for two separate SORT JOIN operations, it typically performs poorly for online users. MERGE JOIN operations are efficient when tables are of equal size; but as table sizes increase, the time required for the sorts to be completed increases dramatically.

Nested Loops

If an index is available for the join conditions, then Oracle may perform a NESTED LOOPS join. NESTED LOOPS join two tables by retrieving data from the first table, and then for each record retrieved, an access is performed on the second table (access by an index of the second table). For example, we will first create an index of Emp:

```
ALTER TABLE Emp
ADD CONSTRAINT Emps_ndx
PRIMARY KEY (Empno);
Table altered.
```

Then we will perform the following NESTED LOOPS operation:

```
SELECT /*+ ORDERED USE_NL */*
FROM emp,job
WHERE emp.jobcode=job.jobc;
```

Output will be:

```
Empno   JobCode   JobC   JobTitle
---------------------------------
  102      ac       ac    accountant
  101      cp       cp    programmer
  103      de       de    dentist


Execution Plan
0    SELECT STATEMENT Optimizer=CHOOSE
1  0 NESTED LOOPS
2  1 TABLE ACCESS (FULL) OF 'JOB'
3  1 TABLE ACCESS (BY ROWID) OF 'EMP'
4  3 INDEX (UNIQUE SCAN) OF 'EMPS_NDX'
```

Note: The /*+ ORDERED USE_NL*/ hint is forcing the optimizer to use the NESTED LOOPS operation.

In our example, since an index has been created for the Emp table, and there is no index available for the Job table, the Job table will be used as the driving table for the query. A TABLE ACCESS FULL operation will select all of the records of the Job table, and for each record retrieved, the Emp table will be checked to determine if it contains an entry for the value of the current record from the Job table. If a match is found, then the RowID for the matching Emp row will be retrieved from the index.

Unlike the Merge Join operation, the NESTED LOOPS operation does not wait for the whole set of records to be selected before returning records to successive operations. NESTED LOOPS return records as soon as they are found, providing the first matching rows quickly to users; hence, NESTED LOOPS are more useful for online users. In NESTED LOOPS joins, the order in which the tables are joined is critical. A NESTED LOOPS join is most useful if the smaller table is used as the driving table, and the larger table is accessed by an index. If multiple indexes are available, then Oracle will select a driving table for the query, unless one is specifically mentioned in the hint.

Hash Joins

In a HASH JOIN, each table is first read into main memory separately by a TABLE ACCESS FULL operation, and then a hashing function is used to compare the second table to the first table. The rows that result in matches are then returned to the user. HASH JOINS use memory (because the two tables that are being compared are kept in the memory), so applications that make extensive use of HASH JOINS may need to increase the amount of memory available in the database's System Global Area (specified in the *init.ora* parameters). If tables are small and can be scanned quickly, then hash joins may be appropriate for queries executed by an online user. The order of execution for the hash join is:

```
SELECT /*+ ORDERED USE_HASH */*
FROM emp,job
WHERE emp.jobcode=job.jobc;
```

Output will be:

```
Empno   JobCode   JobC   JobTitle
--------------------------------
  102       ac      ac   accountant
  101       cp      cp   programmer
  103       de      de   dentist


Execution Plan
0   SELECT STATEMENT Optimizer=CHOOSE
1 0 HASH JOIN
2 1 TABLE ACCESS (FULL) OF 'JOB'
3 1 TABLE ACCESS (FULL) OF 'EMP'
```

Note: The /*+ ORDERED USE_HASH*/ is hinting to the optimizer to use the HASH JOIN operation. Once a HASH JOIN is done, HASH JOIN will be performed by optimizer unless disabled with the initialization parameter *hash_join_enabled*=FALSE.

Summary

This chapter has introduced the outer join — an extension of the normal equi-join of two tables. In constructing outer joins, there are options that allow a programmer to display part or all of the rows in one table, whether or not there are matching rows in the other table. Oracle uses the term "driving table" to designate the table that will be wholly represented in the outer join, whereas the SQL standard uses the terms "left" and "right outer joins." (Driving table is actually more descriptive, useful, and less ambiguous than "left" and "right.") Oracle disallows full outer joins (symmetric outer joins), but such a join can be had using a UNION workaround.

Outer joins seem to act strangely when other constraints are placed on the join in the WHERE clause. Although the "strange" behavior is explainable, the best advice might be to use the outer join in an inline (or other) view so that the outer join product may be handled in a more normal way without worrying about added conditions and syntax restrictions on the "ordinary" outer join.

Finally, a discussion of join tactics is presented. Merge-joins, nested-loops joins, and hashed joins are illustrated to show that Oracle (as would other database systems) chooses an internal method to return results from joins. The point in this chapter is that one can force which of the tables is the driving table in both inner (normal equi-joins) and outer joins and that outer joins, are not necessarily faster or slower than ordinary equijoins.

> Beware of COST-based joins in Oracle7. Beware of a known problem with Oracle cost-based optimizer in n-way joins in Oracle7. Whenever three or more tables are joined using first_rows or all_rows, Oracle will perform a full-table scan against one of the tables, even if indexes are available for alleviate the full table scan. Hence, carefully check all n-way joins in Oracle7 and ensure that the execution plan only does a full-table scan on very small tables. Otherwise, change the execution plan with a /+* rule */ hint.

Now that we've covered how the optimizer works, let's look at what YOU can control – what your SQL looks like. Donald K. Burleson, noted SQL Tuning expert has provided in-depth insight into tips on tuning SQL:

Using Hash Joins

As noted above, in the recent releases of Oracle, hash joins often outperform the other join types.

Other tips on using hash joins have been provided by Oracle Tuning expert Don Burleson:

Increasing Hash Joins – Donald K. Burleson

To force hash joins you must perform two steps. It may not be enough to increase the *hash_area_size* if the CBO is stubborn, and usually you must force the hash join with a hint.

Step 1 - Increase the hash_area_size maximum

```
alter session set workarea_size_policy=manual;
alter session set hash_area_size=1048576000;
```

Step 2 - Add a use_hash hint to the SQL

```
select /*+ use_hash(a, b)*/
from . . .
```

Whenever considering join types, you must also consider how Oracle is sorting, as Don Burleson describes:

Increasing RAM sorting

In Oracle9i, the sorting default is that no single task may consume more than 5% of the *pga_aggregate_target* region before the sort pages-out to the TEMP tablespace for a disk sort. For parallel sorts, the limit is 30% of the PGA aggregate, regardless of the number of parallel processes.

You can override the default sorting behavior in two ways:

Option 1 - Manual override:

```
alter session set workarea_size_policy=manual;
alter session set sort_area_size=1048576000;
```

Option 2 - Bounce with special hidden parameter:

In this example, we increase the default amount of RAM available to sort operations from 5% to about 50%:

```
pga_aggregate_target=10g_smm_max_size=4000000;
```

Not that the number for *_smm_max_size* is expressed in k-bytes, so this value is about 4.5 gigabytes.

Remember, hidden parameters are totally unsupported, so use this technique at your own risk.

Conclusion

This chapter provided an overview of the SQL execution internals. Understanding how and when usage of hints is relevant, as well as the different join types and correlated subqueries are important when diagnosing a poorly performing system.

Use of STATSPACK is key when trying to see what is going on in a database. A STATSPACK of a healthy database is a good thing to keep around, so when things begin to go awry, you have something to go back and compare against. Reviewing the STATSPACK output to see what your Top 5 waits are, and your largest SQL resource utilizers is the first step in trying to troubleshoot a system with performance issues.

SQL Extensions for Performance

Analytic Functions

Oracle has greatly enhanced their SQL capabilities such that there are many new functions that return complex data quickly. Formerly, coding a simple query to use a ranking of items was quite complex. Now, if you delve into these capabilities, things are much easier. Jonathon Lewis, world-renowned Oracle expert, provides a great introduction into these functions in the following excerpt:

Analytic Functions

In Oracle version 8.1.6, Oracle Corp. introduced a whole new layer of functionality to its implementation of SQL: the analytic functions. This article provides a brief introduction to these functions, describing their use, and then demonstrating the benefit in clarity and brevity of the code that they offer. This article is based on material previously presented to the U.K. Oracle User Group at their annual conference in December 2000.

The Way Things Were

Assume you have a data warehouse describing the sales for a chain of shops selling computer games. One of your main data tables, describing sales by location and title sold per week, may look something like the following:

```
create table game_sale (
    title varchar2(30),
    store varchar2(30),
```

```
   sales number(10,2),
   week_ending date
);
```

How would you deal with the requirement for an end-user report showing the two best-selling games in each store this week? There are two traditional approaches: procedural and nonprocedural.

In the procedural case, we simply write a piece of SQL that sorts the data for a given week by store and period, then use a 3GL to walk through it one row at a time, making sure we print only the first two rows for each store. Consider, for example, this very simple PL/SQL solution that produces output which is correct but perhaps not entirely aesthetically satisfactory:

```
declare
    cursor c1 is
        select store, title, sales
        from game_sale
        where week_ending = '21-Jan-2001'
        order by store, sales desc
    ;
    m_last_row c1%rowtype;
    m_out_ct number := 0;

begin
for r1 in c1 loop
    if (m_last_row.store != r1.store) then
        m_out_ct := 0;
        dbms_output.new_line;
    end if;

    if m_out_ct != 2 then
        dbms_output.put_line (
            r1.store || ' - ' ||
            r1.title || ' - ' || r1.sales
        );
        m_out_ct := m_out_ct + 1;
    end if;
    m_last_row := r1;
end loop;
end;
/
Glasgow - Crash Simulator - 1934
```

```
Glasgow - Manic the Gerbil - 913

London - Dome - 2167
London - Portal Combat - 1824

PL/SQL procedure successfully completed.
```

The following nonprocedural solution is rather more compact. On the plus side, if we are using SQL*Plus, it does allow us to produce a much tidier output without resorting to more fiddly little bits of code. On the minus side, the style of thinking required to produce this code is not really "natural;" thus, it is not immediately obvious that the SQL is appropriate to the requirement. More significantly, perhaps, this second solution requires Oracle to perform a correlated subquery for each row we examine to check how many items sold more than the current item in the current store this week — this could be a very resource-intensive query.

```
select      store, title, sales
from        game_sale gs1
where       week_ending = '21-Jan-2001'
and         2 > (
    select      count(*)
    from        game_sale gs2
    where       gs2.week_ending =
                gs1.week_ending
    and         gs2.store = gs1.store
    and         gs2.sales > gs1.sales
    )
order by
    store, sales desc;

STORE       TITLE               SALES
----------  ------------------  ---------
Glasgow     Crash Simulator      1934
            Manic the Gerbil      913

London      Dome                 2167
            Portal Combat        1824
```

In fact, both solutions also suffer from logical defects, partly because the requirement was not specified with sufficient precision, but also because the code in both cases is too simplistic.

Look at the PL/SQL code and ask yourself what would happen if Glasgow happened to sell 913 copies of Dome — it wouldn't be reported although it appears to qualify for second place. (In fact, two users running the same query with a different set of *init.ora* parameters might get different answers, depending solely on a minor variation in their *init.ora* parameters such as *sort_area_size*). Anyway, if there is a draw for second place, should both items be reported or should neither item be reported? The requirement was for the two best-selling games — we have no indication of how we should handle draws which result in more than two candidate titles.

The SQL option suffers from similar problems. Take the same scenario where Dome ties with Manic in Glasgow. As it stands, the SQL solution will automatically return three lines for Glasgow. At least there is no risk of the results changing randomly and you can choose to control the result by changing the inequalities in the SQL, substituting '>' for '>=', but you do need to think very carefully about how you are supposed to handle tied places.

One final point to consider with these solutions is the next, simple refinement of the requirement. The top two sales in London total 3991, whereas the top two sales in Glasgow total 2847; surely the marketing director will want to see the stores sorted in descending order by volume of sales. How do you do that in PL/SQL or SQL?

An Analytic Solution

The analytic functions offer a cleaner and simpler solution at the SQL level. We can solve (one version of) our requirement using the *rank()* function. This function behaves like all the other analytic functions: after any initial selection, manipulation and grouping of the data, but before applying an order by clause, it will:

- Break the data into partitions (nothing to do with partitioned tables or partition views)

- Optionally sort the data within each partition for further processing

- Optionally define "windows" within each partition (not shown in this example)

- Add value to the output based on the partitions and windows.

All this extra processing is cued by the *over()* clause as follows:

```
select      store, title, sales, in_store_rank
            ranked
from (
select
store, title, sales,
            rank()over (
                partition by store
                order by sales desc
            ) as in_store_rank
    from game_sale
where week_ending = '21-Jan-2001'
    )
where in_store_rank <= 2
order by
store, in_store_rank;


STORE    TITLE               SALES   IN_STORE_RANK
-------  ----------------    ------- ---------
Glasgow  Crash Simulator      1934       1
         Manic the Gerbil      913       2

London   Dome                 2167       1
         Portal Combat        1824       2
```

You will note that I have used an in-line view as part of the query. There are two reasons for this. First, you cannot use an analytic function in a where clause but we want to test the value of the generated rank, so we have wrapped our SQL in a pair of parentheses and made it an in-line view. The second reason is for clarity: if you use a complex SQL statement to generate the basic solution, it is convenient to improve clarity by pushing it into an in-line view before applying the analytic functions to something that now looks like a simple table. I frequently use in-line views when applying analytic views. (Be warned, however, that I have found a few exotic cases in which this causes dramatic changes to execution paths; in particular, when mixing partitioned tables with partition views. The current status of this problem is "possibly a bug.")

In examining the highlighted (i.e., bold faced) code that demonstrates the use of the *rank()* function, we see the partition clause that breaks the data set into separate sections, each section is then sorted in descending order by the sales column. When this phase of sorting is complete, Oracle applies a ranking to the intermediate data and the job is nearly finished. Because we want to report only the top two rows for each store (partition), we wrap the query into an in-line view, and restrict our selection to those rows in which the generated rank is less than or equal to 2. Note that we then sort the final result set; it is likely, but not guaranteed, that the data for this example would coincidently appear in the correct order, but it is important to remember that any application of analytic functions takes place before, and independently of, the final order by clause. Do not rely on side-effects; always include an explicit closing order by if you want your output sorted.

In case you are wondering about tied places, the *rank()*function leaves gaps. If sales of Dome in the Glasgow store had matched those of Manic, then both games would have been ranked 2, and the next placed game would have been ranked 4, with no game in third place. There is an alternative ranking function, *dense_rank()*

that would give the results 1,2,2,3,4…, but there is no function for generating the ordering 1,3,3,4,5….

We can be a lot more fanciful than this simple example, however. We note that London clearly sells more games than Glasgow. Perhaps we would like to list the store not alphabetically, but by total sales. We can do this by introducing another style of analytic function, partitioning the data again by store, and sorting on the result of that function.

```
select store, title, sales
from (
    select
        store, title, sales,
        rank()over (
            partition by store
            order by sales desc
        ) as in_store_rank,
        sum(sales) over (
            partition by store
        ) as store_totals
    from game_sale
    where week_ending = '21-Jan-2001'
)
where
    in_store_rank <= 2
order by
    store_totals desc, in_store_rank;
```

In the highlighted (bold faced) code this time, we have taken the familiar *sum()* function, and used it in its new analytic form, demonstrating that analytic functions can use existing columns as parameters and are not restricted to generating new values as the parameterless *rank()*function does. In this case, we only have a *partition* clause, which splits the data by *store* again and thereby sums the *sales* by *store* without the need for the "traditional" *group by* clause. In this way, we can get "raw data" and summaries on the same line of a report without having to run two versions of the query or joining a table to itself. By the way, the example above sorts the store by total sold in each store; it is left as useful and interesting exercise to sort the stores by the totals of just the games listed in the report.

The savings in processing can be significant, but do remember that each time we do any partitioning we are introducing more work, typically sorting. However, the *v$sysstat* and *v$sesstat* views do not appear to report in all the work that Oracle is doing, so be a little cautious as you investigate the possibilities on offer from analytic functions.

There are numerous functions, old and new, that can be used in this analytic way. The existing functions, like *sum()* above are *count()*, *avg()*, *min()*, *max()*, *variance()*, and *stddev()*. Apart from the *rank()* function introduced above, we have the new *dense_rank()*, *percent_rank()*, and *row_number()*. There are also a number of new statistical functions, such as *corr()*, *var_pop()*, *var_samp()*, *covar_pop()*, *covar_samp()*, *stddev_pop()*, *stddev_samp()*, and an entire host of regression functions. There are also the *cume_dist()* and *ntile()* functions (the latter allowing data to be split into percentiles, quartiles, etc.). Finally, under the heading of "miscellaneous but useful" we have the functions *first_value()*, *last_value()*, *ratio_to_report()*, *lead()*, and *lag()*.

Common Requirements

Take a look at a couple of the new functions and see how they answer some of the most commonly asked questions about SQL. How do I report the difference between one row and the next? How do I report a figure as the percentage of the total for a report? How do I make one column report a running total of the figures in another column?

First, the *lead()* function can used to return the data from the following row in the output. *lead()* and *lag()* take as their parameters the name of the column you want to report, and the distance, (expressed as a number of rows) between the current row and the row you want to report alongside it. In my case, the distance is just one row; hence, the value 1 appearing in the function in this example.

```
select
    title, this_sale, next_sale,
    this_sale - next_sale delta
from (
    select title, sales this_sale,
        lead(sales,1) over (
            partition by store
            order by sales desc
        ) as next_sale
    from game_sale
where week_ending = '21-Jan-2001'
);
```

```
TITLE               THIS_SALE  NEXT_SALE DELTA
----------------    ---------- --------- --------
Crash Simulator          1934        913     1021
Tonic the Gerbil          913        482      431
Dome                      482        315      167
Portal Combat             315         72      243
Age of Umpires             72
```

Next, to report one column as a percentage of the total data, we use the *ratio_to_report()* function. This function is named somewhat modestly, as it can be used not only to report the data as a percentage of the report total, but can also be used to report the data as a ratio of a partition. I demonstrate this by showing how a query can be simultaneously partitioned in many ways (bear in mind that this does mean more sorting, however).

Note how this report does not need to use an in-line view, because I am not using the result of an analytic function as the basis for a subsequent *where* clause. Note also how an empty *over()* clause shows that I am treating the entire data set as the partition.

```
select
    store, title, sales,
    ratio_to_report(sales) over (
        partition by store
```

```
    ) store_ratio,
    ratio_to_report(sales) over (
    ) country_ratio
from game_sale
where week_ending = '21-Jan-2001'
order by
    store, sales desc;

Store    Title               Sale  St %  Co %
-------  ----------------    ----- ----  ----
Glasgow  Crash Simulator     1934  .52   .24
         Tonic the Gerbil     913  .25   .11
         Dome                 482  .13   .06
         Portal Combat        315  .08   .04
         Age of Umpires        72  .02   .01

London   Dome                2167  .49   .27
         Portal Combat       1824  .41   .22
         Crash Simulator      247  .06   .03
         Age of Umpires       110  .03   .01
         Tonic the Gerbil      52  .01   .01
```

Finally we come to the example of a running total, which also introduces the final feature of analytic functions, and the *over()* clause, which is the *range* or *rows* clause. Thus far, our analytic functions have been associated with either a single row from a partition (e.g., *rank()*) or with the entire set of data within the partition (e.g., *ratio_to_report()*). It is possible, however, to specify that a function should be applied to a range within the partition. There are several types of range specification, such as "within 3 rows of the current row," "within 10 days of the date in the current row," "the week (yes, analytic functions do know what a week is) preceding the date in the current row," etc. In this example, we use one of the simplest options, which is "this row and all the preceding rows in the partition," to make a function produce the running total of the partition. Note that if you use the *range* or *rows* clause, you must have an *order by* clause in the *over()* clause to allow the ranging calculation to have a consistent, reproducible meaning.

```
select
    store, week_ending, sales,
        sum(sales) over(
        partition by store
        order by week_ending
        range unbounded preceding
    ) running
from game_sales
where store = 'Glasgow'
order by store, week_ending;
```

STORE	WEEK ENDING	SALES	RUNNING
Glasgow	07-May-2000	4,000	4,000
	14-May-2000	5,000	9,500
	21-May-2000	6,000	15,000
	28-May-2000	7,000	22,000
	04-Jun-2000	8,000	30,000
	11-Jun-2000	7,802	37,802
	18-Jun-2000	7,636	45,438
	25-Jun-2000	8,134	53,572
	2-Jul-2000	7,815	61,387
	9-Jul-2000	8,023	69,410

This is a wonderful demonstration of how a very clean and simple piece of SQL can now be used to produce a result that previously required some heavy-duty calculation from the database engine or a carefully tested piece of procedural code. In this particular case, we also have an example in which the analytic function appears to be applied with virtually no overhead to produce a commonly requested form of output.

Conclusion

Analytic functions are very powerful and allow you to produce useful tabular results with very little programming, but it helps to use in-line views to increase the clarity of code.

Be careful about performance; some of the functions available clearly require Oracle to do a lot of sorting. But because the sort statistics are not reported; you should only apply analytic functions to relatively small result sets.

One final warning, PL/SQL does not yet recognize the syntax of analytic functions in static code, so you will need to resort to *ref cursors* and dynamic SQL to implement analytic functions inside PL/SQL packages.

But, what if you want to do more than that? What if you want to use a function, but still want to use the index? Often, in the past, use of functions meant a full-table scan, as the optimizer would often opt to ignore the index, if you had a function present. Enter Function Based Indexes – build your index using the function, and low and behold – now you are back to using your index. Also, there are a wealth of other functions present, in addition to ranking, things like 'top n' which will return your top 5 or top 10 (or top x) items from a table, or group by functionality that can now do cubes and roll ups, essentially totaling all the data for you, for each major category.

Pete Cassidy provides some highlights of this new functionality, as well as another key feature – descending indexes - in his recent publication:

Advanced Analytical SQL Functions

Dropping Columns

With the advent of Oracle8i or Oracle 8.1.5, you can now drop a column from a table. You can both mark the column as unused and drop the column later, or you can just drop the column from the table. However, if the table contains many rows, you may prefer to mark the column as unused and drop it later. Or, you can drop the column without marking it as unused, but committing after so many rows. In the following code, the infamous DEPT table has a column named HEAD_COUNT added. The DESCRIBE command shows HEAD_COUNT is now a column in the DEPT table. Then, the HEAD_COUNT column is marked as unused. The data dictionary view, *user_unused_col_tabs*, indicates there is one column marked as unused in the DEPT table. Notice that unused columns are not displayed when using the DESCRIBE command. The ALTER TABLE DEPT DROP UNUSED COLUMNS command drops all unused columns in the DEPT table. *user_unused_col_tabs* does not contain any unused columns for the DEPT table, because they have all been dropped. I think it very fair to say, *"It's about time!"*

Add the column HEAD_COUNT to the DEPT table:

```
SQL> ALTER TABLE DEPT ADD HEAD_COUNT NUMBER;
Table altered.
```

By describing the DEPT table, you can see the new column HEAD_COUNT.

```
SQL> DESC DEPT
      Name            Null?           Type
      DEPTNO          NOT NULL        NUMBER(2)
      DNAME                           VARCHAR2(14)
      LOC                             VARCHAR2(13)
      HEAD_COUNT                      NUMBER
```

Now mark the column HEAD_COUNT as unused.

```
SQL> ALTERTABLEDEPT
  2      SETUNUSED COLUMN HEAD_COUNT;
Table altered.
```

Using the data dictionary view *user_unused_col_tabs*, you can determine the number of unused columns in a particular table. In this example, only the HEAD_COUNT column is flagged as unused.

```
SQL> SELECT       TABLE_NAME,
  2               COUNT
  3    FROM       USER_UNUSED_COL_TABS
  4  * WHERE      TABLE_NAME = 'DEPT';

TABLE_NAME                               COUNT
----------------------------------- ---------
DEPT                                         1
```

Notice that the DESCRIBE command does not display the unused column HEAD_COUNT:

```
SQL> DESC DEPT
 Name               Null?        Type
 DEPTNO             NOT NULL     NUMBER(2)
 DNAME                           VARCHAR2(14)
 LOC                             VARCHAR2(13)
```

Drop all of the unused columns in the DEPT table:

```
SQL> ALTER       TABLE DEPT
  2    DROP       UNUSED COLUMNS;
Table altered.
```

Notice that the query below indicates no rows are selected from the data dictionary view *user_unused_col_tabs*:

```
SQL> SELECT       TABLE_NAME,
  2               COUNT
  3    FROM       USER_UNUSED_COL_TABS
  4*   WHERE      TABLE_NAME = 'DEPT';
no rows selected
```

The Old Way

The following DESCRIBE command shows the DEPT table with four columns: DEPTNO, DNAME, LOC, and HEAD_COUNT. The goal is to eliminate the HEAD_COUNT column from the DEPT table.

```
SQL> DESC  DEPT
      Name              Null?  Type
-----------------------------------
  DEPTNO      NOT NULL      NUMBER(2)
  DNAME                     VARCHAR2(14)
  LOC                       VARCHAR2(13)
  HEAD_COUNT                NUMBER
```

First, create a table with the desired columns that is identical to the DEPT table. However, this new table only contains the structure and data from the DEPT table. No indexes, grants, database triggers, or constraints get copied. However, any NOT NULL constraints do get copied.

```
SQL> CREATETABLE  ALMOST_LIKE_DEPT AS
  2    SELECT        DEPTNO,- Notice The Column
                          HEAD_COUNT Is Not Included
  3                  DNAME,
  4                  LOC
  5    FROM          DEPT;
Table created.
```

Now drop the table DEPT and rename the table ALMOST_LIKE_DEPT to DEPT:

```
SQL> DROP TABLE DEPT;
Table dropped.

SQL> RENAME ALMOST_LIKE_DEPT TO DEPT;
Table renamed.
```

You should now have four departments in the DEPT table:

```
SQL> SELECT*
  2    FROM          DEPT;

DEPTNO     DNAME        LOC
-----------------------------------
  10         ACCOUNTING   NEW YORK
  20         RESEARCH     DALLAS
  30         SALES        CHICAGO
  40         OPERATIONS   BOSTON
```

Adding Insult to Injury

You may have to do some or all of the following for the DEPT table:

- Grant the necessary privileges.
- Create indexes.
- Create constraints.
- Create database triggers.

Thanks be to Oracle Corporation for adding the new DROP COLUMN enhancement to Oracle8i. It's about time!

Top N Queries

In Oracle8i you can write the following TOP N query to identify the top salaried employees. This example shows the top three salaried employees. Using a query in the FROM clause, you can restrict the number of rows in the active set by using the pseudo-column ROWNUM. Because ROWNUM is less than four in this example, then only three rows are returned. If you prefer not to see the "old" and "new" lines, enter SET VERIFY OFF.

```
SQL> SELECT      ENAME, SAL
  2    FROM      (SELECTENAME, SAL
  3              FROM EMP
  4              ORDERBY SAL DESC)
  5*   WHERE     ROWNUM < &TOP;

Enter value for top: 4
Old 5:    WHERE  ROWNUM < &TOP
New 5:    WHERE  ROWNUM < 4

ENAME               SAL
-------------------  ----
KING               5000
SCOTT              3000
FORD               3000
```

The Old Way

Before Oracle8i you could write the following query to return the top salaried employees using a correlated sub-query. Visualize two tables: an outer table called the candidate table EMP and the inner table S. For every row in the outer candidate table EMP, the inner query fires, counting the number of employees whose salary in the inner table S is more than the salary in the candidate's EMP.SAL column. If the count is less than the value entered for &N, the employee is returned. For example, if KING is the candidate row in the EMP table, the inner query returns a count of zero. Because KING is the president and earns more than anyone else, his salary is not less than any of the monthly salaries. When prompted for N, if you enter 3, as in the following example, 3 is greater than 0 so KING is returned.

```
SQL> SELECT ENAME, SAL
  2  FROM    EMP
  3  WHERE   &N >(SELECTCOUNT(*)
  4                 FROM    EMP S
  5                 WHERE   EMP.SAL < S.SAL)
  6  ORDER BY SAL DESC;

Enter value for n: 3
Old 3: WHERE      &N > (SELECT COUNT(*)
New 3: WHERE      3 > (SELECT COUNT(*)

ENAME       SAL
------------------
KING        5000
SCOTT       3000
FORD        3000
```

Group By Cube

The GROUP BY CUBE clause produces a subtotal line for each department number, and calculates a total for each job in each department, a grand total at the end of the query, and a total for each job in the following example. The GROUP BY ROLLUP does not return the totals for each job, but does return everything else like the GROUP BY CUBE.

```
SQL> SELECT       DEPTNO, JOB, COUNT(*)
     FROMEMP
     GROUP BY CUBE(DEPTNO,JOB);

DEPTNO     JOB        COUNT(*)
--------------------------------
10         CLERK         1
10         MANAGER       1
10         PRESIDENT     1
10                       3
20         ANALYST       2
20         CLERK         2
20         MANAGER       1
20                       5
30         CLERK         1
30         MANAGER       1
30         SALESMAN      4
30                       6
           ANALYST       2
           CLERK         4
           MANAGER       3
           PRESIDENT     1
           SALESMAN      4
                        14
18 rows selected.
```

Group By Rollup

The GROUP BY ROLLUP clause produces a subtotal line for each department number, the number of jobs in each department, and calculates a grand total at the end of the query.

```
SQL> SELECT       DEPTNO, JOB, COUNT(*)
  2  FROM         EMP
  3  GROUP        BY    ROLLUP(DEPTNO, JOB);
```

```
DEPTNO      JOB        COUNT(*)
--------------------------------
10          CLERK             1
10          MANAGER           1
10          PRESIDENT         1
10                            3
20          ANALYST           2
20          CLERK             2
20          MANAGER           1
20                            5
30          CLERK             1
30          MANAGER           1
30          SALESMAN          4
30                            6
                             14
13 rows selected.
```

Function-Based Indexes

You can now create function-based indexes. In previous versions
of Oracle this was impossible. As long as you remember to issue
both ALTER SESSION commands, the Oracle optimizer may
decide to use the function-based index when retrieving rows, as
the following example suggests. You can either enter the
following two ALTER SESSION commands, or you can have
the Oracle database administrator make the entries in the
parameter file: *query_rewrite_enabled* = true and *query_rewrite_integrity*
= trusted.

```
SQL> ALTER SESSION SET QUERY_REWRITE_ENABLED = TRUE;
Session altered.

SQL> ALTER SESSION SET QUERY_REWRITE_INTEGRITY = TRUSTED;
Session altered.
```

Now create your function-based index. The following example
creates a function-based index on the sum of the two columns
SAL and COMM. You would consider creating this index when
many queries use SAL+COMM in the WHERE clause.

```
SQL> CREATE INDEX INDEX_FB_MANY_EMPS_TOT_SAL
  2          ON    MANY_EMPS(SAL+COMM)
  3   TABLESPACE INDX;
Index created.
```

To view the function-based index you just created, write a query using USER_INDEXES similar to the following example. Notice that the INDEX_TYPE column indicates it is a normal function-based index.

```
SQL> SELECT       INDEX_NAME,INDEX_TYPE,UNIQUENESS
  2   FROM        USER_INDEXES
  3*  WHERE       TABLE_NAME = UPPER('&TN');

Enter value for tn: MANY_EMPS

INDEX_NAME                    INDEX_TYPE            UNIQUENES
--------------------------------------------------------------
INDEX_FB_MANY_EMPS_TOT_SAL FUNCTION-BASED NORMAL NONUNIQUE
```

To determine if the Oracle optimizer uses the function-based index, use Explain Plan on a query referencing SAL+COMM in the WHERE clause.

```
SQL> EXPLAIN      PLAN   FOR
  2   SELECT      *
  3   FROM        MANY_EMPS    — Oracle May Now Use
                               The Function-Based Index
  4   WHERE       SAL+COMM = 2100;
Explained.
```

Another nice feature in Oracle8i is that you don't have to write your own SQL scripts to extract data from the table *plan_table*. Instead, Oracle provides you with two new scripts: *utlxpls.sql* and *utlxplp.sql*. The example in Exhibit 1 uses *utlxpls.sql*. Notice that Oracle would use the function-based index if you actually executed the SQL statement without using the Explain Plan.

```
SQL> @C:\ORACLE8I\RDBMS\ADMIN\UTLXPLS

Plan Table
-----------------------------------------------------------------------------
|Operation                  |Name         |Rows |Bytes |Cost |Pstart |Pstop|
-----------------------------------------------------------------------------
|SELECT STATEMENT           |             | 1K  | 26K  | 2 |       |     |
| TABLE ACCESS BY INDEX ROW | MANY_EMPS   | 1K  | 26K  | 2 |       |     |
|  INDEX RANGE SCAN         | INDEX_FB_   | 1K  |      | 1 |       |     |
-----------------------------------------------------------------------------
```

Exhibit 1 - *Using utlxpls.sql to Extract Data from the Table plan_table*

Descending Indexes

Descending indexes can be very useful for concatenated indexes when the ORDER BY clause requires one column of the concatenated index columns to be sorted ascending, and the other concatenated index column to be sorted descending.

```
SQL> CREATE INDEX job_sal_plus_comm
  2    ON SCOTT.emp(job ASC, (sal + nvl(comm,0)) DESC)
  3*   TABLESPACE indx;
Index created.
```

The above descending index can be used to speed up queries such as the following:

```
SQL> BREAK ON JOB SKIP 1
SQL> SELECT job, ename, sal + nvl(comm,0) TOT_SAL
  2    FROM scott.emp
  3*   ORDER BY job ASC, TOT_SAL DESC;
```

```
JOB        ENAME      TOT_SAL
---------  ---------- ---------
ANALYST    SCOTT         3000
           FORD          3000
CLERK      MILLER        1300
           ADAMS         1100
           JAMES          950
           SMITH          700
MANAGER    JONES         2975
           BLAKE         2850
           CLARK         2450
PRESIDENT  KING          5000
SALESMAN   MARTIN        2650
           ALLEN         1900
           WARD          1750
           TURNER        1500

14 rows selected.
```

Materialized Views

For very large tables in a data warehousing application, materialized views (MVs) are used to drastically improve performance. The MVs are really tables that are refreshed on a regular basis. The following example is an MV on an 880,000-row table. A better example would be a MV with 300 million rows, but disk space is tight for this article.

The following DESCRIBE command shows there are just two columns in the STATS table.

```
SQL> DESC STATS

Name     Null?     Type
-------  --------  -------
STAT_NO            NUMBER
RESULT             CHAR(1)
```

There are 880,000 rows in the STATS table, and the average for the STAT_NO column is 440,001. The STAT_NO column contains values from 1 to 880,000. Notice that it requires nearly five seconds to return this average.

```
SQL> SELECT AVG(STAT_NO)— 880,000 Rows
  2    FROM STATS;

AVG(STAT_NO)
============
      440001

real: 4953(Requires 4.953 Seconds)
```

To avoid possible Oracle errors, from SYS grant the system privilege query rewrite to SYSTEM.

```
SQL> GRANT QUERY REWRITE TO SYSTEM;
Grant succeeded.
SQL> CONNECT SYSTEM/MANAGER
```

The query rewrite feature can only be used by the cost-based optimizer, so set your session to either *all_rows* or *first_rows* to use the cost-based optimizer:

```
SQL> ALTER SESSION SET OPTIMIZER_GOAL = ALL_ROWS;
Session altered.
```

Just to be safe, before creating the MV, enable the query rewrite feature for your session:

```
SQL> ALTER SESSION SET QUERY_REWRITE_ENABLED = TRUE;
Session altered.
```

Again, as a safety valve, set query rewrite integrity to the setting of TRUSTED:

```
SQL> ALTER SESSION SET QUERY_REWRITE_INTEGRITY = TRUSTED;
Session altered.
```

So that you can see how long the following commands require executing, set timing on for your session.

```
SQL> SETTIMING ON
```

Now you are ready to create the MV named MV_STATS on your
880,000-row table STATS.

```
SQL> CREATE        MATERIALIZED VIEW mv_stats
2                  BUILD IMMEDIATE
3                  REFRESH COMPLETE — Truncates And Inserts.
                              Also FAST, FORCE, or NEVER
4                  ENABLE QUERY REWRITE
5  AS
6  SELECT  avg(stat_no) avg_statno,
7          min(stat_no) min_statno,
8          max(stat_no) max_statno
9* FROM    stats;
Materialized view created.
real: 9688 (Requires 9.688 Seconds)
```

The materialized view *mv_stats* might be used when writing the
query shown in Exhibit 2. Use Explain Plan to determine if the
Oracle optimizer would rewrite your query and use your
materialized view *mv_stats*. The NAME column in the table
plan_table indicates that Oracle would rewrite the statement using
your MV instead of performing a full table scan of the 880,000-
row STATS table.

```
SQL> EXPLAIN       PLAN FOR
  2    SELECT      avg(stat_no) avg_statno,
  3                min(stat_no) min_statno,
  4                max(stat_no) max_statno
  5*   FROM        stats;
Explained.

SQL> @F:\V8I\RDBMS\ADMIN\UTLXPLS

Plan Table
```

Operation	Name	Rows	Bytes	Cost	Pstart	Pstop
SELECT STATEMENT		21	819	1		
TABLE ACCESS FULL	MV_STATS	21	819	1		

Exhibit 2 - *Query Using MV Instead of a Full Table Scan*

The following query uses your MV and returns the information
you need from an 880,000-row table in less than 0.4 seconds.

Well, actually, your query is rewritten to use the MV containing one row.

```
SQL> SELECT       avg(stat_no) avg_statno,
  2               min(stat_no) min_statno,
  3               max(stat_no) max_statno
  4*  FROM        stats;

AVG_STATNO MIN_STATNO MAX_STATNO
========== ========== ==========
    440001          1     880000
real: 391 (Only Requires .391 Of A Second Using Your MV!)
```

Now try executing the same query not using your MV by setting the optimizer goal to RULE. Wow! It requires Oracle a whopping 6.657 seconds to return the information you need when not using your materialized view. Using your MV only requires less than 0.4 seconds! What a great enhancement Oracle Corporation!

```
SQL> SELECT       avg(stat_no) avg_statno,
  2               min(stat_no) min_statno,
  3               max(stat_no) max_statno
  4*  FROM        stats;

AVG_STATNO MIN_STATNO MAX_STATNO
========== ========== ==========
    440001          1     880000
real: 6657
```

For applications that often do an order by on a field in lower case, the descending index is an important feature. Prior to this, the order by would not use the index, would force a sort (hopefully in memory, and worst case to disk), for each query. But, the descending index avoids that:

```
create index emp1 on scott.emp (hire_date desc, emp_name );
```

In this case, the index is on *hire_date* in descending order, but for those rows with the same *hire_date*, *emp_name* is in ascending order.

Oracle SQL Tuning & CBO Internals

Also, SQL coders need to be careful that their where clauses match the high order columns in the index, or the index won't be used as you'd think, as tuning guru Mike Ault demonstrates:

Index Column Order Does Matter

I have heard it said that because Oracle will reorder the WHERE clause statements to ensure that the leading edge of an index will be used if possible and, that because the new skip-scan index search method is available, it is not required to try to properly order the columns in a concatenated index. In tests against an Oracle9i database (9.0.1), I found this assertion, that the order of columns in a concatenated index is not important, to be false and can result in poorly performing queries. This chapter shows the results from some basic tests to try to disprove this statement.

Index Order and Structure

In a standard concatenated B-tree index, the first level will be based on the initial column values, and subsequent levels on the following columns. If the index is properly built, then the mapping from these levels into the source table will be fairly linear; that is, the index clustering factor will be close to the number of dirty blocks in the table. Exhibit 1 shows a properly ordered index in relation to its table.

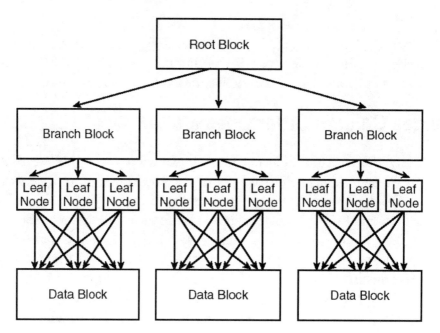

Exhibit 1 - *A Well-Ordered Index with a Low Clustering Factor*

If, on the other hand, an improper order is selected for the columns in the index, then the index will not be a linear match to the source table and a large clustering factor that is closer to the number of rows in the table will result. A large clustering factor results in more table reads to process the same amount of data as a small clustering factor. A poorly ordered index is shown in Exhibit 2.

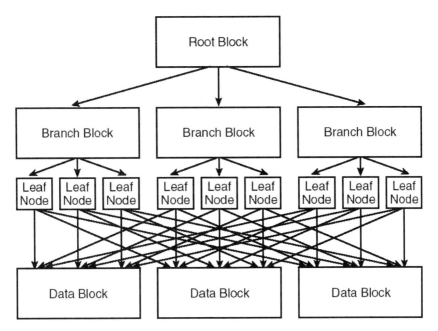

Exhibit 2 - *A Poorly Ordered Index with a High Clustering Factor*

A clustering factor can be equated to the number of table block reads that would be required to perform a full table scan based on reads from the index. A large clustering factor indicates that table blocks would be required to be accessed more than once for a particular index scan operation.

The order in which a table's columns are specified in a concatenated B-tree index can make a significant difference in the indexes ordering, and hence in its efficiency. Let's examine some examples.

Examples Using Various Column Orders in an Index

When I need a test table, I use the DBA series of views to provide input to a CTAS (create table as select). For this example I will use the *dba_objects* view because it has an easy structure to use for indexing. Exhibit 3 shows the CTAS and various statistics for the table TEST created as an image of the *dba_objects* view.

```
CTAS to Create TEST Table
SQL> create table test as select * from dba_objects;
Table created.
SQL> select count(*) from test;

COUNT(*)
----------
   31472

SQL> SELECT 'test',COUNT( DISTINCT( SUBSTR(
       dbms_rowid.rowid_to_restricted(ROWID,1),1,8))) blocks
  2  FROM    test;

TEST BLOCKS
---- ------
test    434

SQL> desc test

Name              Null?  Type
--------------    ------ --------------
OWNER                    VARCHAR2(30)
OBJECT_NAME             VARCHAR2(128)
SUBOBJECT_NAME         VARCHAR2(30)
OBJECT_ID              NUMBER
DATA_OBJECT_ID        NUMBER
OBJECT_TYPE           VARCHAR2(18)
CREATED              DATE
LAST_DDL_TIME      DATE
TIMESTAMP          VARCHAR2(19)
STATUS             VARCHAR2(7)
TEMPORARY          VARCHAR2(1)
GENERATED          VARCHAR2(1)
SECONDARY          VARCHAR2(1)
```

Exhibit 3 *CTAS to Create TEST Table*

Notice the number of blocks and the number of rows (434 and 31472), these will be important once we have our index clustering factors. Now that we have our table, let's create several indexes using the same columns but placing them in different orders, the columns we will use are the OBJECT_TYPE, OWNER, and OBJECT_NAME. The possible orders for these columns are:

- OBJECT_TYPE, OWNER, OBJECT_NAME

- OBJECT_TYPE, OBJECT_NAME, OWNER

- OBJECT_NAME, OWNER, OBJECT_TYPE

- OBJECT_NAME, OBJECT_TYPE, OWNER

- OWNER, OBJECT_NAME, OBJECT_TYPE

- OWNER, OBJECT_TYPE, OBJECT_NAME

Let's select a couple of these orders and create some example indexes. Exhibit 4 shows the create statements for these indexes. Also shown in Exhibit 4 are the various clustering factors for the indexes, but let's pull them all together in one spot and compare them; see Exhibit 5.

```
SQL> create index test_ord1 on
     test(object_type,owner,object_name)
SQL> /
Index created.

SQL> analyze index test_ord1 compute statistics;
Index analyzed.

SQL> select clustering_factor from user_indexes where
     index_name='TEST_ORD1';
CLUSTERING_FACTOR
----------------
             925

SQL> create index test_ord2 on
     test(object_name,owner,object_type);
Index created.

SQL> analyze index test_ord2 compute statistics;
Index analyzed.

SQL>    select   clustering_factor    from    user_indexes    where
index_name='TEST_ORD2';
CLUSTERING_FACTOR
----------------
           25289
```

```
SQL> create index test_ord3 on
     test(owner,object_name,object_type);
Index created.

SQL> analyze index test_ord3 compute statistics;
Index analyzed.

SQL> select clustering_factor from user_indexes where
     index_name='TEST_ORD3'
SQL> /
CLUSTERING_FACTOR
-----------------
              451

SQL> create index test_ord4 on
     test(owner,object_type,object_name);
Index created.

SQL> analyze index test_ord4 compute statistics;
Index analyzed.

SQL> select clustering_factor from user_indexes where
     index_name='TEST_ORD4';
CLUSTERING_FACTOR
-----------------
              908
```

Exhibit 4. *Creation of Various Indexes with Different Column Orders*

```
SQL> select index_name,
            clustering_factor
     from   user_indexes
     where  index_name like'TEST%';

INDEX_NAME               CLUSTERING_FACTOR
------------------------ -----------------
TEST_ORD1                              925
TEST_ORD2                            25289
TEST_ORD3                              451
TEST_ORD4                              908
```

Exhibit 5. *The Clustering Factors for the Indexes*

As you can see, the clustering factors range from a low of 451 for TEST_ORD3 to a high of 25289 for TEST_ORD2. So, based on the clustering factor TEST_ORD3 is the best ordered index and TEST_ORD2 is the worst ordered index. Let's do some example queries and see how the various indexes fare as far as cost in the cost-based optimizer (CBO).

```
SQL> analyze table test compute statistics;
Table analyzed.
Elapsed: 00:00:04.05
```

Now let's issue a SELECT that will use one of the indexes, the one chosen by the CBO (see Exhibit 6). As you can see, the CBO used the index with the higher clustering factor based on the right-to-left read of the WHERE clause leading column rule. The overall cost of the operation was 2. Let's force the optimizer to use a different index and see what the cost becomes. First, let's use the lowest clustering factor index, TEST_ORD3. We will force the query to use the index through use of the index hint (Exhibit 7).

```
SQL> select count(*) from test
  2  where
  3  owner='DBAUTIL' and object_type='TABLE';

COUNT(*)
--------
     338

Elapsed: 00:00:00.02

Execution Plan
-------------------------------------------
0   SELECT STATEMENT Optimizer=
    CHOOSE (Cost=2 Card=1 Bytes=13)
1 0   SORT (AGGREGATE)
2 1     INDEX (RANGE SCAN) OF 'TEST_
        ORD1' (NON-UNIQUE) (Cost=2
    Card=65 Bytes=845)
```

```
Statistics
-----------------------------------------------
      0  recursive calls
      0  db block gets
      4  consistent gets
      0  physical reads
      0  redo size
    384  bytes sent via SQL*Net to client
    503  bytes received via SQL*Net from client
      2  SQL*Net roundtrips to/from client
      0  sorts (memory)
      0  sorts (disk)
      1  rows processed
```

Exhibit 6.*Issuing a SELECT Using One of the Indexes*

```
SQL> select /*+ index(test test_ord3) */
     count(*) from test
  2  where
  3  owner='DBAUTIL' and object_type='TABLE';

COUNT(*)
--------
     338

Elapsed: 00:00:00.02

Execution Plan
-----------------------------------------------
0    SELECT STATEMENT Optimizer=CHOOSE
     (Cost=14 Card=1 Bytes=13)
1 0     SORT (AGGREGATE)
2 1        INDEX (RANGE SCAN) OF 'TEST_
           ORD3' (NON-UNIQUE) (Cost=14
     Card=65 Bytes=845)
```

```
Statistics
-------------------------------------------
      0  recursive calls
      0  db block gets
      8  consistent gets
      0  physical reads
      0  redo size
    384  bytes sent via SQL*Net to client
    503  bytes received via SQL*Net from client
      2  SQL*Net roundtrips to/from client
      0  sorts (memory)
      0  sorts (disk)
      1  rows processed
```

Exhibit 7. *Forcing the Query to Use the Index through Use of the INDEX Hint*

Note that the cost (14) was seven times the cost of our first query (2). The use of the TEST_ORD3 index resulted in a higher cost because the query had to traverse more of the index since the OWNER column was not the leading column.

Let's examine the results form using the highest clus- tering cost index, TEST_ORD2 (Exhibit 8). Wow! A whopping 110 times higher cost (221) over the lowest cost (2) so far. Have you noticed a quasi-correlation between the consistent gets statistics and the cost factors?

```
SQL>  select /*+ test(test_ord2) */ count(*)
      from test
  2   where
  3*  owner='DBAUTIL' and object_type='TABLE'
SQL> /


COUNT(*)
---------
     338

Elapsed: 00:00:00.02
```

```
Execution Plan
----------------------------------------------
0   SELECT STATEMENT Optimizer=CHOOSE
    (Cost=221 Card=1 Bytes=13)
1 0   SORT (AGGREGATE)
2 1     INDEX (FULL SCAN) OF 'TEST_
        ORD2' (NON-UNIQUE) (Cost=221
Card=65 Bytes=845)


Statistics
----------------------------------------------
      0 recursive calls
      0 db block gets
    221 consistent gets
      0 physical reads
      0 redo size
    384 bytes sent via SQL*Net to client
    503 bytes received via SQL*Net from client
      2 SQL*Net roundtrips to/from client
      0 sorts (memory)
      0 sorts (disk)
      1 rows processed
```

Exhibit 8. *Using TEST_ORD2 to View Results*

Now look at TEST_ORD4 (Exhibit 9). TEST_ORD4 performs
as well as the other two low-cost indexes. Let's try the query with
no index by using the full hint (Exhibit 10) and see what happens.

```
aultdb1>select /*+ index(test test_ord4) */
count(*) from test
  2 where
  3 owner='DBAUTIL' and object_type='TABLE';

COUNT(*)
--------
     338

Elapsed: 00:00:00.02
```

```
Execution Plan
-------------------------------------------
0    SELECT STATEMENT Optimizer=CHOOSE
     (Cost=2 Card=1 Bytes=13)
1 0    SORT (AGGREGATE)
2 1      INDEX (RANGE SCAN) OF 'TEST_
         ORD1' (NON-UNIQUE) (Cost=2
Card=65 Bytes=845)


Statistics
-------------------------------------------
     0 recursive calls
     0 db block gets
     4 consistent gets
     0 physical reads
     0 redo size
   384 bytes sent via SQL*Net to client
   503 bytes received via SQL*Net from client
     2 SQL*Net roundtrips to/from client
     0 sorts (memory)
     0 sorts (disk)
     1 rows processed
```

Exhibit 9. *TEST_ORD4*

```
SQL> select /*+ full(test) */ count(*) from test
  2  where
  3* owner='DBAUTIL' and object_type='TABLE'
SQL> /

COUNT(*)
--------
     338


Elapsed: 00:00:00.02

Execution Plan
-------------------------------------------
0    SELECT STATEMENT Optimizer=CHOOSE
     (Cost=67 Card=1 Bytes=13)
1 0    SORT (AGGREGATE)
2 1      TABLE ACCESS (FULL) OF 'TEST'
         (Cost=67 Card=65 Bytes=845)
```

```
Statistics
---------------------------------------------
     0  recursive calls
    36  db block gets
   446  consistent gets
     0  physical reads
     0  redo size
   384  bytes sent via SQL*Net to client
   503  bytes received via SQL*Net from client
     2  SQL*Net roundtrips to/from client
     0  sorts (memory)
     0  sorts (disk)
     1  rows processed
```

Exhibit 10. *Using the FULL Hint*

As you can see, the indexes are making a difference as far as cost. However, if you improperly arranged the index columns as in TEST_ORD2, and you had no other column orders to compare to, from these statistics you would choose to use a full table scan, increasing your cost by up to a factor of 30 based on the best performing index.

But what about a situation that requires an index scan? Lets change our query to use a like operation (Exhibit 11) and see what the CBO does with it.

```
SQL> select count(*) from test
  2  where
  3* owner='DBAUTIL' and object_name like 'DBA%'
SQL> /

COUNT(*)
--------
       6

Elapsed: 00:00:00.02
```

```
Execution Plan
-------------------------------------------
0   SELECT STATEMENT Optimizer=CHOOSE
    (Cost=2 Card=1 Bytes=29)
1 0   SORT (AGGREGATE)
2 1     INDEX (RANGE SCAN) OF 'TEST_
        ORD2' (NON-UNIQUE) (Cost=2
        Card=1 Bytes=29)

Statistics
-------------------------------------------
      0 recursive calls
      0 db block gets
      5 consistent gets
      0 physical reads
      0 redo size
    383 bytes sent via SQL*Net to client
    503 bytes received via SQL*Net from client
      2 SQL*Net roundtrips to/from client
      0 sorts (memory)
      0 sorts (disk)
      1 rows processed
```

Exhibit 11. *Using a LIKE Operation*

Not what we expected was it? In this case it looks like the CBO chose TEST_ORD2 although it has the highest clustering factor.

Let's look at some of the other indexes and see why. First, our lowest clustering factor index, TEST_ORD3 (Exhibit 12). As you can see, this index also produced a cost of 2, so the optimizer probably chose the TEST_ORD2 index based on column order. Now look at our previous queries' high performer, TEST_ORD1 (Exhibit 13). There is our 221 cost again, and 221 consistent gets. Obviously, the TEST_ORD1 index would not be a good candidate for this query. How about TEST_ORD4? (See Exhibit .14.) Again, this demonstrates your columns you can reduce the cost of processing. For TEST_ORD4, we would have increased our cost by a factor of 7 over TEST_ORD2 or TEST_ORD3 by using the column order in TEST_ORD4 and by a factor of 110 using the order from TEST_ORD1. What would the cost be for a full table scan in this case? See Exhibit 15.

```
SQL> select /*+ index(test test_ord3) */
     count(*) from test
  2  where
  3* owner='DBAUTIL' and object_name like 'DBA%'
SQL> /

COUNT(*)
--------
       6

Elapsed: 00:00:00.02

Execution Plan
----------------------------------------------
0   SELECT STATEMENT Optimizer=CHOOSE
    (Cost=2 Card=1 Bytes=29)
1 0    SORT (AGGREGATE)
2 1      INDEX (RANGE SCAN) OF 'TEST_
         ORD3' (NON-UNIQUE) (Cost=2
         Card=1 Bytes=29)

Statistics
----------------------------------------------
      0 recursive calls
      0 db block gets
      2 consistent gets
      0 physical reads
      0 redo size
    383 bytes sent via SQL*Net to client
    503 bytes received via SQL*Net from client
      2 SQL*Net roundtrips to/from client
      0 sorts (memory)
      0 sorts (disk)
      1 rows processed
```

Exhibit 12. *TEST_ORD3*

```
SQL> select /*+ index(test test_ord1) */
     count(*) from test
  2  where
  3* owner='DBAUTIL' and object_name like 'DBA%'
SQL> /

COUNT(*)
--------
       6
```

```
Elapsed: 00:00:00.02

Execution Plan
----------------------------------------------
0   SELECT STATEMENT Optimizer=CHOOSE
    (Cost=221 Card=1 Bytes=29)
1 0   SORT (AGGREGATE)
2 1     INDEX (FULL SCAN) OF 'TEST_
        ORD1' (NON-UNIQUE) (Cost=221
        Card=1 Bytes=29)

Statistics
----------------------------------------------
    0 recursive calls
    0 db block gets
  221 consistent gets
    0 physical reads
    0 redo size
  383 bytes sent via SQL*Net to client
  503 bytes received via SQL*Net from client
    2 SQL*Net roundtrips to/from client
    0 sorts (memory)
    0 sorts (disk)
    1 rows processed
```

Exhibit 13. *TEST_ORD1*

```
SQL> select /*+ index(test test_ord4) */
     count(*) from test
  2  where
  3* owner='DBAUTIL' and object_name like 'DBA%'
SQL> /

COUNT(*)
--------
       6

Elapsed: 00:00:00.02

Execution Plan
----------------------------------------------
0   SELECT STATEMENT Optimizer=CHOOSE
    (Cost=14 Card=1 Bytes=29)
1 0   SORT (AGGREGATE)
2 1     INDEX (RANGE SCAN) OF 'TEST_
        ORD4' (NON-UNIQUE) (Cost=14
        Card=1 Bytes=29)
```

```
Statistics
---------------------------------------------
    0 recursive calls
    0 db block gets
    8 consistent gets
    0 physical reads
    0 redo size
  383 bytes sent via SQL*Net to client
  503 bytes received via SQL*Net from client
    2 SQL*Net roundtrips to/from client
    0 sorts (memory)
    0 sorts (disk)
    1 rows processed
```

Exhibit 14. *TEST_ORD4*

```
SQL> select /*+ full(test) */ count(*) from test
  2  where
  3* owner='DBAUTIL' and object_name like 'DBA%'
SQL> /

COUNT(*)
--------
       6

Elapsed: 00:00:00.02

Execution Plan
---------------------------------------------
0   SELECT STATEMENT Optimizer=CHOOSE
    (Cost=67 Card=1 Bytes=29)
1 0   SORT (AGGREGATE)
2 1     TABLE ACCESS (FULL) OF 'TEST'
        (Cost=67 Card=1 Bytes=29)
```

```
Statistics
----------------------------------------------
     0  recursive calls
    36  db block gets
   446  consistent gets
     0  physical reads
     0  redo size
   383  bytes sent via SQL*Net to client
   503  bytes received via SQL*Net from client
     2  SQL*Net roundtrips to/from client
     0  sorts (memory)
     0  sorts (disk)
     1  rows processed
```

Exhibit 15. *Full Table Scan*

As we could have anticipated, the same as with the other query, but, had we used the column order in TEST_ORD1 for our index, based solely on the results from our analysis of the first query, we would choose a full table scan for this query and again increased our cost by up to a factor of 30 over the best performing indexes.

These examples show that the index column order should be analyzed for all of the major queries and a matrix showing cost prepared. Using the matrix in Exhibit 16, the index with the lowest overall average cost for all queries should be used instead of just blindly choosing a column order.

Query	TEST_ORD1	TEST_ORD2	TEST_ORD3	TEST_ORD4FTS
Q1	2	221	14	267
Q2	221	2	2	1467
Average	111.5	111.5	8	867

Exhibit 16. *Matrix Showing Cost Prepared*

So, for our indexes, the TEST_ORD3 or TEST_ORD4 column orders are the best choices, assuming that the queries have equal weight in our applications. However, if Q1 was performed thousands of times a day and Q2 only a few, then TEST_ORD1 would be a better choice; while if Q2 were the predominate query, then TEST_ORD2 would be a better choice.

All of this goes to show that you must take into consideration the ordering of index columns and the predominant queries that will access those indexes in order to make a logical and rational choice of index column order.

Summary

We have examined the effects of concatenated index column order on clustering factor and query performance for some simple test cases. In your environment preparation of a query/index performance matrix for concatenated indexes and your predominant queries is a must to ensure that you choose the proper index column order.

Materialized Views

In addition to functions and function-based indexes, there are many other enhancements to SQL. We've had snapshots for years, but in recent Oracle versions, we now have materialized views to take the place of snapshots (think of them as newer and better snapshots). Materialized views have several uses:

- Copy data from one instance to another in the identical format, and code SQL against the materialized view directly

- Copy data from one instance to another in a summarized format, and code SQL against the materialized view directly

- Create a summarized version of a table, and code SQL against the base table, and the SQL will automatically be 'rewritten' to use the materialized view

Let's take a look at each of these examples.

For the first example, all the code is in one local database – ORCL. Somewhere else, there is an employee table in a Human Resources database (HRDB) that is highly secured, and no one has access. However, one time per day our materialized view wakes up, dips into the HRDB and grabs the data, and brings it over to ORCL. The data is brought never in its existing format, i.e. no summarization.

So, queries can be written locally on the ORCL database, without ever having to access the HRDB database.

In Oracle database ORCL:

```
create materialized view emp_mview1
refresh complete
start with sysdate
next sysdate+1 as
select emp_name, dept_name from emp@hrdb_far_away;

select * from emp_mview1;
```

Next, let's look at a summary table example. Again, all code is in the ORCL database. We have an employee table in a Human Resources database (HRDB), and this data is summarized daily – getting the total number of employees per department, as well as the average salary in that department.

Again, queries are written against our local copy of the database, with no dynamic access of HRDB, aside from refreshing the materialized view daily.

In Oracle database ORCL:

```
create materialized view emp_mview2
refresh complete
start with sysdate
next sysdate+1 as
select dept_name, count(*), avg(salary)
```

```
from emp@hrdb_far_away
group by dept_name;

select * from emp_mview2;
```

Now, the third example is the most amazing one. A materialized view is built, summarizing data. SQL Is coded against the base table, and the optimizer is smart enough to realize that the data has already been aggregated in a materialized view, and will switch gears and go after the data in the view.

In Oracle database ORCL:

```
create materialized view emp_mview2
refresh complete
start with sysdate
next sysdate+1 as
select dept_name, count(*), avg(salary)
from emp
group by dept_name;

select dept_name, count(*)
from emp
group by dept_name;
```

Now, even though the SQL is coded to query the *emp* table, at execution time, Oracle will realize there is a materialized view with the information already aggregated, and will then use *emp_mview2* instead.

Be advised, that for this sort of 'query rewrite on the fly' to take place, there are several *init.ora* parameters that need to be set (or alter system / session commands to be executed):

- *query_rewrite_enabled* needs to be set to true, or Oracle will not rewrite queries on the fly. You also must have the 'query rewrite' system privilege.

- If the materialized view needs to refresh based on a schedule, it is going to be using *dbms_job* to do so, so *job_queue_processes* needs to be > 0.

There are 3 types of refresh strategies - fast, complete, and force.

With the complete refresh (which was used above), the rows in the view are completely removed, and it is reloaded. This can be time-consuming, especially if the volume is large.

With a fast refresh, only rows that changed since the last refresh are updated/inserted. This requires a log to be kept of all the changes to the table, using the following:

In database HRDB:

```
create materialized view log on emp;
```

The force strategy is a combination of both – it will try to use a fast refresh if possible, and if not, will switch to a complete refresh.

There are certain restrictions on the types of refreshes as well. For example, in 2 of the examples above, I had to use the complete refresh strategy, because I had aggregates – a group by precludes the use of a fast refresh.

To force a refresh of a materialized view, you can use the following:

```
exec dbms_refresh.refresh ('scott', 'emp');
```

Continuing in Pete Cassidy's publication, Advanced SQL Analytical Functions, we'll see examples of using materialized views, as well as *dbms_stats* and transportable tablespaces:

DBMS_STATS

This fantastic package allows you to gather statistics for cost-based optimization. You can store the statistics either in the data dictionary or in a table. You can then export the statistics and import them into another database to simulate production statistics in a development database. You can use this new package to perform any of the following:

- Populate statistics used with stored outlines

- Generate statistics in parallel

- Move statistics between a table and the data dictionary

- Retrieve individual statistics

- Create or drop statistics tables

The following example gathers statistics for the 880,000-row table STATS

```
SQL> EXECUTE dbms_stats.gather_table_stats ('SYSTEM','STATS')
PL/SQL procedure successfully completed
```

Transportable Tablespaces

With Oracle8i it is now possible to transport a tablespace from one database to another. It appears, at the time of this writing, that there is an "undocumented feature" when using the IMP utility in 8.1.5, however. The idea is to transport the RACE_CARS tablespace from the Oracle database V8I to the Oracle database INDY. First, create the tablespace RACE_CARS in the database V8I:

```
SQL> CREATE TABLESPACE RACE_CARS
  2         DATAFILE 'F:\V8I\ ORADATA\V8I\RACE_CARS01.DBF'
  3         SIZE 2M;
Tablespace created.
```

Next, create a table named IRL in the tablespace you just created, RACE_CARS:

```
SQL> CREATE TABLE IRL(car_noVARCHAR2(4),
  2                   car_ownerVARCHAR2(15) )
  3* TABLESPACE RACE_CARS;
Table created.
```

Then, insert a couple of rows into the IRL table in the tablespace RACE_CARS in the database V8I.

```
SQL> INSERT INTO IRL VALUES(99,'BELINGER');
1 row created.

SQL> INSERT INTO IRL VALUES(14,'VUKY');
1 row created.

SQL> COMMIT;
Commit complete.
```

Next, place the tablespace RACE_CARS in READ ONLY mode.

```
SQL> ALTER TABLESPACE RACE_CARS READ ONLY;
Tablespace altered.
```

Now you are ready to export the metadata of the tablespace RACE_CARS in the V8I database. Metadata suggests that the object creation statements are exported and not the actual data. The actual data gets copied in a later step. Notice the new parameters *transport_tablespace* and *tablespaces*. The statement in Exhibit 3 tells the EXP utility to transport the tablespace RACE_CARS from the V8I database.

```
C:\>EXP SYSTEM/MANAGER@V8I TRANSPORT_TABLESPACE=Y
                         TABLESPACES=RACE_CARS
Export: Release 8.1.5.0.0-Production on Mon Apr 17 14:37:27
2000

(c) Copyright 1999 Oracle Corporation. All rights reserved.
```

```
Connected to: Oracle8i Enterprise Edition Release 8.1.5.0.0—
Production
With the Partitioning and Java options
PL/SQL Release 8.1.5.0.0—Production
Export done in WE8ISO8859P1 character set and WE8ISO8859P1
NCHAR
  character set
Note: table data (rows) will not be exported
About to export transportable tablespace metadata...
For tablespace RACE_CARS ...
. exporting cluster definitions
. exporting table definitions
. . exporting tableIRL
. exporting referential integrity constraints
. exporting triggers
. end transportable tablespace metadata export
Export terminated successfully without warnings.
```

Exhibit 3. *EXP Utility Transporting the Tablespace RACE_CARS from the V8I Database*

For those of you with a curious nature, or perhaps you are from the "Show Me State" Missouri, Exhibit 4 shows a major portion of the EXPDAT.DMP file created by the above command executing the Export utility. Notice the command EXECTRP. This must represent EXECUTE TRANSPORTABLE TABLESPACE. Normally, you "EXECUTE" packages.

```
C:\> NOTEPAD EXPDAT.DMP
EXPORT:V08.01.05
Mon Apr 17 14:37:28 2000EXPDAT.DMP
EXECTRP sys.dbms_plugts.beginImport
('8.1.5.0.0',31,NULL,NULL,'NULL',14118,20001,1);
EXECTRP sys.dbms_plugts.checkCompType('DROPCOL','8.1.0.0.0');
EXECTRP
sys.dbms_plugts.checkCompType('NWIMGFMT','8.1.0.0.0');
EXECTRP sys.dbms_plugts.checkCompType('PLUGTS','8.1.0.0.0');
EXECTRP sys.dbms_plugts.checkCompType('TEMPTAB','8.1.0.0.0');
EXECTRP sys.dbms_plugts.checkUser('SYSTEM');
EXECTRP
sys.dbms_plugts.beginImpTablespace('RACE_CARS',7,'SYS',1,0,
2048,1,1187937,1,121,5,5,0,
50,1,0,0,2285095923,1,0,1187899,NULL,0,0,
NULL,NULL);
EXECTRP
sys.dbms_plugts.checkDatafile(NULL,2285095923,8,1024,7,8,0,0,
```

Oracle SQL Tuning & CBO Internals

```
1187905,1187937,1, NULL,NULL,NULL,NULL);
EXECTRP sys.dbms_plugts.commitPluggable;
TABLE "IRL"
CREATE TABLE "IRL" ("CAR_NO" VARCHAR2(4), "CAR_OWNER"
VARCHAR2(15))
PCTFREE 10 PCTUSED 40 INITRANS 1 MAXTRANS 255 LOGGING
STORAGE(SEG_FILE
8 SEG_BLOCK 2 OBJNO_REUSE 14115 INITIAL 10240 NEXT 10240
MINEXTENTS 1
MAXEXTENTS 121 PCTINCREASE 50 FREELISTS 1 FREELIST GROUPS 1
BUFFER_POOL DEFAULT) TABLESPACE "RACE_CARS"
ENDTABLE
CONNECT SYS
EXIT
EXIT
```

Exhibit 4.*Portion of the EXPDAT.DMP File*

Now you can connect to the target Oracle database INDY and
display the current tablespaces and their related files (see Exhibit
5).

```
C:\>SET ORACLE_SID=INDY

C:\>SQLPLUS SYSTEM/MANAGER

SQL*Plus: Release 8.1.5.0.0—Production on Mon Apr 17 16:25:35
2000

(c) Copyright 1999 Oracle Corporation. All rights reserved.

Connected to:
Oracle8i Enterprise Edition Release 8.1.5.0.0—Production
With the Partitioning and Java options
PL/SQL Release 8.1.5.0.0—Production

SQL> SELECT TABLESPACE_NAME FROM DBA_TABLESPACES;
```

```
TABLESPACE_NAME
==============================
SYSTEM
RBS
USERS
TEMP
INDX
OEM_REPOSITORY
6 rows selected.
```

Exhibit 5. *Displaying the Current Tablespaces and Their Related Files*

To display the physical operating system files in the database
INDY, write a query using *v$dbfile*:

```
SQL> SELECT SUBSTR(NAME,1,40)
  2  FROM   V$DBFILE;

SUBSTR(NAME,1,40)
==================================
F:\V8I\ORADATA\INDY\SYSTEM01.DBF
F:\V8I\ORADATA\INDY\RBS01.DBF
F:\V8I\ORADATA\INDY\USERS01.DBF
F:\V8I\ORADATA\INDY\TEMP01.DBF
F:\V8I\ORADATA\INDY\INDX01.DBF
F:\V8I\ORADATA\INDY\OEMREP01.DBF
6 rows selected.
```

To determine the file(s) comprising the RACE_CARS tablespace
in the database V8I, connect to the V8I database and write a
query using *v$dbfile* (see Exhibit 6).

```
SQL> EXIT
Disconnected from Oracle8i Enterprise Edition Release
8.1.5.0.0
With the Partitioning and Java options
PL/SQL Release 8.1.5.0.0—Production

C:\>SET ORACLE_SID=V8I
C:\>SQLPLUS SYSTEM/MANAGER@V8I

SQL*Plus: Release 8.1.5.0.0—Production on Mon Apr 17 16:32:27
2

(c) Copyright 1999 Oracle Corporation. All rights reserved.
```

Oracle SQL Tuning & CBO Internals

```
Connected to:
Oracle8i Enterprise Edition Release 8.1.5.0.0—Production
With the Partitioning and Java options
PL/SQL Release 8.1.5.0.0—Production

SQL> SELECT  SUBSTR(NAME,1,40)
  2  FROM    V$DBFILE
  3* WHERE   NAME LIKE '%RACE_CARS%';

SUBSTR(NAME,1,40)
==================================
F:\V8I\ORADATA\V8I\RACE_CARS01.DBF
```

Exhibit 6. *Writing a Query Using v$dbfile*

Next, ftp or copy the physical operating system files from the
RACE_CARS tablespace to the target machine as well as the
exported file EXPDAT.DMP from the V8I database. From the
above output from *v$dbfile*, you need to copy or ftp the operating
system file F:\V8I\ORADATA\V8I\RACE_CARS01.DBF:

```
C:\>F:

F:\>CD V8I\ORADATA\INDY

F:\V8I\ORADATA\INDY>COPY F:\V8I\ ORADATA\V8I\RACE_CARS01.DBF
*.*
1 file(s) copied.

F:\V8I\ORADATA\INDY>COPY C:\EXPDAT.DMP *.*
1 file(s) copied.
```

Now you have the physical file in the RACE_CARS tablespace of
database V8I copied, and you have the exported file
EXPDAT.DMP on your target machine. So, try to import, or
transport the tablespace RACE_CARS from the V8I database to
the INDY database (see Exhibit 7). Import using SYS as your
import username.

```
F:\V8I\ORADATA\INDY>SET ORACLE_SID=INDY

F:\V8I\ORADATA\INDY>IMP FILE=TRANS.DMP TRANSPORT_TABLESPACE=Y
DATAFILES=F:\V8I\O
```

```
RADATA\INDY\RACE_CARS01.DBF

Import: Release 8.1.5.0.0—Production on Mon Apr 17 16:58:32
2000

(c) Copyright 1999 Oracle Corporation. All rights reserved.

Username: SYS
Password:

Connected to: Oracle8i Enterprise Edition Release 8.1.5.0.0—
Production
With the Partitioning and Java options
PL/SQL Release 8.1.5.0.0—Production

Export file created by EXPORT:V08.01.05 via conventional path
About to import transportable tablespace(s) metadata...

Warning: the objects were exported by SYSTEM, not by you

import done in WE8ISO8859P1 character set and WE8ISO8859P1
NCHAR
character set
. importing SYSTEM's objects into SYS
IMP-00000: Import terminated successfully
```

Exhibit 7. *Import Using SYS as the Import Username*

You can write the following query to view your new plugged in(transported) tablespace.

```
SQL> COL     PLUGGED_INFORMAT A20
SQL> SELECT TABLESPACE_NAME,
            PLUGGED_IN
     FROM   DBA_TABLESPACES;
```

Because the transported tablespace, RACE_CARS, is read-only, alter it to read-write.

```
SQL> ALTERTABLESPACE RACE_CARS READ WRITE;
```

To verify that the transported tablespace is self-con- taining, execute the package *dbms_tts*:

```
SETEXEC DBMS_TTS.TRANSPORT_SET_CHECK(TS_LIST
   =>'ADMIN', INCL_CONSTRAINTS => TRUE);
SQL>  SELECT  *
      FROM    TRANSPORT_SET_VIOLATIONS;
DECLARE X BOOLEAN;
   BEGIN
       X:=DBMS_TTS.ISSELFCONTAINED(TS_LIST
         =>'ADMIN',INCL_CONSTRAINTS => TRUE);
       IF X THENDBMS_OUTPUT.PUT_LINE('SELF CONTAINED IS
TRUE');
       ELSE DBMS_OUTPUT.PUT_LINE('SELF CONTAINED IS FALSE');
       END IF;
END;
/
```

Restrictions on Transporting Tablespaces

The following restrictions must be observed to success- fully
transport a tablespace from one Oracle database to another:

- Must be Oracle 8.1.5 or later

- Both databases must use the same operating system

- Both databases must have the same Oracle block size.
  (*db_block_size*)

Locally Managed Tablespaces

Instead of using Oracle's data dictionary for dynamic allocation
of extents, you can now create locally managed tablespaces. A
locally managed tablespace contains a bit- map in the data file.
The bit settings indicate a block or group of blocks eligible for
row insertion. The following command creates a locally managed
tablespace named LOCAL with one file. The size of the file is 2
MB and each extent is 64K. You cannot include a storage clause
when using locally managed tablespaces.

```
SQL> CREATE  TABLESPACE  LOCAL
  2            DATAFILE   'C:\LOCAL1.DBF'
  3            SIZE       2M
  4  EXTENT  MANAGEMENT  LOCAL UNIFORM SIZE 64K;
Tablespace created.
```

You can still view available space in your local tablespaces just like non-local tablespaces.

```
SQL> SELECT *
     FROM    DBA_FREE_SPACE
     WHERE   TABLESPACE_NAME = 'LOCAL';

TABLESPACE_NAME FILE_ID BLOCK_ID BYTES     BLOCKS RELATIVE_FNO
=============== ======= ======== =======   ======= =============
LOCAL                 7        9 2031616      248             7
```

Oracle Corporation recommends using local tablespaces.

LogMiner

Someone has deleted Mr. Ford from Scott's EMP table, and everyone disavows any knowledge of the event. However, you are very suspicious of one of your users, who has a tendency of bending the truth at times. So, you decide to use LogMiner to track down the guilty party.

First, you edit your parameter file entering *utl_fil_dir*=C:\ORACLASS\LOGS. LogMiner can now create an operating system file in this path.

```
SQL> SHOW USER
USER is "SYS"

SQL> SHOW PARAMETER utl

NAME          TYPE    VALUE
------------- ------- ----------------
utl_file_dir  string  C:\ORACLASS\LOGS
```

Next, you execute the BUILD procedure in the DBMS_LOGMNR_D package to create an operating sys- tem file MINER2.DAT. This file will contain information taken from the specified redo log files.

```
SQL> CONNECT SYS/CHANGE_ON_INSTALL@DBA
Connected.

SQL> BEGIN
  2   dbms_logmnr_d.build ( 'miner2.dat', 'C:\ORACLASS\LOGS'
);
  3   END;
  4   /
PL/SQL procedure successfully completed.
```

Next, switch log files and identify the current log file.

```
SQL> ALTER SYSTEM SWITCH LOGFILE;
System altered.

SQL> column member NEW_VALUE redo
SQL> SELECT member
  2   FROM    v$logfile — IF REDO LOGS ARE MIRRORED,
                          ONLY WANT ONE(ROWNUM<2)
  3   WHERE   group# = ( SELECT group# FROM v$log
                          WHERE status = 'CURRENT' )
  4           AND ROWNUM < 2;

MEMBER
-----------------------------------
C:\ORACLASS\DATA\DISK3\REDO0201.LOG
```

Next, copy the above redo log member to C:\ORA-CLASS\LOGS\redo.log.

```
SQL> host xcopy &redo C:\ORACLASS\LOGS\redo.log
```

Now, indicate to LogMiner that you want information contained in the redo.log file by executing ADD_LOGFILE.

```
SQL> BEGIN
  2  dbms_logmnr.add_logfile('C:\ ORACLASS\ LOGS\redo.log',
  3                          dbms_logmnr.NEW );
  4  END;
  5  /

PL/SQL procedure successfully completed.
```

Now, tell LogMiner to start. LogMiner takes the data in the operating system file miner2.dat and loads it into the dynamic performance views used by LogMiner. One of these views is *v$logmnr_contents*.

```
SQL> BEGIN
  2   dbms_logmnr.start_logmnr ( dictFileName =>
       'c:\ORACLASS\LOGS\miner2.dat' );
  4   END;
  5  /
PL/SQL procedure successfully completed.
```

Now you are ready to write a query (Exhibit 8) using *v$logmnr_contents* to identify the villain in who deleted ford saga. The two columns of interest are SQL_REDO and SQL_UNDO. The SQL_REDO column shows the SQL statement that changes data in a table, and the SQL_UNDO column shows the SQL statement(s) to reverse or undo the SQL statement that changed the table data. It is more than painfully obvious that user LIAR_LIAR deleted Ford and also committed his dastardly deed. Notice the undo of the DELETE command is an INSERT command.

```
SQL> columnsql_redo format a30 word_wrapped
SQL> columnsql_undo format a30 word_wrapped
SQL> columnusername format a12
SQL> SELECT scn,
            username,
            sql_redo,
            sql_undo
     FROM   V$LOGMNR_CONTENTS;
```

```
SCN     USERNAME  SQL_REDO                       SQL_UNDO
------  --------- ------------------------------ ----------------------
232009 LIAR_LIAR  set transaction read write;
232009 LIAR_LIAR  delete from SCOTT.EMP where     insert into
                  EMPNO = 7902 and ENAME =SCOTT  .EMP(EMPNO,ENAME,JOB,MGR,
                  'ford' and JOB = 'ANALYST' and HIREDATE,SAL,COMM,DEPTNO)
                  MGR = 7566 and HIREDATE =      values
                  TO_DATE('03-DEC-2081           (7902,'ford','ANALYST',
                  00:00:00', 'DD-MON-YYYY        7566,TO_DATE('03-DEC-2081
                  HH24:MI:SS') and SAL = 3000    00:00:00','DD-MON-YYYY
                  and COMM IS NULL and DEPTNO =  HH24:MI:SS'),3000,NULL,
                  20 and ROWID =                 20);
                  'AAAAsrAADAAAAF6AAM';
232010 LIAR_LIAR  commit;
```

Exhibit 8. *Query Using v$logmnr_contents to Identify the Villain*

To view the INSERT required to place Mr. Ford back into Scott's EMP table, write a query viewing the SQL_UNDO column of *v$logmnr_contents*:

```
SQL> SELECT sql_undo
     FROM   V$LOGMNR_CONTENTS;

insert into
SCOTT.EMP(EMPNO,ENAME,JOB,MGR,
HIREDATE,SAL,COMM,DEPTNO)
values
(7902,'ford','ANALYST',7566,TO
_DATE('03-DEC-2081 00:00:00',
'DD-MON-YYYY
HH24:MI:SS'),3000,NULL,20);
```

You can cut and paste the INSERT statement and exe- cute it to place Ford back into Scott's EMP table.

```
SQL> insert into
          SCOTT.EMP(EMPNO,ENAME,JOB,MGR,
          HIREDATE,SAL,COMM,DEPTNO)
          values
          (7902,'ford','ANALYST',7566,
          TO_DATE('03-DEC-2081 00:00:00',' DD-MON-YYYY
            HH24:MI:SS'),3000,NULL,20);
1 row created.

SQL> COMMIT;
Commit complete.
```

Finally, end your LogMiner session.

```
SQL> BEGIN
SQL> dbms_logmnr.end_logmnr;
SQL> END;
SQL> /
PL/SQL procedure successfully completed.
```

BMC Corporation has had a product named LogMaster for many years. It is much easier to use than Oracle's LogMiner. You merely enter commands at the operating system prompt. However, it is a good start for Oracle to allow you to read and interpret the binary redo log files. It's about time!

Database Event Triggers

You can now write database triggers that fire when a user logs on or logs off of Oracle. The following example fires whenever someone connects as the Oracle user SYSTEM. Database triggers now permit the COMMIT statement:

```
SQL> SHOW USER
USER is "SYS"
```

The following Oracle8i event trigger fires whenever someone logs on as SYSTEM. The trigger inserts a row into the table *sys.event_log*, which is created manually by the database administrator.

```
SQL> CREATE TABLE EVENT_LOG(WHO_AND_WHEN VARCHAR2(70));
Table Created.
```

```
SQL> CREATE OR REPLACE TRIGGER track_logons
  2          AFTER LOGON ON DATABASE
  3          WHEN (user = 'SYSTEM')
  4  BEGIN
  5    INSERT INTO sys.event_log
  6      VALUES(user || ' Logged On At ' || to_char(sysdate,
  7      'MM/DD/YYYY HH:MI:SS'));
  8    COMMIT;- Can't Do This In Previous Versions
  9* END;
SQL> /
Trigger created.
```

So that you can see the time on the terminal while in SQL*Plus, set the time environmental parameter on.

```
SQL> SHOW TIME
time OFF
```

Notice that someone connects as SYSTEM at 5:49 PM or 17:49 military time.

```
SQL> SET TIME ON
17:49:30 SQL> CONNECT SYSTEM/MANAGER
Connected.

17:49:41 SQL> SET TIME OFF
```

Write a query using *sys.event_log* to test your event trigger tracking log-ons for user SYSTEM. As you can see, your trigger works.

```
SQL> SELECT *
  2  FROM   SYS.EVENT_LOG;

WHO_AND_WHEN
----------------------------------------
SYSTEM Logged On At 01/12/2000 05:49:41
```

To track who drops an object and when, the name of the object and its type, write an event trigger such as the following. First, create a table to contain the required information gleaned from the trigger:

Database Event Triggers   **187**

```
SQL> CREATE TABLE who_dropped_object
  2              (who_done_it VARCHAR2(30),
  3               when_dropped DATE,
  4               obj_name VARCHAR2(30),
  5               obj_type VARCHAR2(30))
  5* TABLESPACE users;
Table created.
```

Use the Oracle provided *dbms_standard* package to determine which user dropped an object, the name of the object, and the object type.

```
SQL> CREATE OR REPLACE TRIGGER track_dropped_ objects
  2          AFTER     DROP
  3          ON        DATABASE—Not Schema But Database
  4   BEGIN
  5     INSERT into who_dropped_object
  6     VALUES(dbms_standard.login_user, sysdate,
  7            dbms_standard.dictionary_ obj_name,
  8            dbms_standard.dictionary_ obj_type);
  9* END;
SQL>/
Trigger created.
```

Write a query using *dba_triggers* to display infor- mation about the database triggers in your database.

```
SQL> DESC DBA_TRIGGERS

Name                  Null? Type
-----------------------------------
OWNER                       VARCHAR2(30)
TRIGGER_NAME                VARCHAR2(30)
TRIGGER_TYPE                VARCHAR2(16)
TRIGGERING_EVENT            VARCHAR2(75)
TABLE_OWNER                 VARCHAR2(30)
BASE_OBJECT_TYPE            VARCHAR2(16)
TABLE_NAME                  VARCHAR2(30)
COLUMN_NAME           VARCHAR2(4000)
REFERENCING_NAMES     VARCHAR2(128)
WHEN_CLAUSE           VARCHAR2(4000)
STATUS                      VARCHAR2(8)
DESCRIPTION           VARCHAR2(4000)
ACTION_TYPE                 VARCHAR2(11)
TRIGGER_BODY                      LONG
```

This query indicates an event trigger associated with the database and not just a specific schema.

```
SQL> SELECT BASE_OBJECT_TYPE,- Database or Schema
  2          TRIGGER_TYPE,- Before or After
  3          TABLE_NAME- Null For Db and Schema
  4   FROM    DBA_TRIGGERS
  5   WHERE   TRIGGER_NAME = 'TRACK_DROPPED_OBJECTS';

BASE_OBJECT_TYPE TRIGGER_TYPE TABLE_NAME
================ ============ ==========
DATABASE         AFTER EVENT
```

User NOT_TOO_BRIGHT connects to Oracle and drops the table SYSTEM.PARTS.

```
SQL> CONNECT NOT_TOO_BRIGHT/NOT_TOO_BRIGHT
Connected.

SQL> DROP TABLE SYSTEM.PARTS;
Table dropped.
```

Applications are failing because a production table is not in the database. So, you connect to Oracle to determine who dropped the PARTS table.

```
SQL> CONNECT SYSTEM/MANAGER
Connected.

SQL> COL WHO_DONE_IT   FORMAT A14
SQL> COL WHEN_DROPPED FORMAT A12
SQL> COL OBJ_NAME     FORMAT A8
SQL> COL OBJ_TYPE     FORMAT A8
```

You can see that user NOT_TOO_BRIGHT is the guilty party.

```
SQL> SELECT *
  2* FROM   WHO_DROPPED_OBJECT;

WHO_DONE_IT    WHEN_DROPPED OBJ_NAME OBJ_TYPE
============== ============ ======== ========
NOT_TOO_BRIGHT 19-APR-00    PARTS    TABLE
```

You can also write event triggers to track when an Oracle database is shut down and when it is started. The following event trigger fires when your Oracle database is shut down:

```
SQL> CREATE TABLE shutdowns
  2                (who_shutdown  VARCHAR2(30)
  3                 when_shutdown DATE)
  4* TABLESPACE   users;
Table created.
```

If you use AFTER SHUTDOWN, your trigger does not compile. You must use BEFORE SHUTDOWN:

```
SQL> CREATE OR REPLACE TRIGGER track_shutdowns
  2         BEFORE      SHUTDOWN — after won't work
  3         ON          DATABASE
  4     BEGIN
  5     INSERT into shutdowns
  6     VALUES(dbms_standard.login_user, sysdate);
  7* END;
SQL>/
Trigger created.
```

To test your event trigger, shut down your database.

```
SQL> SHUTDOWN;
Database closed.
Database dismounted.
ORACLE instance shut down.
```

Now, start up your database.

```
SQL>CONNECT INTERNAL/ORACLE
Connected to an idle instance.

SQL>STARTUP;
ORACLE instance started.
```

```
Total System Global Area   4.3E+07 bytes
Fixed Size                    65484 bytes
Variable Size              1.3E+07 bytes
Database Buffers           3.1E+07 bytes
Redo Buffers                  73728 bytes
Database mounted.
Database opened.
```

To verify your event trigger fired correctly, write a query using the table you created to contain shutdown information. There were two shutdowns on your database today, three minutes apart.

```
SQL> COL WHEN_SHUTDOWN FORMAT A13

SQL> SELECT WHO_SHUTDOWN,
  2          TO_CHAR(WHEN_SHUTDOWN,'MM/DD HH:MI:SS') WHEN
  3   FROM   SHUTDOWNS;

WHO_SHUTDOWN             WHEN
======================== ==============
SYSTEM                   04/19 04:48:44
SYS                      04/19 04:51:14
```

Defragging Non-partitioned Tables

To defrag a table or eliminate chained rows, you normally export the table, drop the table, and import the table. You can also move a table from one tablespace to another to defrag and eliminate row chaining. The following example shows the table EMP_CHAINED_ROWS with 22 chained rows, in tablespace USERS, with one index INDX_SAL. The table is moved from tablespace USERS to DATA, and the index must be rebuilt. The following query shows there are 22 rows chained in the table EMP_CHAINED_ROWS.

```
SQL> SELECT CHAIN_CNT, TABLESPACE_NAME
  2   FROM   USER_TABLES
  3*  WHERE  TABLE_NAME = 'EMP_CHAINED_ROWS';

CHAIN_CNT  TABLESPACE_NAME
---------- ----------------
22         USERS
```

To determine the indexes on table EMP_CHAINED_ROWS table, use the following query. When you defrag a table using the ALTER MOVE command, indexes on the non-partitioned table must be rebuilt.

```
SQL> SELECT INDEX_NAME, TABLESPACE_NAME
  2  FROM    USER_INDEXES
  3* WHERE   TABLE_NAME = 'EMP_CHAINED_ROWS';

INDEX_NAME TABLESPACE_NAME
---------- ----------------
INDX_SAL   INDX
```

Move the table, EMP_CHAINED_ROWS, from the USERS tablespace to the DATA tablespace and also defrag the EMP_CHAINED_ROWS table:

```
SQL> ALTER TABLE EMP_CHAINED_ROWS MOVE TABLESPACE DATA;
Table altered.
```

You can also enter the following command if you want to defrag the table, but keep the table in its current tablespace.

```
SQL> ALTER TABLE EMP_CHAINED_ROWS MOVE;
```

Because an index exists on the EMP_CHAINED_ROWS table, and the table is moved to another tablespace, when the index is used, you receive an error.

```
SQL> SELECT *
  2  FROM    EMP_CHAINED_ROWS
  3  WHERE   SAL = 5000;
     FROM    EMP_CHAINED_ROWS
             *
ERROR at line 2:
ORA-01502: index 'SYSTEM.INDX_SAL' or partition of such index is
     in unusable state
```

Now, you must rebuild the index. In Oracle8i, you can use the ONLINE option, allowing transactions to update the underlying table of the index while the index is being rebuilt.

```
SQL> ALTER INDEX INDX_SAL REBUILD TABLESPACE INDX ONLINE;
Index altered.
```

Reanalyze the table to determine if the chained rows are repaired.

```
SQL> ANALYZE TABLE EMP_CHAINED_ROWS COMPUTE STATISTICS;
Table analyzed.
```

Because the following query shows a chain count of zero, row chaining no longer exists in EMP_CHAINED_ROWS. It's more than about time!

```
SQL> SELECT CHAIN_CNT, TABLESPACE_NAME
  2  FROM   USER_TABLES
  3* WHERE  TABLE_NAME = 'EMP_CHAINED_ROWS';

CHAIN_CNT  TABLESPACE_NAME
---------  ---------------
        0  DATA
```

Explain Plan

Finally, after all of these years and releases (1990 Version 6), Oracle Corporation has written two SQL scripts used to extract and interpret information from the table PLAN_TABLE after using the EXPLAIN PLAN command. The two scripts are named *utlxpls.sql* and *utlx-plp.sql*. On UNIX platforms, the scripts are found in $ORACLE_HOME/rdbms/admin.

After all this time of struggling with LPAD, CONNECT BY, and START WITH, it is now much easier to use Explain Plan. However, you must still create the table *plan_table*.

```
SQL> @f:\v8i\rdbms\admin\utlxplan
Table created.
```

Next, you are ready to run Explain Plan on queries.

```
SQL> EXPLAIN PLAN FOR
  2  SELECT *
  3  FROM    EMP
  4  WHERE   SAL = 5000;
Explained.
```

Now you can use one of the SQL scripts written by Oracle to extract meaningful information from the table *plan_table*. The following example uses *utlx-pls.sql*. Oracle would use a full table scan to retrieve all employees who earn $5000 per month. On a large table with only a few employees earning $5000 per month, you would want to create an index on the SAL column of the EMP table, and use the index to improve performance.

```
SQL> @f:\v8i\rdbms\admin\utlxpls
Plan Table
-------------------------------------------------------------
|Operation            |Name|Rows|Bytes|Cost|Pstart|Pstop|
-------------------------------------------------------------
|SELECT STATEMENT     |    |    |     |    |      |     |
| TABLE ACCESS FULL   |EMP |    |     |    |      |     |
-------------------------------------------------------------
```

The example in Exhibit 9 shows the result of an Explain Plan on a Top N query. Notice the "STOPKEY" in the OPERATION column of the table *plan_table*. Oracle's new script is robust and easy to read. Thanks Oracle!

```
SQL> SET       VERIFY  OFF
SQL> EXPLAIN PLAN      FOR
  2  SELECT  ENAME,  SAL
  3  FROM    (SELECT ENAME, SAL
  4          FROM    EMP
  5          ORDER   BY SAL DESC)
  6* WHERE   ROWNUM< &TOP;
Enter value for top: 3
Explained.

SQL> @C:\ORACLE8I\RDBMS\ADMIN\UTLXPLS
```

```
Plan Table
-------------------------------------------------------------
|Operation                    |Name|Rows|Bytes|Cost|Pstart|Pstop|
-------------------------------------------------------------
|SELECT STATEMENT             |    |    |     |    |      |     |
|  COUNT STOPKEY              |    |    |     |    |      |     |
|    VIEW                     |    |    |     |    |      |     |
|      SORT ORDER BY STOPKEY| |    |    |     |    |      |     |
|        TABLE ACCESS FULL   | EMP|    |     |    |      |     |
-------------------------------------------------------------
8 rows selected.
```

Exhibit 9. *Result of an Explain Plan on a Top N Query*

The Old Way

Previous to Oracle8i, you had to write a query similar to the following. For someone new to the Oracle world, it was always a traumatic experience trying to determine the functionality of LPAD, LEVEL, CONNECT BY, START WITH, and recursion.

```
SQL> get old_explain
  1   COL        "Query Plan" FORMATA40
  2   SELECT     LPAD(` `,2*LEVEL-1) || OPERATION || ` ` ||
  3   OPTIONS    || ` ` || OBJECT_NAME || ` ` ||
  4   OPTIMIZER  "Query Plan", COST
  5   FROM       PLAN_TABLE
  6   START      WITH ID= 0
  7*  CONNECT    BY PRIOR ID= PARENT_ID
SQL> @old_explain

Query Plan                                    COST
--------------------------------------- -----
SELECT STATEMENT CHOOSE                          3
  COUNT STOPKEY
    VIEW                                         3
      SORT ORDER BY STOPKEY                      3
        TABLE ACCESS FULL EMP ANALYZED           1
```

Exporting Selected Rows from a Table

Thanks to the new export parameter, *query*, you can now export particular rows from a table. The example in Exhibit 10 shows an export of all employees in department number 10 from the EMP table.

```
C:\>exp help=yes
Keyword      Description (Default)        Keyword       Description (Default)
-----------  ---------------------------  ------------  ------------------------
USERID       username/password           FULL          export entire file (N)
BUFFER       size of data buffer         OWNER         list of owner usernames
FILE         output files (EXPDAT.DMP)   TABLES        list of table names
COMPRESS     import into one extent (Y)  RECORDLENGTH  length of IO record
GRANTS       export grants (Y)           INCTYPE       incremental export type
INDEXES      export indexes (Y)          RECORD        track incr. export (Y)
ROWSexport   data rows (Y)               PARFILE       parameter filename
CONSTRAINTS  export constraints (Y)      CONSISTENT    cross-table consistency
LOG          log file of screen output   STATISTICS    analyze objects (ESTIMATE)
DIRECT       direct path (N)             TRIGGERS      export triggers (Y)
FEEDBACK     display progress every x rows (0)
FILESIZE     maximum size of each dump file
QUERY        select clause used to export a subset of a table

The following keywords only apply to transportable tablespaces
TRANSPORT_TABLESPACE export transportable tablespace metadata (N)
TABLESPACES list of tablespaces to transport

Export terminated successfully without warnings.

C:\>exp query='where deptno=10' file=emp10.dmp tables=emp
userid=system/manager

Export: Release 8.1.5.0.0—Production on Sun Jan 23 09:55:22 2000

(c) Copyright 1999 Oracle Corporation. All rights reserved.

Connected to: Oracle8i Enterprise Edition Release 8.1.5.0.0—Production
With the Partitioning and Java options
PL/SQL Release 8.1.5.0.0—Production
Export done in WE8ISO8859P1 character set and WE8ISO8859P1 NCHAR character
Set

About to export specified tables via Conventional Path ...
. . exporting tableEMP3 rows exported
Export terminated successfully without warnings.
```

Exhibit 10. *All Employees in Department Number 10 from the EMP Table*

Column Definitions for Data Dictionary Tables

How many times have you needed to know what kind of information is contained in a column of a data dictionary table? It can take anywhere from five minutes to a couple of hours to locate the column definition in Oracle's documentation set. Finally, there is a great solution to this old problem: the data dictionary view *dict_columns*. The query in Exhibit 11 prompts for a data dictionary name and returns the column and a description of the column contents for all columns in the data dictionary view.

```
SQL> COL     COLUMN_NAMEFORMAT A30
SQL> COL "Description Of Column Contents" FORMAT A40
SQL> SELECT column_name,
  2       comments "Description Of Column Contents"
  3  FROM   DICT_COLUMNS
  4* WHERE  TABLE_NAME = UPPER('&DD');
Enter value for dd: DBA_USERS


COLUMN_NAME                    Description Of Column Contents
-------------------------------------------------------------
USERNAME                       Name of the user
USER_ID                        ID number of the user
PASSWORD                       Encrypted password
ACCOUNT_STATUS
LOCK_DATE
EXPIRY_DATE
DEFAULT_TABLESPACE             Default tablespace for data
TEMPORARY_TABLESPACE           Default tablespace for temporary
                                 tables
CREATED                        User creation date
PROFILE                        User resource profile name
INITIAL_RSRC_CONSUMER_GROUP    User's initial consumer group
EXTERNAL_NAME                  User external name
12 rows selected.
```

Exhibit 11. *Data Dictionary Query*

Notice that not all columns are defined. No work has apparently been done in the area of dynamic performance views, as the next example illustrates.

```
SQL> SELECT column_name,
  2       comments "Description Of Column Contents"
  3  FROM   DICT_COLUMNS
  4* WHERE  TABLE_NAME = UPPER('&DD');

Enter value for dd: v$dbfile

COLUMN_NAME      Description Of Column Contents
--------------- ------------------------------
FILE#
NAME
```

At any rate, Oracle Corporation is on the right track. It's about darn time!

Init.ora Parameter Definitions

There are times when even developers need to know the definitions and settings of parameters in the parameter file. This file is under the lock and key of the Oracle database administrator. If you have been granted privileges to view the *v$parameter* dynamic performance view, you can write a query such as the following example. You want to see all parameters containing the string "LARGE" and the definition or description of the parameter. You can see that there is one parameter containing the string "LARGE", *large_pool_size*. By the output in the DESCRIPTION column, you can see *large_pool_size* is the size of the large pool in bytes.

```
SQL> COL NAME FORMAT A20
SQL> COL DESCRIPTION FORMAT A58
SQL> SELECT name,
  2          description
  3   FROM   V$PARAMETER
  4*  WHERE  name like '%' || lower ('&Parameter') || '%';

Enter value for parameter: LARGE

NAME                DESCRIPTION
---------------     ------------------------------------------
large_pool_size     size in bytes of the large allocation pool
```

So now you don't have to spend a lot of valuable time looking up the definition of an *init.ora* parameter. After all, Oracle continues to add parameters with each release. The following query indicates that there are presently 195 parameters in Oracle 8.1.5.

```
SQL> SELECT count(*)
  2   FROM   V$PARAMETER;

COUNT(*)
---------
195
```

```
SQL> DEF
DEFINE _SQLPLUS_RELEASE = "801050000" (CHAR)
DEFINE _EDITOR          = "Notepad" (CHAR)
DEFINE _O_VERSION       = "Oracle8i Enterprise Edition
Release
                              8.1.5.0.0
With the Partitioning and Java options
PL/SQL Release 8.1.5.0.0-Production" (CHAR)
DEFINE _O_RELEASE       = "801050000" (CHAR)
DEFINE _RC              = "1" (CHAR)
```

I think it is very safe to say that all Oracle database administrators are saying "Amen" to this enhancement. It's about time!

Conclusion

Oracle8i contains many sought-after enhancements. This chapter is just a "tip of the iceberg." To learn most of the new Oracle8i enhancements, take Oracle Corporation's "Oracle8i New Features" class. Of all the features, this author appreciates the DROP COLUMN feature the most; and now it's about time to end this chapter.

External Tables

Not only are all these fancy functions and materialized views available to access Oracle data. They can also be used to access non-Oracle data, via external tables. An external table is a file that lives outside of the database, yet you can use DML to access the data in the table, as if it lives inside the database. Mike Ault, tuning guru, describes their access below.

Using External Tables in Oracle9i

In Oracle we are used to using internal tables; in fact, that, for many years, was the only option available to Oracle users. In later versions, the *utl_file* utility provided access for read and write to external files but not directly from SQL; you had to use PL/SQL to move the data into internal tables before it could be easily accessed by Oracle users. External data files had to be loaded using SQL*Loader or UTL_FILE into internal tables before SQL access was allowed. In Oracle8, the concept of BFILEs was introduced. BFILEs allow access to external files such as bitmaps, jpegs, PDF, and other formats as a single data column in a table; however, once again, SQL access was not possible and the columns had to be read by specialized PL/SQL routines.

Now in Oracle9i, DBAs have been given the external table. Combining the best features of BFILEs, UTL_FILE, and SQL*Loader, external tables allow direct SQL access to data contained in external data files. Once the DBA defines the data map into the external data file, users can directly access the data through SQL. However, the true strength of external tables will be in simplifying and streamlining data loading. An external table only has to be defined once and can be reused many times against multiple versions of the external data file.

Many applications use data from external sources to feed tables in an Oracle database. In previous releases (prior to Oracle9i), this data feed would require you to:

1. Collect data from an external source such as a mainframe or telephony switch.

2. Move file to Oracle system using FTP or other file transfer protocols.

3. Convert data to a recognizable format.

4. Load into Oracle using:

   - SQL*Loader routine
   - 3GL routine
   - UTL_FILE and PL/SQL

- Multiple SQL insert commands

5. Manipulate data inside Oracle using SQL or PL/SQL.

6. Parse data to multiple tables (if required) using SQL or PL/SQL.

The scripts and processes involved in this data import from external files where usually complex and prone to failures.

Oracle9i has added the capability to use external tables as sources for data in an Oracle database. The data will still reside in the external tables but will be accessible to users from inside the database.

Using External Tables

Using external tables with Oracle9i is actually a very easy process. In fact, if you are using SQL*Loader to perform Step 4, you have already performed the most difficult part of using external tables.

To use external data tables, they must be compatible for use with SQL*Loader. Oracle will support other loading routines; but until the APIs are written to use third-party routines, we are stuck with SQL*Loader. The new process flow for using external data in an Oracle database will be:

1. Collect data from an external source such as mainframe.

2. Move file to Oracle system.

3. Convert data to recognizable format.

4. Create external table call.

5. Manipulate data inside Oracle.

6. Parse data to multiple tables (if required).

With new features in Oracle9i we can simplify Steps 4, 5, and 6; that is all the steps that require access to the Oracle database.

As long as the external data file is named the same, is of the same format, and is placed in the same location each time, the external table call only has to be created once; there is no hard connection between the external file and the external table call other than the location and file name. Also, the definition of an external table can be modified without being dropped to point to new data locations on-the-fly. This ability to re-point the data file locations means that you will not have to re-grant permissions, recompile packages and procedures, or re-compile views because you had to drop and recreate the external table definition.

The general format for accomplishing this connection between an external data file and a table defined as ORGANIZATION EXTERNAL in the database is:

```
CREATE TABLE [schema.]table_name
[relational_properties]
ORGANIZATION EXTERNAL external_table_clause;
```

Where

```
Relational_properties are:
(column datatype constraint list)
[table constraints]
[logging clauses]
  external_table_clause is:
  ([TYPE external_driver_type]
external_data_properties)
[REJECT LIMIT n|UNLIMITED]
external_data_properties are:
DEFAULT DIRECTORY directory
[ACCESS PARAMETERS (opaque_format_spec)| USING
  CLOB subquery]
LOCATION ([directory:]'location specifier')
```

The definitions for the various parts of the above clauses are:

TYPE . TYPE *access_driver_type* indicates the access driver of the external table. The access driver is the API that interprets the external data for the database. If you do not specify TYPE, Oracle uses the default access driver, ORACLE_LOADER. Currently, ORACLE_LOADER is the only access driver available.

DEFAULT DIRECTORY. Allows you to specify one or more default directory objects corresponding to directories on the file system where the external data sources may reside. Default directories can also be used by the access driver to store auxiliary files such as error logs. Multiple default directories are permitted to facilitate load balancing on multiple disk drives using parallel access streams.

ACCESS PARAMETERS. The optional ACCESS PARAMETERS clause lets you assign values to the parameters of the specific access driver for this external table:

- The *opaque_format_spec* lets you list the parameters and their values. Use the Oracle Utilities manual to help you define the opaque format specification for your data. Essentially, it will be identical to an SQL*Loader control file for the same data

- The USING CLOB subquery lets you derive the parameters and their values through a subquery. The subquery cannot contain any set operators or an ORDER BY clause. It must return one row containing a single item of datatype CLOB.

- Whether you specify the parameters in an *opaque_format_spec* or derive them using a subquery, Oracle does not interpret anything in this clause. It is up to the access driver to interpret this information in the context of the external data.

LOCATION. The LOCATION clause lets you specify one external locator for each external data source. Usually, the *location_identifier* is a file, but it need not be. Oracle does not interpret this clause. It is up to the access driver to interpret this information in the context of the external data.

REJECT LIMIT. The REJECT LIMIT clause lets you specify how many conversion errors can occur during a query of the external data before an Oracle error is returned and the query is aborted. The default value is 0. The value of UNLIMITED is also allowed.

You use the *external_table_clause* to create an external table, which is a read-only table whose metadata is stored in the database but whose data is stored outside the database. External tables let you query data without first loading it into the database, among other capabilities.

Because external tables have no data in the database, you define them with a small subset of the clauses normally available when creating tables.

- Within the *relational_properties* clause, you can specify only column, datatype, and column_constraint. Further, the only constraints valid for an external table are NULL, NOT NULL, and CHECK constraints.

- Within the *table_properties* clause, you can specify only the *parallel_clause* and the enable-disable clause:

- The *parallel_clause* lets you parallelize subsequent queries on the external data.

- The enable-disable clause lets you either enable or disable a NULL, NOT NULL, or CHECK constraint. You can specify only ENABLE or DISABLE, and CONSTRAINT *constraint_name*. No other parts of this clause are permitted.

Restrictions on external tables include:

- No other clauses are permitted in the same CREATE TABLE statement if you specify the *external_table_clause*.

- An external table cannot be a temporary table.

- An external table cannot be indexed.

- An external table cannot be analyzed.

- No DML is allowed against an external table.

Example Creation of an External Table

We have a listing of all of the SQL scripts we use to manage Oracle databases. This listing has been generated on a Linux box using the ls–l>file.dat command and the resulting listing file cleaned up using system editors looks like the following (the actual file has over 400 entries):

```
'-rw-r--r--';1;oracle;dba;626;
  Apr 17 18:25;accept.sql;
'-rw-r--r--';1;oracle;dba;11103;
  Apr 17 18:25;access.sql;
'-rw-r--r--';1;oracle;dba;3295;
  Apr 18 01:19;act_size8.sql;
'-rw-r--r--';1;oracle;dba;918;
  Apr 17 18:25;active_cursors.sql;
'-rw-r--r--';1;oracle;dba;63;
  Aug 21 12:35;afiedt.buf;
'-rw-r--r--';1;oracle;dba;273;
  Apr 17 18:25;alter_resource.sql;
'-rw-r--r--';1;oracle;dba;5265;
  Apr 17 18:25;alter_views.sql;
'-rw-r--r--';1;oracle;dba;401;
  Apr 17 18:25;anal_tab.sql;
'-rw-r--r--';1;oracle;dba;374;
  Apr 17 18:25;analyze_all.sql;
'-rw-r--r--';1;oracle;dba;244;
  Apr 17 18:25;analz_sch.sql;
'-rw-r--r--';1;oracle;dba;989;
  Apr 17 19:25;auto_chn.sql;
'-rw-r--r--';1;oracle;dba;1861;
  Apr 17 18:25;auto_defrag.sql;
'-rw-r--r--';1;oracle;dba;167;
  Apr 17 18:25;awt.sql;
'-rw-r--r--';1;oracle;dba;481;
```

```
  Apr 18 01:20;backup.sql;
'-rw-r--r--';1;oracle;dba;405;
  Apr 18 01:20;block_usage.sql;
'-rw-r--r--';1;oracle;dba;960;
  Apr 18 01:21;blockers.sql;
'-rw-r--r--';1;oracle;dba;940;
  Apr 17 18:25;blockers2.sql;
'-rw-r--r--';1;oracle;dba;1002;
  Apr 18 01:21;bound2.sql;
'-rw-r--r--';1;oracle;dba;1299;
  Apr 18 01:22;bound_ob.sql;
'-rw-r--r--';1;oracle;dba;1742;
  Apr 17 18:25;brown.sql;
```

To match this external file we create a CREATE TABLE command that matches up the columns in the internal representation with the external file using standard SQL*LOADER control file syntax (first, we must create the DIRECTORY object that points to the external file location):

```
CREATE DIRECTORY sql_dir as '/home/
oracle/sql_scripts';
```

For the directory to be used by more than just the creator, we have to grant READ and WRITE to other users, in this case, public:

```
GRANT READ ON DIRECTORY sql_dir TO public;

GRANT WRITE ON DIRECTORY sql_dir TO public;

CREATE TABLE sql_scripts (permissions
  VARCHAR2(20),
filetype NUMBER(3),owner VARCHAR2(20),
group_name VARCHAR2(20), size_in_bytes NUMBER,
date_edited DATE , script_name VARCHAR2(64))
ORGANIZATION EXTERNAL
(TYPE ORACLE_LOADER
DEFAULT DIRECTORY sql_dir
```

```
ACCESS PARAMETERS
(FIELDS TERMINATED BY ';' OPTIONALLY ENCLOSED BY "'"
(permissions, filetype,owner,group_name,size_in_bytes,
date_edited DATE(17) "Mon dd hh24:mi",
script_name))
LOCATION ('file.dat'))
/
```

Once the table is created, we grant SELECT permission so others can also use it:

```
GRANT SELECT ON sql_scripts TO public;
```

The syntax of the statement is not verified for accuracy concerning the existence of the specified directory or file, or that the format specification for the load is correct, until the table is actually executed. Exhibit 1 shows what it actually looked like during the creation.

To verify that the table is accessing the data correctly, you need to do more than just verify that a COUNT(*) works. You need to access each data item in each row. I suggest doing a COUNT of each column to verify that it is accessible. I then used multiple Linux copy (cp) commands to make three additional copies of the file.dat file, used the Linux concatenation (cat) command to combine them with the original to make the file four times larger, and then renamed the larger file using the Linux move (mv) command to the name of the original file. Without changing a thing inside Oracle, I was able to reselect from the new external table:

```
SQL> /
  COUNT(*)
----------
      1764
Elapsed: 00:00:00.37
```

```
Execution Plan
-------------------------------------------------
0   SELECT STATEMENT Optimizer=CHOOSE
1 0    SORT (AGGREGATE)
2 1       EXTERNAL TABLE ACCESS (FULL)
          OF 'SQL_SCRIPTS'
```

Hints and External Tables

External tables also support the use of hints to affect join and access methods. Of course, any hints involving features not able to be used by external tables, such as indexes, will be ignored. From a lecture by Richard Niemiec of TUSC:

```
SQL> l
  1   select /*+ use_hash(a) */ a.empno, b.job, a.job
  2   from   emp_external4 a, emp_external5 b
  3   where  a.empno = b.empno
  4   and    a.empno = 7900
  5*  and    b.empno = 7900;
400 rows selected.

Elapsed: 00:00:02.65

Execution Plan
-------------------------------------------------
0   SELECT STATEMENT Optimizer=CHOOSE
    (Cost=33 Card=81 Bytes=2754)
1 0    HASH JOIN (Cost=33 Card=81 Bytes=2754)
2 1       EXTERNAL TABLE ACCESS (FULL) OF 'EMP_EXTERNAL4'
3 1       EXTERNAL TABLE ACCESS (FULL) OF 'EMP_EXTERNAL5'
```

Notice how we forced it to use a HASH join operation?

External Table Performance

To get an idea of the performance of these external tables, I kept quadrupling the size of the external table until I reached 1,806,336 rows. Exhibit 2 shows the results from the full table scans of the external table compared against a full table scan of an identical internal table created from a SELECT * FROM *sql_tables* command of the largest external table. The actual data is shown in Exhibit 3.

You must remember that external tables cannot be analyzed or indexed; thus, their performance will always be identical to that for a full table scan. In addition, if you have a syntax error in your SQL*LOADER command file section, it will not show itself until an attempt is made to access that row. In my initial specification, I had an error in the date conversion. I was able to select columns without the dates and do row counts and value counts; but as soon as I did anything that attempted to access the date_edited column, I would get an OCI error. This indicates that you should always verify that you can access all rows before turning over an external table for general use. Another thing to watch is that, by default, a log identical to an SQL*LOADER log will be generated and will be inserted into each time a user accesses the external table unless you specify that no log be generated.

We will now look at using external tables in parallel and using some of the new, advanced features of Oracle9i, the multi-table INSERT and the MERGE command with the external table as a source for our data.

If we are to use external tables to replace the data loads from other data sources, then we must have a means to load data quickly and easily into multiple internal tables. Additionally, we must be able to provide conditional INSERT and UPDATE based on existence of rows in existing tables and the actual column values in existing rows. By using the new multi-table INSERT and MERGE commands, these tasks become easier than ever before.

Using External Tables in Parallel

If you have a multiple-file external file, you can use parallel access to speed performance. For example, suppose we have our script list in three files and we want to utilize parallel processing to speed access to these lists. We would redefine the external table as follows:

```
SQL> CREATE TABLE sql_scripts (permissions
         VARCHAR2(20),
   2  filetype NUMBER(3),owner VARCHAR2(20),
   3  group_name varchar2(20), size_in_bytes number,
   4  date_edited date , script_name
         VARCHAR2(64))
   5  ORGANIZATION EXTERNAL
   6  (TYPE ORACLE_LOADER
   7  DEFAULT DIRECTORY sql_dir
   8  ACCESS PARAMETERS
   9  (FIELDS TERMINATED BY ';' OPTIONALLY ENCLOSED BY "'"
  10  (permissions, filetype,owner,group_name,size_in_bytes,
  11  date_edited DATE(17) "Mon dd hh24:mi",
  12  script_name))
  13  LOCATION
         ('file1.dat',sql_dir2:'file2.dat',
         sql_dir3: 'file3.dat'))
  14  PARALLEL 3
  15* REJECT LIMIT UNLIMITED
SQL>/
```

The major difference between the above command and the standard command we saw earlier is in the LOCATION line; there are three data files listed. In the data file specifications, notice that there are two additional directories specified: the additional directories would have to exist and, of course, the specified files would have to reside in them. If no additional directories are specified, then Oracle assumes that the files in the LOCATION qualifier reside in the same directory. Also notice the PARALLEL keyword. If no integer argument is specified with the PARALLEL keyword, the default degree of parallel will be used. In the example, a parallel degree of 3 will be used to read the data from the external tables into Oracle. You should also make sure that your system is properly set up for parallel query by verifying the settings of the *min_parallel_servers* and *max_parallel_servers* initialization parameters. Other initialization parameters that you may want to check include *db_file_multiblock_read_count, sort_area_size*, as well as others dealing with how efficiently Oracle reads data to and from disk (because access to external tables will be by full-table scan only).

If the external data files are located on different disk assets or are spread to minimize contention, then performance increases will be realized from using parallel processes to access the external data files. However, if they contend for each other, a performance penalty may occur.

Using External Tables to Export Data

According to early documentation, external tables can also be used to export data out of Oracle. The following example using the EMP and DEPT tables in the SCOTT schema shows how all employees working in the MARKETING and ENGINEERING departments can be exported in parallel using the default degree of parallelism. *Note*: This example was listed in the Oracle9i Beta documentation but removed for the production release. The Oracle concepts manual still states that the external table can be used to perform parallel data export but no examples are given anywhere in the documentation that I can find. I have to assume the capability was yanked at the last minute but may be available in future releases.

```
#
# Export employees working in the departments
  'MARKETING' and
# 'ENGINEERING'
#
CREATE TABLE emp_ext
    (empno NUMBER, ename VARCHAR2(100), ...)
     ORGANIZATION EXTERNAL
    (
        TYPE ORACLE_INTERNAL
        DEFAULT DIRECTORY private2
        LOCATION(export_dir:'/emp_data/emp1.exp',
```

```
          export_dir:'/emp_data/emp2.exp')
...)
PARALLEL
AS SELECT e.*, d.dname
   FROM   emp e, dept d
   WHERE  e.deptno = d.deptno
   AND    d.dname IN ('MARKETING','ENGINEERING');
```

At this point, you will have an external table that contains all of the records corresponding to the MARKETING and ENGINEERING departments that can be used by other programs if desired. Once changes are made to the data, it can be re-imported into the external table specification and then moved easily from there back into its parent tables. Notice that the TYPE becomes ORACLE_INTERNAL rather than ORACLE_LOADER and that no conversion specification is required.

```
#
# Re-import the employees that are working in
  the 'ENGINEERING' department
#
CREATE TABLE emp_import
   PARALLEL
   AS SELECT *
      FROM   emp_ext
      WHERE  dname = 'ENGINEERING';
```

This example illustrates how the external table feature can help to export (and import) a selective set of records.

Multi-Table Insert Using External Tables

Once the external data source is made into an external table that is accessible by SQL, the DBA will usually need to parse the data into one or more internal database tables for it to be in a truly useful form. In prior Oracle releases, after loading the data into a staging table, a PL/SQL procedure or SQL script with multiple SQL statements would have been required. In Oracle9i, the new

---

Oracle SQL Tuning & CBO Internals

multi-table insert capability will reduce the complexity of data parsing.

Using the new multi-table insert capability with Oracle9i and external tables, many lines of code in older versions can be compressed into a few statements with a resulting improvement in reliability and performance. For example, let's pull all of the scripts with tab in their names (assuming that all with tab in the name are for tables) into a *table_scripts* table and all of the scripts with ind in their names into a *index_scripts* table, the scripts left over will go into an *other_scripts* table.

First we need to create our empty tables. You cannot create them as a select off of the external table, so we will use the internal table we created as a template:

```
SQL> create table table_scripts as select * from
  2  sql_scripts_int where rownum<1;
Table created.

SQL> create table index_scripts as select * from
  2  sql_scripts_int where rownum<1;
Table created.

SQL> create table other_scripts as select * from
  2  sql_scripts_int where rownum<1;
Table created.
```

Now do the multi-table INSERT (see Exhibit 1).

```
SQL> INSERT FIRST
  2  WHEN script_name like '%tab%' THEN
  3  INTO table_scripts
  4  VALUES (PERMISSIONS, FILETYPE ,OWNER,
       GROUP_NAME, SIZE_IN_BYTES,
  5  DATE_EDITED, SCRIPT_NAME )
  6  WHEN script_name like '%ind%' THEN
  7  INTO index_scripts
  8  VALUES (PERMISSIONS, FILETYPE, OWNER,
       GROUP_NAME, SIZE_IN_BYTES,
  9  DATE_EDITED,SCRIPT_NAME)
 10  ELSE
```

```
 11  INTO other_scripts
 12  VALUES(PERMISSIONS, FILETYPE, OWNER,
        GROUP_NAME, SIZE_IN_BYTES,
 13  DATE_EDITED,SCRIPT_NAME)
 14  SELECT * FROM sql_scripts;
1806336 rows created.

Elapsed: 00:03:36.50

SQL> select count(*) from table_scripts;
COUNT(*)
----------131072

SQL> select count(*) from index_scripts;
COUNT(*)
----------20480

SQL> select count(*) from other_scripts;
COUNT(*)
----------1654784
```

Exhibit 1. *The Multi-Table INSERT*

Was this faster than doing the tables individually? Let's see. We will truncate the tables we just placed data into and reload them using standard INSERT commands (see Exhibit 2).

```
Them Using Standard INSERT Commands

SQL> truncate table table_scripts;

Table truncated.

SQL> truncate table index_scripts;

Table truncated.

SQL> truncate table other_scripts;

Table truncated.
SQL> INSERT
  2  INTO table_scripts (
  3  PERMISSIONS, FILETYPE ,OWNER,
  4  GROUP_NAME, SIZE_IN_BYTES, DATE_EDITED,
       SCRIPT_NAME)
```

```
    5  SELECT * FROM sql_scripts
    6  WHERE script_name like '%tab%';

131072 rows created.

Elapsed: 00:00:46.05

SQL> INSERT
    2  INTO index_scripts (
    3  PERMISSIONS, FILETYPE ,OWNER,
    4  GROUP_NAME, SIZE_IN_BYTES,
    5  DATE_EDITED, SCRIPT_NAME )
    6  SELECT * FROM sql_scripts
    7  WHERE script_name like '%ind%';

20480 rows created.

Elapsed: 00:00:27.21

SQL> INSERT
    2  INTO other_scripts (
    3  PERMISSIONS, FILETYPE ,OWNER,
    4  GROUP_NAME, SIZE_IN_BYTES,
    5  DATE_EDITED, SCRIPT_NAME )
    6  SELECT * FROM sql_scripts
    7  WHERE script_name not like '%tab%'
    8  AND script_name not like '%ind%';

1654784 rows created.

Elapsed: 00:03:45.64
```

Exhibit 2. *Truncating the Tables and Reloading*

Now compare the results. First we need to sum the times required for the multiple statements:

```
         46.05
         27.21
        3:45.64
        ----------
total    4:58.90
```

A total of 4:58.90 versus 3:36.50 for the multi-table insert. A 25 percent improvement in speed! Some complex examples have up to a reported 400 percent improvement in speed. I repeated the test several times with similar results.

Using the MERGE Command with External Tables

In many situations, data might have to be inserted into a table if it does not already exist; but if the key portions of data are already in the table, the changed data columns have to be updated instead. In earlier versions of Oracle, this would have been done with an INSERT and UPDATE command. Now we have a new Oracle9i feature called the MERGE command. The MERGE command allows for what is euphemistically known as an UPSERT. The MERGE command allows for the conditional INSERT or UPDATE of data based on the values in the data being manipulated. Because the INSERT and UPDATE are combined into a single command, the requirement for multiple scans in SQL or decision trees in PL/SQL is eliminated, thus allowing better performance and less complex code.

For example, we want to update all of the values for the DATE_EDITED column in our OTHER_SCRIPTS table based on the script name. If the script does not exist in OTHER_SCRIPTS, we want the entire new row inserted. Here is the UPDATE and INSERT required in SQL to do this operation without the MERGE command:

```
SQL> UPDATE other_scripts a
  2   SET    a.date_edited = (SELECT distinct
               b.date_edited FROM sql_scripts b
  3   WHERE  a.script_name = b.script_name);
492 rows updated.

Elapsed: 00:00:01.01
```

```
Execution Plan
------------------------------------------------
0   UPDATE STATEMENT Optimizer=CHOOSE
1 0    UPDATE OF 'OTHER_SCRIPTS'
2 1       TABLE ACCESS (FULL) OF
             'OTHER_SCRIPTS'
3 1       SORT (UNIQUE)
4 3          EXTERNAL TABLE ACCESS (FULL)
                OF 'SQL_SCRIPTS'
```

And

```
SQL> INSERT INTO other_scripts a
  2  SELECT * FROM sql_scripts b
  3  WHERE  b.script_name not in (
  4  select b.script_name from other_scripts b);
28 rows created.

Elapsed: 00:00:00.01

Execution Plan
------------------------------------------------
0   INSERT STATEMENT Optimizer=CHOOSE
1 0    FILTER
2 1       EXTERNAL TABLE ACCESS (FULL) OF
             'SQL_SCRIPTS'
3 1       TABLE ACCESS (FULL) OF
             'OTHER_SCRIPTS'
```

With the new MERGE command, this becomes like the code in
Exhibit 3.

```
SQL> MERGE INTO other_scripts a
  2  USING (SELECT * FROM sql_scripts) b
  3  ON (a.script_name = b.script_name)
  4  WHEN MATCHED THEN
  5  UPDATE SET a.date_edited =
       b.date_edited
  6  WHEN NOT MATCHED THEN
  7  INSERT (a.permissions, a.filetype,
       a.owner, a.group_name,
  8  a.size_in_bytes,
       a.date_edited,a.script_name )
  9  VALUES (b.permissions, b.filetype,
       b.owner, b.group_name,
 10  b.size_in_bytes, b.date_edited,
       b.script_name );

12770 rows merged.
```

Example Creation of an External Table

```
Elapsed: 00:00:05.01

Execution Plan
---------------------------------------------
0   MERGE STATEMENT Optimizer=CHOOSE
    (Cost=7874 Card=4018656 Bytes=598779744)
1 0   MERGE OF 'OTHER_SCRIPTS'
2 1     HASH JOIN (OUTER)(Cost=26
            Card=211508 Bytes=32995248)
3 2       EXTERNAL TABLE ACCESS (FULL)
            OF'SQL_SCRIPTS' (Cost=16
            Card=8168 Bytes=857640)
4 2       TABLE ACCESS (FULL) OF
            'OTHER_SCRIPTS' (Cost=2
            Card=492 Bytes=25092)
```

Exhibit 3. *New MERGE Command*

Thus, we were able to perform both the UPDATE and the INSERT using a single command and a single transaction that performs both operations. Oddly, the performance seems to be worse using the MERGE command in Oracle 9.0.1.1 and there are certain oddities with the statistics reported.

Examples of the oddities in the reported statistics are the CARD (cardinality) reported against the external table SQL_SCRIPTS; the external table only contains 520 rows, not the 8168 reported by the cardinality. In addition, only 520 rows were subject to the combined INSERT and UPDATE operations, not the 12770 reported by the summary for the command. This seems to indicate that multiple, instead of single scans of the external table are being done, followed by multiple UPDATE of rows (because the final row count on the table was only 520). This has been reported to Oracle support and perhaps in future releases the expected better performance will materialize.

I also attempted to force index usage on the internal table using hints, but the hints, although supported by the MERGE command according to documentation, were steadfastly ignored.

Summary

We have examined the creation and general usage of external tables. We have also examined the performance characteristics. We can conclude that DBAs now have several new, powerful tools to add to their toolboxes. The capability to access external tables directly from SQL will allow easier data loading and use of data from other systems without the time-intensive loading and parsing that was previously required. The new multi-table INSERT command makes it much easier to spread data from both external tables and internal tables to several sub-tables. The new MERGE command allows easier INSERT and UPDATE activities.

Stored Outlines

Stored outlines can be very useful, especially when the SQL can't be changed (packaged applications).

In order to use them, you need to capture the SQL statement, and then create an outline with exactly the same SQL statement that uses an alternative access path (perhaps via a hint).

Initially, set up security to create the outlines:

```
connect 'sys/xxx as sysdba'
grant create any outline to scott;
grant execute on dbms_outln to scott;
grant execute on dbms_outln_edit to scott;
grant select on dba_outlines to scott;
```

To begin with, set up the session to allow stored outlines, or to ensure that the *init.ora* parameter *create_stored_outlines* is set accordingly.

```
connect scott/tiger
alter session set create_stored_outlines =  TRUE
```

```
create or replace outline first_outline
on select a.emp_id, a.name, b.dependent_id, b.name
from emp a,
dependent b
where a.empid_id = b.emp_id
```

Now a public outline has been created, but in order to test it, make a private outline (personal copy). In order to do this, you need to create the tables to hold the private outline first:

```
execute dbms_outln_edit.create_edit_tables;
create private outline first_private_outline from
first_outline;

--- check out what is in the outline table by default,
--- just from creating the private outline
select * from ol$hints
where ol_name = 'first_private_outline';

--- change which ever access path we are interested in
--- for example, could change a nested_lop join to
--- a hash join

update ol$hints set hint_text='USE_HASH(B)'
where hint#=5;
commit;

--- check the result, and be sure the update worked
select * from ol$hints
where ol_name = 'first_private_outline';

--- resync the outline

execute dbms_outline_edit.refresh_private_outline
('first_private_outline')

--- test it out
alter session set use_private_outlines=true;

set autotrace on explain
select a.emp_id, a.name, b.dependent_id, b.name
from emp a,
dependent b
where a.empid_id = b.emp_id
;

--- if new access plan is correct, make the outline public
```

```
--- for use by everyone

create or replace second_outline from private
first_private_outline;
```

Now, whenever the original SQL is executed, it will use the revised access plan instead of the original (assuming the *init.ora* parameter *use_stored_outlines* is set to true).

Note that the SQL used to create the stored outline and the SQL that is run after the outline is created, must be IDENTICAL, or it won't use the outline. Identical means the text must be in the same case, same amount of white space, etc. Oracle 9i and 10g are more forgiving on this requirement than Oracle 8i.

The catalog tables *dba_outlines* and *dba_outline_hints* contain relevant information about the outlines. They are based on catalog tables OUTLN.OL$ and OUTLN.OL$HINTS.

Stored Outlines have been greatly enhanced with the new Oracle 10g features of SQL Profiles.

Oracle 10g New SQL Language Features

We are going to discuss the new features involving the SELECT command. The SELECT command has been greatly expanded (although there are only a few new clauses added). The expansions come mostly in the form of adding functionality to existing features. The new SELECT features include:

- Grouped Table Outer Join
- Increased Number of Aggregates per Query
- Remote Stored Functions in SELECT Statements
- Case-Insensitive and Accent-Insensitive Query and Sort
- Enhanced CONNECT BY Support

- Oracle Expression Filter
- SQL Regular Expressions
- Row Timestamp

We will start by examining the grouped table outer join enhancement.

Grouped Table Outer Join

This new SELECT feature, known as the "Grouped Table Outer Join", is an extension to the standard ANSI join syntax. The new syntax is used to improve performance and simplify SQL queries for Oracle10*g* time-based calculations. The WITHIN GROUP clause must reference a column or columns used in a GROUP BY statement in the source SELECT statement.

The grouped table outer join clause syntax is:

```
<Table_reference> WITHIN GROUP (<expr>[,])
```

You use a grouped table outer join to fill in sparse data; sparse data is data that doesn't have rows for all possible values of a dimension, such as time or department. This is known as the process of data densification.

The example below shows the use of a grouped table outer join in a *subquery_factoring_clause*. A *subquery_factoring_clause* allows you to assign a name to a subquery block. The subquery block can then be referenced from multiple locations in your query simply by specifying the name. This type of query is optimized by Oracle in the same way as an in-line view. The subquery_factoring_clause can be used in top-level SELECT statements and subqueries.

The subquery factoring clause comes before the normal SELECT in the command syntax.

```
WITH X AS (
SELECT time_id, loader_id, sum(loaded_weight) total_weight
FROM shipments
WHERE loader_id = 165432
GROUP BY time_id, loader_id)
SELECT X.loader_id, t.time_id,
SUM(total_weight) OVER
(partition by loader_id, t.calendar_year
ORDER BY T.time_id) as YTD_tonnes
FROM X WITHIN GROUP (loader_id)
RIGHT OUTER JOIN TIMES T
ON (x.time_id = t.time_id);
```

Grouped tables can be used singly, or as a target of a JOIN. The grouped table clause is usually a sub-section of the joined_table clause as a sub-section of the table_reference clause.

The next new feature is the increased number of aggregates per query.

Increased Number of Aggregates per Query

In previous releases of Oracle, the number of aggregate functions that could be used in a SELECT statement was limited to the constraints imposed by the limit on GROUP BY clauses, in other words, the GROUP BY expression and all of the non-distinct aggregate functions (for example, SUM, AVG) had to fit within a single database block. There is no longer a limitation on the number or size of aggregations in a single SQL statement. This was also tied to the 64K size limitation on SQL statements, which has also been removed.

Next, let's talk about the use of remote stored functions in select statements.

Remote Stored Functions in SELECT Statements

You can now refer to remote functions stored in a non-Oracle database within the SELECT statement. The *hs_call_name* parameter refers to this feature. Detailed information about this parameter can be found on page A-3 in the manual: Oracle10*i* Heterogeneous Connectivity Administrator's Guide.

The *hs_call_name* parameter is specified in the heterogeneous services initialization parameter file. This file contains configuration settings stored as a text file. The heterogeneous services initialization parameters serve two functions:

- They give the DBA a means of fine-tuning to optimize performance and memory utilization for the gateway and the Heterogeneous Services component.

- They enable the DBA to tell the gateway services (and thereby, heterogeneous services) how the non-Oracle system has been configured.

These parameters give heterogeneous services information about the configurable properties of the non-Oracle database system.

You use the view *v$hs_parameter* to monitor the heterogeneous services initialization parameters. Users can set initialization parameters in the gateway initialization files. There is a heterogeneous services initialization file for each gateway instance. The name of the file is *initsid.ora*, where sid is the Oracle system identifier used for the gateway.

For generic connectivity, the heterogeneous services initialization file is located in the directory $ORACLE_HOME/hs/admin.

In case of specific non-oracle database system transparent gateways, they are located in directories named with the naming convention:

```
$ORACLE_HOME/product_name/admin
```

where the product_name variable is the name of the database system. So, for example, the Sybase gateway initialization file is located in the directory $ORACLE_HOME/tg4sybs/admin.

The heterogeneous services initialization files contain a list of initialization parameter settings, each of which should be on an individual line. The syntax to set the initialization parameters is:

```
[set] [private] parameter = parameter_value
```

The *set* and *private* keywords are optional. When the *set* keyword is present, the variable will also be set in the environment. When the *private* keyword is present, the parameter will not be uploaded to the server. In general, it is recommended by Oracle that the *private* keyword not be used. The only exception is if the initialization parameter value contains sensitive information (such as a password) that shouldn't be sent over the network.

In the initialization parameter syntax, the following rules apply:

- All keywords (SET, PRIVATE, and IFILE) are case insensitive.

- Initialization parameter names and values are case sensitive. Most initialization parameter names are uppercase.

- String values for heterogeneous services parameters must be lowercase.

Note: Exceptions to these rules are explicitly noted.

For this section, the only parameter we are interested in is the *hs_call_name* parameter.

---

hs_call_name

The *hs_call_name* parameter specifies the list of remote functions that a developer can reference in SQL statements to a specific database, through a specific gateway. The value for *hs_call_name* contains a list of remote functions and their owners, separated by semicolons, in the following format:

```
owner_name.function_name
```

For example:

```
owner1.F1;owner2.F2;owner3.F3
```

If no owner name is specified for a remote function, then the default owner name is used to connect to the remote database (the default owner name is specified when the HS database link is created). The entries for the owner names and the function names are case-sensitive.

Case-Insensitive and Accent-Insensitive Query and Sort

You use the *nls_sort* session parameter to specify a case-insensitive or accent-insensitive sort, this is accomplished by:

- Appending a " _CI" to an Oracle sort name for a case-insensitive sort.
- Appending an "_AI" to an Oracle sort name for an accent-insensitive and case-insensitive sort.

For example, you can set *nls_sort* to the following types of values:

- SPANISH becomes SPANISH_AI
- DUTCH becomes DUTCH_CI

Binary sorts can also be case-insensitive or accent-insensitive. When you specify *binary_ci* as a value for *nls_sort*, it designates a sort that is accent-sensitive and case-insensitive. *binary_ai* designates an accent-insensitive and case-insensitive binary sort. You may want to use a binary sort if the binary sort order of the character set is appropriate for the character set you are using.

For example, with the *nls_lang* environment variable set to *american_america.we8iso8859p1*, to use an example right out of the Oracle Database 10g manual, you can create a table called test1 and populate it as follows:

```
SQL> CREATE TABLE test1 (letter VARCHAR2(10));
SQL> INSERT INTO test1 VALUES('ä');
SQL> INSERT INTO test1 VALUES('a');
SQL> INSERT INTO test1 VALUES('A');
SQL> INSERT INTO test1 VALUES('Z');
SQL> SELECT * FROM test1;

LETTER
------
ä
a
A
Z
```

Since the default value of *nls_sort* is BINARY you don't need to specify anything extra to use a binary sort. Use the following statement to do a binary sort of the characters in table test1:

```
SELECT * FROM test1 ORDER BY letter;
```

To change the value of *nls_sort*, you would enter a statement like (only using your sort specifier):

```
ALTER SESSION SET NLS_SORT=BINARY_AI;
```

When *nls_sort=binary*, uppercase letters come before lowercase letters. Letters with diacritics appear last. If the sort considers diacritics but ignores case (*binary_ci*), the letters with diacritics will appear last. When both case and diacritics are ignored (*binary_ai*), the "ä" is sorted with the other characters whose base letter is "a". All characters whose base letter is "a" occur before any occurrence of the letter "z". You should use binary sorts for better performance when the character set is US7ASCII, or any other character set that has the same sort order as the binary sorts.

The following table shows the results from setting *nls_sort* to *binary, binary_ci, and binary_ai.*

BINARY	BINARY_CI	BINARY_AI
A	a	ä
Z	A	a
a	Z	A
ä	ä	Z

The next table shows the sort orders that result from German sorts for the table. A German sort places lowercase letters before uppercase letters, and a "ä" occurs before a "Z". When the sort ignores both case and diacritics (using *nls_sort=german_ai*), the "ä" appears with the other characters whose base letter is an "a".

GERMAN	GERMAN_CI	GERMAN_AI
a	a	ä
A	A	a
Ä	ä	A
Z	Z	Z

The next feature we will discuss is the enhanced CONNECT BY support.

Enhanced CONNECT BY Support

Additions to the CONNECT BY clause enhance queries of hierarchical data by returning all ancestor-dependent pairs (not just parent-child pairs); a new set of pseudo-columns is provided in Oracle Database 10*g*:

- *connect_by_iscycle*
- *connect_by_isleaf*
- *connect_by_root*

These specify whether or not a given node is a leaf of a hierarchy, a cycle in a hierarchy triggers an error message with information about the rows involved in the cycle, and the CONNECT BY clause is now supported for simple subqueries.

Hierarchical Query Pseudo-columns

The new hierarchical query pseudo-columns are valid only in hierarchical queries. The specific hierarchical query pseudo-columns are:

- *connect_by_iscycle*
- *connect_by_isleaf*

connect_by_iscycle

The purpose of the *connect_by_iscycle* pseudo-column is to return 1 if the current row has a child which is also its ancestor. If there is no relation, it returns a 0 value. This information can then be used to further expand the hierarchy.

connect_by_iscycle can only be used if you have specified the *nocycle* parameter of the CONNECT BY clause. The NOCYCLE clause enables Oracle to return the results of a query that would fail because of a CONNECT BY loop.

connect_by_iscycle Example

In the standard Oracle example table, scott.emp, provided for this purpose in all Oracle databases, the employee King is the ultimate boss and has no manager (no entry for the mgr column). One of his employees is Clark, who is the manager of department 10. If we update the employees table to set Clark as King's manager, we can create a loop in the data to show the use of the CONNECT_BY_ISCYCLE pseudo-column:

Without the update the SELECT:

```
SQL> SELECT ename "Employee",
  2 LEVEL, SYS_CONNECT_BY_PATH(ename, '/') "Path"
  3 FROM scott.emp
  4 WHERE level <= 3 AND deptno = 10
  5 START WITH ename = 'KING'
  6 CONNECT BY PRIOR empno = mgr AND LEVEL <= 4;
```

Generates:

```
Employee          LEVEL Path
-------------- --------- ------------------
KING                  1 /KING
CLARK                 2 /KING/CLARK
MILLER                3 /KING/CLARK/MILLER
```

Now, let's give Clark a really big promotion (don't we all dream about becoming our boss's boss?).

```
SQL> UPDATE scott.emp SET mgr = 7782
  2 WHERE empno = 7939;

1 row updated.
```

Now let's check out the hierarchy again:

```
SQL> SELECT ename "Employee",
  2 LEVEL, SYS_CONNECT_BY_PATH(ename, '/') "Path"
  3 FROM scott.emp
  4 WHERE level <= 3 AND deptno = 10
  5 START WITH ename = 'KING'
  6 CONNECT BY PRIOR empno = mgr AND LEVEL <= 4;
```

```
ERROR:
ORA-01436: CONNECT BY loop in user data

no rows selected
```

By adding the *nocycle* parameter in the CONNECT BY condition, we can cause Oracle to return the rows despite the loop. The *connect_by_iscycle* pseudo-column will show you which rows contain the cycle:

```
SQL> SELECT ename "Employee", CONNECT_BY_ISCYCLE "Cycle",
  2 LEVEL, SYS_CONNECT_BY_PATH(ename, '/') "Path"
  3 FROM scott.emp
  4 WHERE level <= 3 AND deptno = 10
  5 START WITH ename = 'KING'
  6 CONNECT BY NOCYCLE PRIOR empno = mgr AND LEVEL <= 4;

Employee        CYCLE     LEVEL Path
-------------- ----- --------- ------------------
KING                0         1 /KING
CLARK               1         2 /KING/CLARK
MILLER              0         3 /KING/CLARK/MILLER
```

connect_by_isleaf

The pseudo-column, *connect_by_isleaf,* returns 1 if the current row is a leaf in the tree defined by the CONNECT BY condition. If the current row is not a leaf in the current tree, it returns 0. This information indicates whether a given row can be further expanded to show more of the hierarchy.

connect_by_isleaf Example

The following example shows the first three levels of the scott.emp table, indicating for each row whether it is a leaf row (which is indicated by 1 in the Leaf column) or whether it has child rows (which is indicated by 0 in the Leaf column):

```
SQL> SELECT ename "Employee", CONNECT_BY_ISLEAF "Leaf", LEVEL,
  2  SYS_CONNECT_BY_PATH(ename,'/') "Path" FROM scott.emp
  3  WHERE level <= 3 AND deptno = 10 START WITH ename ='KING'
  4*  CONNECT BY nocycle  PRIOR empno = mgr AND LEVEL <= 4
```

```
Employee          Leaf      LEVEL
Path

KING               0          1
/KING

CLARK              1          2
/KING/CLARK

MILLER             1          3
/KING/CLARK/MILLER
```

There is one more new clause, *connect_by_root*. Let's discuss this additional clause before we go on to the next new feature.

connect_by_root

The unary operator *connect_by_root* is only valid in hierarchical queries. When a column is qualified with this operator, Oracle returns the column value using data from the root row. This operator is intended to extend the functionality of the CONNECT BY [PRIOR] condition of hierarchical queries.

There is one restriction on the *connect_by_root* clause - this operator cannot be specified in the START WITH condition or the CONNECT BY condition.

```
SQL> SELECT ename "Employee", CONNECT_BY_ROOT empno "Root", LEVEL,
  2  SYS_CONNECT_BY_PATH(ename,'/')  "Path" FROM scott.emp
  3  WHERE level <= 3 AND deptno = 10 START WITH ename='KING'
  4* CONNECT BY NOCYCLE PRIOR empno = mgr AND LEVEL <= 4

Employee        Root     LEVEL Path
-------------- ----- --------- ------------------
KING            7839          1 /KING
CLARK           7839          2 /KING/CLARK
MILLER          7839          3 /KING/CLARK/MILLER
```

Oracle Expression Filter

The Oracle Expression Filter allows application developers to manage and evaluate conditional expressions that describe users' interests in data. The feature consists of: an Expression datatype, a SQL EVALUATE operator, and an index (Enterprise Edition only).

The Oracle Expression Filter allows you to store conditional expressions in a column, which you can then use in the WHERE clause of a database query.

You can use the EVALUATE operator to identify the conditional expressions that return true for a given data item. For example, the following query can be issued to return all the boaters who are interested in a given boat (Model='Sunray', Length=32, Year=2002):

```
SELECT Name, Email FROM Boaters
WHERE EVALUATE (Boat4Sale,
'Model=>''SunRay'', Length=>32, Year=>2002') = 1;
```

To speed up such queries, you can create an optional Expression Filter index on the INTEREST column, this is only available in the Enterprise edition of Oracle.

The Oracle Expression Filter is an internal set of functions and procedures that enables conditional expressions to be stored, managed, and evaluated efficiently in Oracle Database 10*g*.

The conditional expressions, referred to as *Expressions*, are a useful way of describing the interest of a user regarding some expected data.

The Oracle Expression Filter provides a SQL schema and PL/SQL and Java packages that facilitate the storage, retrieval, update, and query of collections of *Expressions* in Oracle Database 10*g*. The Expression Filter consists of the following components:

- The EXFSYS schema that determines the storage, syntax, and semantics of the *Expression* datatypes

- The Expression Filter indexing mechanism

- A set of operators and functions that evaluate the *Expressions* stored in user tables for a given data item

- The Administrative utilities to validate and give advice about correct index structure

The Expression Filter feature can be installed on an Oracle 10*g* Standard or Enterprise Edition database. It is provided as a set of PL/SQL packages, a Java package, a set of dictionary tables, and catalog views. All these objects are created in a dedicated schema named EXFSYS. This schema is not part of the typical installation of the database and will not exist before the Expression Filter is installed. For these initial Oracle Database 10*g* releases, you'll need to manually install the feature, in a future release, you will not need to do so.

> In the preconfigured example database templates provided by the dbca utility, this feature is already installed.

The script to install the Expression Filter feature is available as *catexf.sql*, under the $ORACLE_HOME/rdbms/admin/ directory. This script should be executed from a SQL*Plus session while connected as SYSDBA. The catexf.sql script performs the following actions:

- Creates the exfsys schema owner using exfsys.exe

- Loads information about the exfsys schema into the *dbms_registry* package

- Creates the Java Expresssion library, using *initexf.sql*

- Creates the exfsys objects, using *exftyp.sql*

- Creates the Expression Filter Dictionary, using *exftab.sql*

- Creates the public PL/SQL packages with *exfpbs.sql*

- Creates the Expression filter catalog views, using *exfview.sql*
- Creates the sys owned private package, using *exfsppvs.plb*
- Creates the Expression filter APIs, using *exfeapvs.plb*
- Creates the Expression filter indextype and operators, using *exfimpvs.plb*
- Creates the Xpath Expression filter support, using *exfxppvs.plb*
- Creates the indextype definition for the EXPFilter indextype
- Associates the statistical methods with the appropriate functions

The Expression Filter feature is uninstalled using the *catnoexf.sql* script, which is found in the $ORACLE_HOME/rdbms/admin directory, or its equivalent on your operating system. The functionality of the Expression Filter is the same in both the Standard and Enterprise Edition however, the support for indexing *Expressions* is only available in the Enterprise Edition.

Expressions are Boolean conditions that characterize the interest of a user in some data or information. It is required that the *Expressions* adhere to standard SQL WHERE clause format, and only reference variables and built-in or user-defined functions in their predicates.

For example, the following expression captures the interest of a user in a boat (the data item) with the model, price, and year as attributes.

```
UPPER(Model) = 'POLAR' and Price < 10000 and Year > 2000
```

Expressions are stored in a column of the *Expression* datatype in an Oracle 10*g* database table. *Expressions*, stored in an *Expression* datatype can be inserted, updated, and deleted using standard DML statements. For queries projecting the columns holding expressions, the expressions are displayed in string format.

A set of *Expressions* stored in an *Expression* column of a database table shares a common list of variables that can be used in their predicates. Additionally, these *Expressions* can reference any built-in function or an approved user-defined function in their predicates. The list of variable names along with their datatypes and the list of built-in and approved user-defined functions constitute the metadata for a set of *Expressions* stored in a column. This metadata, referred to as the Attribute Set, determines the evaluation context (scope) for the corresponding expressions. When a new expression is added or an existing expression is modified (using INSERT or UPDATE), it is validated against the attribute set.

Let's look at how the attribute set is specified for an *Expression*.

The Expression Attribute Set

An *Expression's* attribute set is defined as a special Oracle object type that carries all the valid variables for the set. Implicitly, the attribute set includes all the built-in functions as valid references. If desired, you can add user-defined functions to the attribute set as well.

The user-specified attributes for the attribute set can be added one at a time, using the packages and procedures provided, or you can use a type definition as the source of the attribute set for an *Expression*. If you don't use an object type definition for the elementary attributes, the system automatically creates an object type using the name of the attribute set as the object type's name.

The following PL/SQL commands create an attribute set named Boat4Sale with a list of required elementary attributes (variables used in the expressions). First, we will look at using the method provided by the Expressions packages and procedures:

```
BEGIN
dbms_expfil.create_attribute_set(attr_set => 'Boat4Sale');
dbms_expfil.add_elementary_attribute(
attr_set => 'Boat4Sale',
attr_name => 'Model',
attr_type => 'VARCHAR2(20)');
dbms_expfil.add_elementary_attribute(
attr_set => 'Boat4Sale',
attr_name => 'Year',
attr_type => 'NUMBER');
dbms_expfil.add_elementary_attribute(
attr_set => 'Boat4Sale',
attr_name => 'Price',
attr_type => 'NUMBER');
dbms_expfil.add_elementary_attribute(
attr_set => 'Boat4Sale',
attr_name => 'EngineHours',
attr_type => 'NUMBER');
dbms_expfil.add_elementary_attribute(
attr_set => 'Boat4Sale',
attr_name => 'Length',
attr_type => 'NUMBER');
END;
/
```

Personally, I find using the provided packages and procedures a bit cumbersome and complex; it is much easier to simply define a type and use that as the source for the attribute set as is shown below:

```
CREATE OR REPLACE TYPE Boat4Sale AS OBJECT
(Model VARCHAR2(20),
Year NUMBER,
Price NUMBER,
EngineHours NUMBER
Length NUMBER);
/
BEGIN
dbms_expfil.create_attribute_set(attr_set => 'BOAT4SALE',
from_type => 'YES');
END;
/
```

Both methods result in a datatype that can be used to create a table for storing *Expressions*, using the specified *Expression* datatype.

Note: You cannot create an Expression and associated tables in the SYS schema, as the creation builds a trigger and triggers

cannot be built on SYS-owned objects. Any attempt will fail with
an error stack similar to:

```
BEGIN
*
ERROR at line 1:
ORA-38465: failed to create the privilege checking trigger due to:
ORA-4089
ORA-06512: at "EXFSYS.DBMS_EXPFIL_DR", line 24
ORA-06512: at "EXFSYS.DBMS_EXPFIL_DR", line 370
ORA-06512: at "EXFSYS.DBMS_EXPFIL", line 602
ORA-06512: at line 2
```

The ORA-409 error is thrown when you attempt to create a
trigger on a SYS-owned object.

Expression Datatype and Expressions

An *Expression* datatype is always a VARCHAR2 column with an
associated attribute set. Any VARCHAR2 column in a user table
can be converted into a column of *Expression* datatype by
assigning a defined *Expression* attribute set to it. This assignment
constrains the values stored in the specified column to be valid
SQL WHERE clause expressions that reference only the
specified *Expresssion* datatype attributes (elementary attributes and
approved functions).

For example, the Boaters table, which stores a buyer's interest in
buying pre-owned boats, would be defined as follows:

```
CREATE TABLE Boaters (BId NUMBER,
Zipcode NUMBER,
Phone VARCHAR2(12),
Interest VARCHAR2(200));
```

```
BEGIN
dbms_expfil.assign_attribute_set (
attr_set => 'Boat4Sale',
expr_tab => 'BOATERS',
expr_col => 'INTEREST');
END;
/
```

For DML purposes, the column storing the expression is treated as a VARCHAR2 column with a data constraint on it. Attempts to insert invalid expressions in such columns are rejected. A boat buyer's interest in trading cars can be added to the Boaters table using standard DML INSERT statements. For example:

```
INSERT INTO boaters VALUES (1, 32611, '917 768 4633',
'Model=''Sea ray'' and Price < 10000
and EngineHours < 250');
INSERT INTO Boaters VALUES (2, 03060, '603 983 3464',
'Model=''Bayliner'' and Year > 2001 and Price < 13000');
Email column is missing
```

What happens if we attempt to insert a non-approved function into an *Expression*? Let's see:

```
SQL> INSERT INTO Boaters VALUES (3, 03060, '603 484 7013',
   2 'SeaRating(Model, Year) > 5 and Price < 15000');
INSERT INTO Boaters VALUES
                  *
Error at line 1:
ORA-00904: "SEARATING": invalid identifier
ORA-06512: at "EXFSYS.EXF$VALIDATE_3", line 17
ORA-04088: error during execution of trigger 'EXFSYS.EXF$VALIDATE_3'
```

So, what can we do about this?

If the expressions need to reference additional user-defined functions, they can be added to the corresponding attribute set as shown in the following examples:

```
CREATE or REPLACE FUNCTION HorsePower(Model VARCHAR2, Year VARCHAR2)
return NUMBER is
BEGIN
-- Just for example since this returns same value each time
return 150;
END HorsePower;
/
```

```
CREATE or REPLACE FUNCTION SeaRating(Model VARCHAR2, Year VARCHAR2)
return NUMBER is
BEGIN

-- Just for example since this returns same value each time
return 5;
END SeaRating; ( you mean SeaRating!!!)
/
BEGIN
dbms_expfil.add_functions (attr_set => 'Boat4Sale',
funcs_name => 'HorsePower');
dbms_expfil.add_functions (attr_set => 'Boat4Sale',
funcs_name => 'SeaRating');
END;
/
```

Once the user-defined function SeaRating is registered for the expression set, the following *Expression* is now legal for insertion:

```
INSERT INTO Boaters VALUES (3, 03060, '603 484 7013',
'SeaRating(Model, Year) > 5 and Price < 15000');
```

Stored *Expressions* can contain predicates, conjunctions, and disjunctions. *Expressions* cannot contain subqueries. *Expression* data can also be loaded using SQL*Loader.

An individual attribute set can be used to create multiple columns of *Expression* datatypes in multiple tables. The tables with columns referencing an attribute set must be in the same schema as the attribute set. For example, an attribute set created in the NAUTICAL schema cannot be used to create an *Expression* datatype column in another schema.

All of this is well and good, but how do you use these expressions once they exist? This is the purpose of the EVALUATE operator.

The EVALUATE Operator

The EVALUATE operator is used to evaluate an *Expression* set for a given data item. The *Expressions* to be evaluated must be stored in a column of *Expression* datatype, which is created by associating an attribute set to a VARCHAR2 column in a user table, as we saw in the previous sections.

Format for EVALUATE

```
EVALUATE (expression_column, <dataitem>)
<dataitem> := <varchar_dataitem> | <anydata_dataitem>
<varchar_dataitem> := attribute_name => attribute_value
{, attribute_name => attribute_value}>
<anydata_dataitem> := AnyData.convertObject(attribute_set_instance)
```

KEYWORDS AND PARAMETERS	DESCRIPTIONS
Expression_column	Name of the column storing the expressions.
attribute_name	Name of an attribute from the corresponding attribute set.
attribute_value	Value for the attribute.
attribute_set_instance	Instance of the object type associated with the corresponding attribute set.

Table 1 *EVALUATE Keywords and Attributes*

The EVALUATE operator returns 1 for an expression that evaluates to true for the data item and 0 otherwise.

The EVALUATE operator is used in the WHERE clause of a standard SQL query or DML (UPDATE or DELETE) statement. The name-value pairs for a data item can be generated using the *getVarchar()* method, defined for the object type associated with the corresponding attribute set.

When an Expression Filter index is defined on a column storing expressions (only in Enterprise versions), the EVALUATE operator on such a column may use the index for the expression set evaluation based on its usage cost. The EVALUATE operator can be used as a join predicate between a table storing expressions and a table storing corresponding data items.

The VARCHAR form of data item cannot be used for an attribute set with one or more binary typed attributes. For example, if one of the attributes is of CLOB type or an object type (embedded object), the AnyData form of the data item should be used.

Related views:

- *user_expfil_attribute_sets*

- *user_expfil_attributes*

- *user_expfil_expression_sets*

Some example queries against these views are:

```
SQL> select * from user_expfil_attribute_sets;

ATTRIBUTE_SET_NAME
--------------------
BOAT4SALE
BOAT4SALE2

SQL> select * from user_expfil_attributes;

ATTRIBUTE_SET_NAME    ATTRIBUTE      DATA_TYPE        ASSOCIATED_TABLE
--------------------  ------------   ---------------  ----------------
BOAT4SALE             MODEL          VARCHAR2(20)
BOAT4SALE             YEAR           NUMBER
BOAT4SALE             PRICE          NUMBER
BOAT4SALE             ENGINEHOURS    NUMBER
BOAT4SALE2            MODEL          VARCHAR2(20)
BOAT4SALE2            YEAR           NUMBER
BOAT4SALE2            PRICE          NUMBER
BOAT4SALE2            ENGINEHOURS    NUMBER

8 rows selected.


SQL> col expr_table format a10
SQL> col expr_column format a12
SQL> column attribute_set format a15
SQL> select * from user_expfil_expression_sets
```

```
EXPR_TABLE EXPR_COLUMN  ATTRIBUTE_SET   LAST_ANAL NUM_EXPRESSIONS
PREDS_PER_EXPR NUM_SPARSE_PREDS
---------- ----------- --------------- --------- --------------- --
----------- ----------------
BOATER     INTEREST    BOAT4SALE       30-AUG-03               3
2               0
```

Let's look at an example using the EVALUATE operator.

Example use of the EVALUATE Operator

The following example query uses the VARCHAR form of data item generated by the *getVarchar( )* function:

```
SQL> SELECT * FROM Boaters WHERE
   2 EVALUATE (Boaters.Interest,
   3 Boat4Sale('Sea ray', 2002, 9000, 0).getVarchar ()) = 1;

 BID ZIPCODE PHONE        INTEREST
---- ------- ------------ -----------------------------
-----------------------
   1   32611 917 768 4633 Model=>'Sea ray' and Price<10000 and
EngineHours<250
```

For the previous query, the data item can be passed in the AnyData form with the following syntax:

```
SQL> SELECT * FROM Boaters WHERE
EVALUATE (Boaters.Interest,
AnyData.convertObject (
Boat4Sale ('Sea ray',2002,9000,0))) = 1;
BID ZIPCODE PHONE        INTEREST
---- ------- ------------ ----------------------------------------
----------
   1   32611 917 768 4633 Model=>'Sea ray' and Price<10000 and
EngineHours<250
```

When a large set of *Expressions* are stored in a table, the table storing the Expressions can be joined with the table storing data items to be evaluated. For example, let's say we have a used boats table that looks like so:

```
SQL> DESC USED_BOATS

Name          Datatype
---------     ----------
SELLER_ID     NUMBER
MODEL         VARCHAR2(20)
YEAR          NUMBER
PRICE         NUMBER
ENGINEHOURS   NUMBER
LENGTH        NUMBER
```

We could compare our list of Boaters and their expressed desires to our list of used boats using the following syntax:

```
SELECT u.seller_id, b.bid, b.Phone
FROM Boaters c, Used_boats u
WHERE
EVALUATE (b.Interest,
Boat4Sale(u.Model, u.Year, u.Price, u.EngineHours).getVarchar()) = 1
ORDER BY u.seller_id;
```

Of course, if we have a bunch of data and a bunch of Expressions, the comparisons can get pretty complicated and performance can suffer. To help with this, the Expressions can be indexed. Lets look at the concept of the Expression Index next.

Using CREATE INDEX for Expressions

The CREATE INDEX statement can be used to create an Expression Filter index for a set of expressions stored in a column. The column being indexed should be configured to store expressions (that is, it must have an attribute set assigned to it), and the index should be created in the same schema as the table (the table that is storing the expressions).

Format for CREATE INDEX for Expressions

```
CREATE INDEX [schema_name.]index_name ON
[schama_name.].table_name (column_name) INDEXTYPE IS
EXFSYS.EXPFILTER
[ PARAMETERS (' <parameters_clause> ' ) ...;
<parameters_clause>:= [ADD TO DEFAULTS | REPLACE DEFAULTS]
[<storeattrs_clause>] [<indexattrs_clause>][< predstorage _clause>]
```

```
<storeattrs_clause> := STOREATTRS [ ( attr1, attr2, ..., attrx ) |
TOP n ]
<indexattrs_clause> := INDEXATTRS [ ( attr1, attr2, ..., attry ) |
TOP m ]
<predstorage_clause> := PREDSTORAGE (<storage_clause>)
```

The various clauses and parameters for the CREATE INDEX command for Expressions are shown in the following table.

KEYWORDS AND PARAMETERS	DESCRIPTION
EXFSYS.EXPFILTER	This is the name of the Index type that implements the Expression Filter index.
ADD TO DEFAULTS	If this parameter is specified, the attributes listed in the STOREATTRS and INDEXATTRS clauses are added to the defaults associated with the corresponding attribute set. This is the default behavior.
REPLACE DEFAULTS	If this parameter is specified, the index is created using only the list of stored and indexed attributes specified after this clause. In this case, the default index parameters associated with the corresponding attribute set are ignored.
STOREATTRS	Parameter is used to list the stored attributes for the Expression Filter index.

KEYWORDS AND PARAMETERS	DESCRIPTION
INDEXATTRS	Parameter is used to list the indexed attributes for the Expression Filter index.
TOP	This parameter can be used for both STOREATTRS and INDEXATTRS clauses only when the expression set statistics have been collected. The number after the TOP parameter indicates the number of (the most-frequent) attributes to be stored or indexed for the Expression Filter index.
PREDSTORAGE	This is the storage clause for the predicate table.

Table 2 *Expression Index Clauses and Paramters*

Usage Notes for Expression Indexes

For an Expression Filter index, all the indexed attributes are stored. Therefore, the list of stored attributes is derived from those provided in the STOREATTRS and the INDEXATTRS clause. If the REPLACE DEFAULTS clause is not specified, this list is merged with the default index parameters associated with the corresponding attribute set.

If the index parameters are directly assigned to an expression set (column storing expressions), the PARAMETERS clause in the CREATE INDEX statement cannot contain the STOREATTRS or INDEXATTRS clauses. In this case, the Expression Filter index is always created, using the parameters associated with the declared expression set. To find the parameters associated with the attribute set use the *dbms_expfil.index_parameters* and *dbms_expfil.xpindex_parameters* APIs and the *user_expfil_index_parameters* catalog view.

If the REPLACE DEFAULTS clause is not specified, the list of indexed attributes for an Expression Filter index is derived from the INDEXATTRS clause and the default index parameters associated with the corresponding attribute set. If this list is empty, the system picks a maximum of 10 stored attributes and indexes them.

If the PARAMETERS clause is not used with the CREATE INDEX statement and the index parameters are not assigned to the expression set, the default index parameters associated with the corresponding attribute set are used for the Expression Filter index. If the default index parameters list is empty, all the scalar attributes defined in the attribute set are stored and indexed in the predicate table.

Predicate statistics for the expression set must be available, in order to use the TOP clause for the corresponding Expression Filter index when the TOP clause is used for the STOREATTRS clause.

When an attribute is provided in the PARAMETERS clause as well as in the default index parameters, its stored indexed property is determined by the PARAMETERS clause specification.

Examples Using the CREATE INDEX Command for Expressions

To create an index, using the default index parameters specified for the expressions corresponding attribute set, use the following type of syntax for the CREATE INDEX command:

```
CREATE INDEX BoaterInterestIndex ON Boaters (Interest) INDEXTYPE IS
EXFSYS.EXPFILTER;
```

An index can be created with a few additional stored attributes using the following statement.

```
CREATE INDEX BoaterInterestIndex ON Boaters (Interest) INDEXTYPE IS
exfsys.ExpFilter
PARAMETERS ('STOREATTRS (SeaRating(Model, Year))
PREDSTORAGE (tablespace Boater_index_1) ');
```

If you wish to specify the complete list of stored and indexed attributes for an index, you would use a statement similar to the following example.

```
CREATE INDEX BoaterInterestIndex ON Boaters(Interest)
INDEXTYPE IS exfsys.ExpFilter
PARAMETERS ('REPLACE DEFAULTS
STOREATTRS (Model, SeaRating(Model, Year))
INDEXATTRS (Model, Year, Price)
PREDSTORAGE (tablespace tbs_1) ');
```

The TOP clause can be used in the parameters clause when statistics have been computed for the expression set. These statistics are accessible from the *user_expfil_exprset_stats* view.

```
BEGIN
dbms_expfil.get_exprset_stats (expr_tab => 'Boaters',
expr_col => 'Interest');
END;
/
DROP INDEX InterestIndex;
CREATE INDEX BoaterInterestIndex ON Boaters (Interest)
INDEXTYPE IS exfsys.ExpFilter
PARAMETERS ('STOREATTRS TOP 4 INDEXATTRS TOP 3');
```

The Expression Filter uses predefined types, so let's take a quick look at them.

Expression Filter Object Type

The Expression Filter feature is supplied with a set of predefined types and public synonyms for these types. Most of these types are used for configuring index parameters with the Expression Filter procedural APIs. The *exf$table_alias* type is used to support expressions defined on one or more database tables.

All the values and names passed to the types defined in this chapter are case-insensitive. In order to preserve the case, double quotation marks should be used around the values.

The next topic in this section on Expression Filters will discuss the *dbms_expfil* package, the heart of the Expression Filter feature.

The core of the Expression Filter feature is the *dbms_expfil* package. This package contains the various procedures used to manage the Expression datatype and Expression data. The following table describes the procedures in the *dbms_expfil* package.

> All the values and names passed to the packages defined in the DBMS_EXPFIL package are case-insensitive. In order to preserve the case, double quotation marks should be used around the values.

PROCEDURE	DESCRIPTION
add_elementary_attribute	Adds a specified attribute to the attribute set.

PROCEDURE	DESCRIPTION
add_functions	Adds a Function, Type, or Package to the approved list of objects within an attribute set
assign_attribute_set	Assigns an attribute set to the specified table column used for storing expressions.
build_exception_table	Creates an exception table to hold references to invalid expressions.
clear_exprset_stats	Clears the predicate statistics for an expression set.
copy_attribute_set	Makes a copy of the attribute set.
create_attribute_set	Creates an attribute set.
default_index_parameters	Assigns default index parameters to an attribute set.
default_xpindex_parameters	Assigns default XPath index parameters to an attribute set.
defrag_index	Rebuilds the bitmap indexes online to reduce fragmentation.
drop_attribute_set	Drops an unused attribute set.
get_exprset_stats	Collects predicate statistics for an expression set.
grant_privilege	Grants an expression DML privilege to a user.
index_parameters	Assigns index parameters to an expression set.
revoke_privilege	Revokes an expression DML privilege from a user.
unassign_attribute_set	Breaks the association between a column storing expressions and the attribute set.
validate_expressions	Validates expression metadata and the expressions stored in a column.

PROCEDURE	DESCRIPTION
xpindex_parameters	Assigns XPath index parameters to an expression set.

Table 3 *dbms_expfil Procedures*

We have mentioned several views associated with Expressions, let's take a quick look at them as the final topic in this section

Expression Filter Views

The metadata associated with the Expression Filter feature can be viewed using the Expression Filter views. The Expression Filter views are defined with a xxx_EXPFIL prefix, where xxx can be USER or ALL. These views are read-only to the users and are created and maintained by the Expression Filter APIs.

The following Table lists the names of the views and their descriptions.

VIEW NAME	DESCRIPTION
user_expfil_aset_functions	List of functions/packages approved for the attribute set.
user_expfil_attributes	List of elementary attributes of the attribute set.
user_expfil_attribute_sets	List of attribute set.
user_expfil_def_index_params	List of default index parameters.
user_expfil_expression_sets	List of expression sets.
user_expfil_exprset_stats	List of predicate statistics for the expression sets.
user_expfil_index_params	List of index parameters assigned to the expression set.
user_expfil_indexes	List of expression filter indexes.

VIEW NAME	DESCRIPTION
user_expfil_predtab_attributes	List of stored and indexed attributes for the indexes.
user_expfil_privileges	List of all the expression privileges of the current user.

Table 4 *Expression Filter Views*

Next, we will look at the new features in SQL Regular expressions.

SQL Regular Expressions

Oracle Database 10g supports POSIX-compliant regular expressions to enhance search and replace capability in programming environments such as Unix and Java. In SQL, this new functionality is implemented through new functions that are regular expression extensions to existing functions, such as LIKE, REPLACE, and INSTR. This implementation supports multilingual queries and is locale sensitive.

Let's look at the additions to INSTR, LIKE, and REPLACE so you can see what we mean.

Changes to INSTR

The function INSTR has been extended with the new function *regexp_instr*.

regexp_instr extends the functionality of the INSTR function by letting you search a string for a POSIX regular expression pattern. The function evaluates strings using characters, as defined by the input character set. It returns an integer indicating the beginning or ending position of the matched substring, depending on the value of the *return_option* argument. If no match is found, the function returns 0.

An example query using *regexp_instr* would look like:

```
SQL> SELECT
  2 REGEXP_INSTR('5035 Forest Run Trace, Alpharetta, GA',
  3 '[^ ]+', 1, 6) "Test"
  4 FROM dual;

    TEST
      36
```

In this example, we are telling Oracle to examine the string, looking for occurrences of one or more non-blank characters and to return the sixth occurrence of one or more non-blank character.

Changes to LIKE

In versions of Oracle prior to Oracle Database 10*g*, LIKE was the only expression. Now, there is *regexp_like*.

regexp_like resembles the LIKE condition, except *regexp_like* performs regular POSIX and Unicode expression matching, instead of the simple pattern matching performed by LIKE. This condition evaluates strings using characters, as defined by the input character set.

An example query using *regexp_like* would look like:

```
SQL> SELECT ename FROM emp
  2 WHERE
  3 REGEXP_LIKE (ename, '^J.(N|M),S$');

ENAME
-----
JONES
JAMES
```

In this example, we tell Oracle to retrieve any values that start with J, followed by any letter, then N or M, then any letter, then S

Changes to REPLACE

In Oracle Database 10*g*, the REPLACE function has been extended with the *regexp_replace* function.

regexp_replace extends the functionality of the REPLACE function by letting you search a string for a regular expression pattern. By default, the function returns the supplied source_string variable with every occurrence of the regular expression pattern replaced by the supplied replace_string variable. The string returned is either VARCHAR2 or CLOB, and in the same character set as the source_string supplied.

Let's look at an example of *regexp_replace* (note: in this example we added a column to the emp table to allow for *emp_phone*):

```
SQL> SELECT
  2 REGEXP_REPLACE(emp_phone,
  3 '([[:digit:]]{3})\.([[:digit:]]{3})\.([[:digit:]]{4})',
  4 '(\1) \2-\3') "Test"
  5 FROM emp;

Test
----------------
(404) 444-4321
(404) 555-5432
(404) 666-6543

In this eample we search for a pattern of numbers that looks like a
European phone number listing such as 111.222.3333 and convert it to
a normal USA format listing of (111) 222-3333.
```

Changes to SUBSTR

The SUBSTR function has been extended by the *regexp_substr* function provided in Oracle Database 10*g*.

The *regexp_substr* function extends the functionality of the SUBSTR function by letting you search a string for a POSIX or Unicode compliant regular expression pattern. It is also similar to *regexp_instr*, but instead of returning the position of the substring, it returns the substring itself.

The *regexp_substr* function is useful if you need the contents of a match string, but not its position in the source string. The function returns the string as VARCHAR2 or CLOB data in the same character set as the supplied *source_string*.

Here is an example use of the *regexp_substr*:

```
SQL> SELECT
  2 REGEXP_SUPSTR('5035 Forest Run Trace, Alpharetta, GA',
  3 ',[^,]+,') "Test"
  4 FROM dual;

Test
-----------------
, Alpharetta,
```

In this example we search for a comma, followed by one or more characters immediately followed by a comma.

Let's look at the multi-lingual regular expression syntax used in these new functions.

Multilingual Regular Expression Syntax

The next table lists the full set of operators defined in the POSIX standard Extended Regular Expression (ERE) syntax. Oracle follows the exact syntax and matching semantics for these operators, as defined in the POSIX standard for matching ASCII (English language) data. The notes following the table provide more complete descriptions of the operators and their functions, as well as Oracle multilingual enhancements of the operators. The table following the notes summarizes Oracle support for and Multilingual enhancement of the POSIX operators.

OPERATOR	DESCRIPTION
\ (1)	The backslash character can have four different meanings, depending on the context. It can: Stand for itself, Quote the next character, Introduce an operator, Do nothing
*	Matches zero or more occurrences
+	Matches one or more occurrences
?	Matches zero or one occurrence
|	Alternation operator for specifying alternative matches
^ (2)	Matches the beginning-of-line character
$ (2)	Matches the end-of-line character
. (3)	Matches any character in the supported character set except NULL
[ ] (4)	Bracket expression for specifying a matching list that should match any one of the expressions represented in the list. A non-matching list expression begins with a circumflex (^) and specifies a list that matches any character except for the expressions represented in the list.
( )	Grouping expression, treated as a single subexpression
{m}	Matches exactly m times
{m,}	Matches at least m times
{m,n}	Matches at least m times but no more than n times

Table 5 *Regular Expression Operators and Metasymbols*

Notes on the POSIX operators and Oracle enhancements:

- '\': The backslash operator is used to make the character following it normal, if it is an operator. For example, '*' is interpreted as the asterisk string literal.

- '^' and '$': The characters '^' and '$' are the POSIX anchoring operators. By default, they match only the beginning or end of an entire string. Oracle lets you specify '^' and '$' to match the start or end of any line anywhere within the source string. This in turn lets you treat the source string as multiple lines.

- '.': In the POSIX standard, the "match any character" operator ('.') is defined to match any English character, except NULL and the newline character. In the Oracle implementation, the '.' operator can match any character in the database character set, including the newline character.

- '[ ]': In the POSIX standard, a range in a regular expression includes all collation elements between the start and end points of the range in the linguistic definition of the current locale. Therefore, ranges in regular expressions are linguistic ranges, rather than byte values ranges, and the semantics of the range expression are independent of character set. Oracle implements this independence by interpreting range expressions according to the linguistic definition determined by the *nls_sort* initialization parameter.

- '\n': The back-reference expression '\n' matches the same string of characters as was matched by the nth subexpression. The character n must be a digit from 1 to 9, designating the nth subexpression, numbered from left to right. The expression is invalid if the source string contains fewer than n subexpressions preceding the \n.

  For example, the regular expression ^(.*)\1$ matches a line consisting of two adjacent appearances of the same string. Oracle supports the backreference \n e The backreference expression (n is a digit between 1 and 9) matches the nth subexpression enclosed between '(' and ')' preceding the \n.

- [..] Specifies one collation element, and can be a multi-character element (for example, [.ch.] in Spanish).

- [: :] Specifies character classes (for example, [:alpha:]). It matches any character within the character class.

- [==] Specifies equivalence classes. For example, [=o=] matches all characters having base letter 'o' expression in the regular expression pattern and the replacement string of the REGEXP_REPLACE function.

- '[..]': A collating element is a unit of collation and is equal to one character in most cases, but may comprise two or more characters in some languages.

  In the past, regular expression syntax did not support ranges containing multi-character collation elements, such as the range 'a' through 'ch'. The POSIX standard introduces the collation element delimiter '[..]', which lets you delimit multi-character collection elements, such as : '[a-[.ch.]]'. The collation elements supported by Oracle are determined by the setting of the *nls_sort* initialization parameter. The collation element is valid only inside the bracketed expression.

- '[::]': In English regular expressions, range expressions often indicate a character class. For example, '[a-z]' indicates any lowercase character. This convention is ambiguous in many multilingual environments where the first and last character of a given character class might not be the same in all languages. The POSIX standard introduces a portable character class syntax, '[::]'.

  This character class syntax lets you make better use of NLS character definitions to write flexible regular expressions. These character classes are valid only inside the bracketed expression.

- '[==]': Oracle supports the equivalence classes through the POSIX '[==]' syntax.

  A base letter and all of its accented versions constitute an equivalence class. For example, the equivalence class '[=a=]'

matches ä and â. The equivalence classes are valid only inside the bracketed expression.

CHARACTER	CLASS SYNTAX MEANING
[:alnum:]	All alphanumeric characters
[:alpha:]	All alphabetic characters
[:cntrl:]	All control characters (nonprinting)
[:digit:]	All numeric digits
[:lower:]	All lowercase alphabetic characters
[:print:]	All printable characters
[:punct:]	All punctuation characters
[:space:]	All space characters (nonprinting)
[:upper:]	All uppercase alphabetic characters

Restriction on equivalence classes: Composed and decomposed versions of the same equivalence class do not match. For example, "ä" does not match "a" followed by umlaut.

Regular Expression Operator Multilingual Enhancements

When applied to multilingual data, Oracle's implementation of the POSIX operators extend the matching capabilities specified in the POSIX standard.

The table below shows the relationship of the Oracle implementation of the operators in the context of the POSIX standard.

The first column in the table lists the supported operators.

The second and third columns in the table indicate whether the POSIX standard (Basic Regular Expression--BRE and Extended Regular Expression--ERE, respectively) defines the operator.

The fourth column in the table indicates whether Oracle's implementation extends the operator's semantics for handling multilingual data.

If you have a direct input capability, Oracle allows you to enter multi-byte characters directly. If you don't have direct input capability you can use functions to compose the multi-byte characters. However, you can't use the Unicode hexadecimal encoding value of the form '\xxxx'. Oracle evaluates the characters based on the byte values used to encode the character, not the graphical representation of the character.

OPERATOR	POSIX BRE SYNTAX	POSIX ERE SYNTAX	MULTI-LINGUAL ENHANCEMENT
\	Yes	Yes	—
*	Yes	Yes	—
+	—	Yes	—
?	—	Yes	—
|	—	Yes	—
^	Yes	Yes	Yes
$	Yes	Yes	Yes
.	Yes	Yes	Yes
[ ]	Yes	Yes	Yes
( )	Yes	Yes	—
{m}	Yes	Yes	—
{m,}	Yes	Yes	—
{m,n}	Yes	Yes	—
\n	Yes	Yes	Yes
[..]	Yes	Yes	Yes
[::]	Yes	Yes	Yes
[==]	Yes	Yes	Yes

Table 6.6 *POSIX and Multilingual Operator Relationships*

Row Timestamp

Oracle Database 10g provides a new pseudo-column, consisting of the committed timestamp or SCN that provides applications and users the ability to efficiently implement optimistic locking. In previous releases, when posting updates to the database, applications had to read in all column values or user-specified indicator columns, compare them with those previously fetched, and update those with identical values. With this feature, only the row SCN needs to be retrieved and compared to verify that the row has not changed from the time of the select to the update.

The pseudo-column for the committed SCN is called *ora_rowscn* and is one of the version query pseudo-columns.

The *ora_rowscn* pseudo-column returns, for each version of each row, the system change number (SCN) of the row. You cannot use this pseudo-column in a query to a view.

However, you can use it to refer to the underlying table when creating a view. You can also use this pseudo-column in the WHERE clause of an UPDATE or DELETE statement.

Even though this pseudo-column is grouped with the restricted version query pseudo-columns, this pseudo-column can be used like any other pseudo-column. For example:

```
SQL> SELECT ora_rowscn FROM used_boats:

ORA_ROWSCN
----------
    791744
    791744
    791744
    791744
    791744
    791744
    791744
    791744
    791744
```

```
       791744
       791744
       791744
       791744
       791744

13 rows selected.
```

The above query shows us that all of the records in *used_boats* were committed in the same transaction. Let's update some of the rows and see what happens.

```
SQL> UPDATE used_boats SET price=price*1.1 WHERE seller_id=1;

3 rows updated.

SQL> commit;

Commit complete

SQL> SELECT ora_rowscn FROM used_boats:

ORA_ROWSCN
----------
    816673
    816673
    816673
    791744
    791744
    791744
    791744
    791744
    791744
    791744
    791744
    791744
    791744

13 rows selected.
```

Another convenient function allows you to retrieve the actual time that the row was last altered through a conversion function called *scn_to_timestamp*. Let's look at an example usage of this function.

```
SQL> select scn_to_timestamp(ora_rowscn) from used_boats;
```

```
SCN_TO_TIMESTAMP(ORA_ROWSCN)
30-AUG-03 11.06.08.000000000 PM
30-AUG-03 11.06.08.000000000 PM
30-AUG-03 11.06.08.000000000 PM
30-AUG-03 04.33.19.000000000 PM
30-AUG-03 04.33.19.000000000 PM
30-AUG-03 04.33.19.000000000 PM
30-AUG-03 04.33.19.000000000 PM
30-AUG-03 04.33.19.000000000 PM
30-AUG-03 04.33.19.000000000 PM
30-AUG-03 04.33.19.000000000 PM
30-AUG-03 04.33.19.000000000 PM
30-AUG-03 04.33.19.000000000 PM
30-AUG-03 04.33.19.000000000 PM

13 rows selected.
```

The *ora_rowscn* has the following restrictions: This pseudo-column is not supported for external tables or when directly querying views.

The data from the SCN and timestamp pseudo-columns could prove invaluable in a flashback situation.

Review

To recap the enhancements we've reviewed:

- Grouped Table Outer Join

- Increased Number of Aggregates per Query

- Remote Stored Functions in SELECT Statements

- Case-Insensitive and Accent-Insensitive Query and Sort

- Enhanced CONNECT BY Support

- Oracle Expression Filter

- SQL Regular Expressions

- Row Timestamp

Of these, the most important in our opinion are:

- Grouped Table Outer Join

- Oracle Expression Filter

This is because they will provide greater flexibility for web-based environments. Of the two, the Oracle Expression filter will be the most utilized.

Oracle 10g Automatic Database Diagnostics Management

Oracle 10g offers a number of new monitors / advisors to help DBAs tune their databases. In prior releases, we spent much of our time adding indexes, dropping indexes, changing *init.ora* parameters, testing hints, reading TKPROF output, examining explain plans and STATSPACK output, etc., in hopes of improving SQL. Oracle 10g offers mechanisms to do all of that testing for us, so the DBA can focus on implementing.

To begin with, the new Automatic Workload Repository (AWR) replaces what STATSPACK provided, and adds even more functionality. It collects and maintains the statistics, every x minutes (configured by the DBA). The stored data is then used by the Advanced Database Diagnostic Monitor (ADDM, pronounced 'adam').

ADDM provides the analysis that you need to monitor the database and effectively diagnose problems. It gives you the root-cause analysis, along with recommendations on what to do to fix the problem.

These facilities can be accessed either via the command line interface, or through OEM (Oracle Enterprise Manager). Example outputs may be information that there is read / write contention, have a freelist problem, or need to use locally managed tablespaces.

There is also the new SQL Tuning Advisor, to assist with tuning SQL. This is based on changes to the optimizer. The optimizer now has a 'tuning mode' that is used when tuning SQL. The tuning mode causes the optimizer to go through 4 checks:

- Analyze SQL Statistics – check for missing / stale statistics

- SQL Profiling – determine additional information that will make a statement run better, and save it off for use later (similar to a stored outine)

- SQL Access Analysis – verify that the access path is, in fact the most optimal, or make recommendations for a better one

- SQL Structure Analysis – determine if tweaking the SQL will make it run better (changing a NOT IN to a NOT EXISTS, for example)

But, before you tune the problem SQL, you need to find it first. ADDM can identify high-load SQL statements, which can, in turn, be fed into the SQL Tuning advisor below.

ADDM automatically detects all common performance problems, including:

- Excessive I/O

- CPU Bottlenecks

- Contention issues

- High Parsing

- Lock Contention

- Buffer sizing issues

- RAC issues

ADDM wakes up every 30 minutes, or whenever it is configured, and identifies performance issues. It presents a set of findings that identify the cause of performance problems, as well as potential resolutions.

To begin with ADDM and create a new snapshot with information populated in *dba_hist_snapshot*:

```
exec dbms_workload_repository.create_snapshot();
```

To view the output of the snapshot, including recommendations:

```
set long 1000000
set pagesize 50000
column get_clob format a80
select dbms_advisor.get_task_report(task_name, 'TEXT', 'ALL')
as first_ADDM_report
from dba_advisor_tasks
where task_id=(
select max(t.task_id)
from dba_advisor_tasks t, dba_advisor_log l
where t.task_id = l.task_id
and t.advisor_name='ADDM'
and l.status= 'COMPLETED');
```

An example of some output that ADDM might generate:

```
FINDING 3: 5.2% impact (147 seconds)
------------------------------------
The buffer cache was undersized causing significant
additional read I/O.

RECOMMENDATION 1: DB Configuration, 5.2% benefit (147
seconds)
ACTION: Increase SGA target size by increasing the value of
parameter "sga_target" by 24 M.

SYMPTOMS THAT LED TO THE FINDING:
Wait class "User I/O" was consuming significant database
time. (5.3%  impact [150 seconds])
```

Oracle 10g SQL Tuning Advisor

Here is an example of a SQL Tuning session, using all this new functionality:

Step 1: Create a tuning task

You have a SQL statement (perhaps from a packaged application, and you may not be able to change the code).

```
create_tuning_task (
sql_text => 'select * from emp_history
where empid_id = :bnd_var',f
bind_list =>
sql_binds(anydata.ConvertNumber(100)),
usern_name => 'scott',
scope => 'comprehensive',
time_limit => 60,
task_name => 'bad_sql',
description => 'sql that performs poorly');
```

Time limit is 60, so the optimizer will spend up to 60 seconds analyzing this SQL. The 'comprehensive' setting indicated that the optimizer should perform its' additional analysis. Instead of putting the SQL above, we could have used the *sql_id* out of OEM or other catalog tables (sql_advisor_%).

```
create_tuning_task (sql_id =>
'abc123456xyz');
```

Step 2: Execute the tuning task

```
Execute_tuning_task (
Task_name => 'bad_sql');
```

The results of this execution have been put into the new catalog tables, and can be seen by querying *dba_advisor_%* views such as *dba_advisor_findings*, *dba_advisor_recommendations*, etc.

Step 3: See the results

```
set long 10000;
select report_tuning_task (task_name => 'bad_sql') from dual;
```

This will return a complete report of the results, including findings and recommendations. This report can also be run via OEM

Step 4: Determine what is to be implemented, and execute accordingly.

```
accept_sql_profile (tastk_name => 'bad_sql',
name => 'use_this_profile');
```

This will store the profile in the catalog (similar to a stored outline, in previous releases of Oracle). So, when using the optimizer in 'normal' mode, when the 'bad_sql' comes along, instead of using the original access path, this new profile will be used instead.

Conclusion

This chapter provided an overview of some of the unique extensions to SQL that Oracle has provided. From all sorts of new analytical functions like cube and rollup to tanking to top-5, these new functions really make coding much easier.

Certainly, the introduction of materialized views and stored outlines can help performance, especially in circumstances where you can't change the original code (for example, in packaged applications).

And, the new features of Oracle 10g make a DBAs life even easier with the introduction of ADDM – Advanced Database Diagnostic Management.

Now that you have all the background on how the SQL executes, what happens with joins, and Oracle's newer SQL features, let's move on to SQL coding techniques to achieve optimum performance.

Coding for Performance

CHAPTER

5

High Performing SQL – Where Do You Start?

This chapter provides a high-level summary of the rest of the book – now that you know all the things that can be tuned, within the database, where do you start? The answer is, with the code. You can double check all the *init.ora* parameters to start, monitor hit ratios and use operating system monitoring tools, but most often, the issue is in the code. Both Oracle 9i and Oracle 10g have added many new features to assist in tuning SQL to make it run faster. We've already covered some of the major Oracle 10g new functionality, including ADDM, and the advisors.

Before you can start tuning, you need to understand your goals. Oracle has several types of indexes (b-tree, bitmap) all designed to speed-up data retrieval. Index access can be faster than a full-table scan especially when the desired result set is small and when the rows are on adjacent data blocks (as defined by the *clustering_factor* column of the *dba_indexes* view). In certain cases (i.e., a large sorted result set), index access can be more expensive (in terms of logical I/O's) than a full-table scan, but it will start to deliver rows to the requesting program very quickly. Therefore, in order to tune, you need to decide your destination:

- Minimize computing resources – This is Oracle's *all_rows optimizer_mode*, whereby the CBO strives to deliver the desired rows with a minimum of computing resources. The all_rows *optimizer_mode* gives a lower cost to parallel full-table scans.

- Minimize response time – When the goal is to minimize response time, Oracle's *first_rows optimizer_mode* is ideal. The *first_rows optimizer_mode* gives a lower relative weight to index scans, thereby favoring access plans that start returning rows very quickly, even if it means more logical I/O operations and more computing resources. Being flexible, Oracle provides a wealth of optimizer parameters to allow the senior Oracle DBA to change the default behavior of the CBO.

For example, the *optimizer_index_cost_adj* parameter is used to control the relative weigh assigned to index scans. For most databases, the CBO does an excellent job of always choosing the most appropriate access method for the query.

The characteristics of the data have a huge bearing on the CBO's choice of execution plans. These metadata items include:

- Size of the table, partitioning of table

- Number of distinct values within each table column

- Distribution of values (skew) of table columns (from dba_histogram_cols)

- Availability of parallel query servers (from cpu_count)

- Clustering of data rows on data blocks (clustering_factor column in dba_indexes)

- And many, many more

The CBO only makes intelligent decisions when it is provided with accurate metadata statistics. For years, the CBO has been viewed as 'potentially problematic', when in fact, it is the lack of accurate and current statistics that have been the real issue.

Robin Schumacher, performance expert, has identified ways in Oracle 9i to tune SQL, with the new views that have been delivered:

SQL Analysis Made Easy

New Performance Views to Identify Problem SQL

One short path to identifying performance problems in an Oracle database is the following:

- Find the sessions responsible for hogging the most resources (I/O, CPU, etc.).

- Identify the code these sessions are running.

- Peel away the bad code these sessions have executed from the good/acceptable code.

- Highlight the worst SQL and then work to tune it for better performance.

This process has been made much easier in Oracle9i, especially with respect to identifying problem SQL that gets run in a production database. Let's work our way through these four steps and see how several new performance views introduced in Oracle9i can really assist in the process.

Find the Problem Sessions

Even if you don't have a database monitor that offers a "Top Sessions" view, you can easily pinpoint the sessions that are giving your database grief (see Exhibit 1). Keep in mind that different database professionals have their own ideas about what constitutes a "top session." Some feel that the sum total of physical I/O alone tells the story, while others look at CPU, and still others use a combination of physical and logical I/O. Whatever your preference, you can use the script in Exhibit 1 to quickly bubble to your top-twenty sessions in an Oracle9i database. Note that the initial sort is on physical I/O but you can change that to be any other column you'd like.

```
-- ****************************************************
-- Copyright © 2003 by Rampant TechPress
-- This script is free for non-commercial purposes
-- with no warranties.  Use at your own risk.
--
-- To license this script for a commercial purpose,
-- contact info@rampant.cc
-- ****************************************************

SELECT * FROM
(SELECT b.SID SID,
     decode (b.USERNAME,NULL,e.name,b.username) USER_NAME,
     d.spid OS_ID,
     b.machine MACHINE_NAME,
     TO_CHAR(logon_time,'DD-MON-YY HH:MI:SS PM') LOGON_TIME,
     (sum(DECODE(c.NAME,'physical reads',VALUE,0)) +
     sum(DECODE(c.NAME,'physical writes',VALUE,0)) +
     sum(DECODE(c.NAME,'physical writes direct',VALUE,0)) +
     sum(DECODE(c.NAME,'physical writes direct
(lob)',VALUE,0))+
     sum(DECODE(c.NAME,'physical reads direct
(lob)',VALUE,0)) +
     sum(DECODE(c.NAME,'physical reads direct',VALUE,0)))
     total_physical_io,
     (sum(DECODE(c.NAME,'db block gets',VALUE,0)) +
     sum(DECODE(c.NAME,'db block changes',VALUE,0)) +
     sum(DECODE(c.NAME,'consistent changes',VALUE,0)) +
     sum(DECODE(c.NAME,'consistent gets',VALUE,0)) )
     total_logical_io,
     (sum(DECODE(c.NAME,'session pga memory',VALUE,0))+
     sum(DECODE(c.NAME,'session uga memory',VALUE,0)) )
     total_memory_usage,
     sum(DECODE(c.NAME,'parse count (total)',VALUE,0))
parses,
     sum(DECODE(c.NAME,'CPU used by this session',VALUE,0))
     total_cpu,
     sum(DECODE(c.NAME,'parse time cpu',VALUE,0)) parse_cpu,
     sum(DECODE(c.NAME,'recursive cpu usage',VALUE,0))
       recursive_cpu,
     sum(DECODE(c.NAME,'CPU used by this session',VALUE,0)) -
     sum(DECODE(c.NAME,'parse time cpu',VALUE,0)) -
     sum(DECODE(c.NAME,'recursive cpu usage',VALUE,0))
       other_cpu,
     sum(DECODE(c.NAME,'sorts (disk)',VALUE,0)) disk_sorts,
     sum(DECODE(c.NAME,'sorts (memory)',VALUE,0))
memory_sorts,
     sum(DECODE(c.NAME,'sorts (rows)',VALUE,0)) rows_sorted,
     sum(DECODE(c.NAME,'user commits',VALUE,0)) commits,
     sum(DECODE(c.NAME,'user rollbacks',VALUE,0)) rollbacks,
     sum(DECODE(c.NAME,'execute count',VALUE,0)) executions
```

```
FROM sys.V_$SESSTAT a,
     sys.V_$SESSION b,
     sys.V_$STATNAME c,
     sys.v_$process d,
     sys.v_$bgprocess e
WHERE a.STATISTIC#=c.STATISTIC# and
      b.SID=a.SID AND
      d.addr = b.paddr and
      e.paddr (+) = b.paddr and
      c.NAME in ('physical reads',
                 'physical writes',
                 'physical writes direct',
                 'physical reads direct',
                 'physical writes direct (lob)',
                 'physical reads direct (lob)',
                 'db block gets',
                 'db block changes',
                 'consistent changes',
                 'consistent gets',
                 'session pga memory',
                 'session uga memory',
                 'parse count (total)',
                 'CPU used by this session',
                 'parse time cpu',
                 'recursive cpu usage',
                 'sorts (disk)',
                 'sorts (memory)',
                 'sorts (rows)',
                 'user commits',
                 'user rollbacks',
                 'execute count'
)
GROUP BY b.SID,
         d.spid,
         decode (b.USERNAME,NULL,e.name,b.username),
         b.machine,
         TO_CHAR(logon_time,'DD-MON-YY HH:MI:SS PM')
order by 6 desc)
WHERE ROWNUM < 21
```

Exhibit 1. *Finding the Problem Sessions*

You can also modify the above query to exclude Oracle background processes, the SYS and SYSTEM user, etc. The end result should be a current list of your top offending sessions in the database as ranked by various performance metrics, which is the normal way to rank problem user accounts.

Some DBAs feel that this method, while useful, lacks depth. Specifically, because DBAs know that a user's resource consumption is almost always tied to inefficient SQL, they would like to cut to the chase and find the problem sessions in a database that have, for example, caused most of the large table scans on the system or have submitted queries containing Cartesian joins. Such a thing was difficult to determine in earlier versions of Oracle but, fortunately, 9i provides a new performance view that can be used to derive such data. The V$SQL_PLAN view contains execution plan data for all submitted SQL statements. Such a view provides a wealth of information regarding the performance and efficiency of SQL statements and the sessions that submitted them.

For example, if a DBA wants to know what sessions have parsed SQL statements that caused large table scans (with "large" in our example being anything over 1 MB) on a system, along with the total number of large scans by session, he could submit the following query:

```
SELECT c.username username,
       count(a.hash_value) scan_count
FROM sys.v_$sql_plan a,
     sys.dba_segments b,
     sys.dba_users c,
     sys.v_$sql d
WHERE a.object_owner (+) = b.owner
AND   a.object_name (+) = b.segment_name
AND   b.segment_type IN ('TABLE', 'TABLE PARTITION')
AND   a.operation LIKE '%TABLE%'
AND   a.options = 'FULL'
AND   c.user_id = d.parsing_user_id
AND   d.hash_value = a.hash_value
AND   b.bytes / 1024 > 1024
group by c.username
order by 2 desc
```

Output from the above query might look something like the following:

```
USERNAME    SCAN_COUNT
----------  ----------
SYSTEM             14
SYS                11
ERADMIN             6
ORA_MONITOR         3
```

In like fashion, if a DBA wants to uncover what sessions have parsed SQL statements containing Cartesian joins, along with the number of SQL statements that contain such joins, he could run the following query:

```
SELECT username,
       COUNT(DISTINCT c.hash_value) NBR_STMTS
FROM sys.v_$sql a,
     sys.dba_users b,
     sys.v_$sql_plan c
WHERE a.parsing_user_id = b.user_id
AND   options = 'CARTESIAN'
AND   operation LIKE '%JOIN%'
AND   a.hash_value = c.hash_value
GROUP BY username
ORDER BY 2 DESC
```

A result set from this query could look similar to the following:

```
USERNAME    NBR_STMTS
---------   ---------
SYS                 2
SYSMAN              2
ORA_MONITOR         1
```

As you can see, the *v$sql_plan* view adds more meat to the process of identifying problem sessions in a database. When combined with the standard performance metrics query, DBAs can really begin to pinpoint the sessions that are wreaking havoc inside their critical systems.

Identify the Resource-Intensive Code

After identifying the top resource-hogging sessions in a database, you can then turn your attention to the code they (and others) are executing that is likely causing system bottlenecks. As with Top Session monitors, many decent database monitors have a "Top SQL" feature that can help you ferret out bad SQL code. If you don't have access to such tools, a script like the one shown in Exhibit 2 can be used.

```
-- ************************************************
-- Copyright © 2003 by Rampant TechPress
-- This script is free for non-commercial purposes
-- with no warranties.  Use at your own risk.
--
-- To license this script for a commercial purpose,
-- contact info@rampant.cc
-- ************************************************

SELECT SQL_TEXT ,
       USERNAME ,
       DISK_READS_PER_EXEC,
       BUFFER_GETS ,
       DISK_READS,
       PARSE_CALLS ,
       SORTS ,
       EXECUTIONS ,
       ROWS_PROCESSED ,
       HIT_RATIO,
       FIRST_LOAD_TIME ,
       SHARABLE_MEM ,
       PERSISTENT_MEM ,
       RUNTIME_MEM,
       CPU_TIME,
       ELAPSED_TIME,
       ADDRESS,
       HASH_VALUE
FROM
(SELECT SQL_TEXT ,
        B.USERNAME ,
 ROUND((A.DISK_READS/DECODE(A.EXECUTIONS,0,1,
 A.EXECUTIONS)),2)
       DISK_READS_PER_EXEC,
       A.DISK_READS ,
       A.BUFFER_GETS ,
       A.PARSE_CALLS ,
```

```
        A.SORTS ,
        A.EXECUTIONS ,
        A.ROWS_PROCESSED ,
        100 - ROUND(100 *
        A.DISK_READS/GREATEST(A.BUFFER_GETS,1),2) HIT_RATIO,
        A.FIRST_LOAD_TIME ,
        SHARABLE_MEM ,
        PERSISTENT_MEM ,
        RUNTIME_MEM,
        CPU_TIME,
        ELAPSED_TIME,
        ADDRESS,
        HASH_VALUE
FROM SYS.V_$SQLAREA A,
     SYS.ALL_USERS B
WHERE A.PARSING_USER_ID=B.USER_ID AND
      B.USERNAME NOT IN ('SYS','SYSTEM')
ORDER BY 3 DESC)
WHERE ROWNUM < 21
```

Exhibit 2. *Identifying the Resource-Intensive Code*

The code in Exhibit 2 will pull the top-twenty SQL statements as ranked by disk reads per execution. You can change the ROWNUM filter at the end to show more or all SQL that has executed in a database. You can also add WHERE predicates that just show the SQL for one or more of the top sessions that you previously identified. Note that in 9i, Oracle has added the CPU_TIME and ELAPSED_TIME columns, which provide more data that can be used to determine the overall efficiency of an SQL statement.

The new 9i *v$sql_plan* view can also help with identification of problem SQL. For example, a DBA may want to know how many total SQL statements are causing Cartesian joins on a system. The following query can answer that:

```
select count(distinct hash_value) carteisan_
   statements,
     count(*) total_cartesian_joins
from  sys.v_$sql_plan
where options = 'CARTESIAN'
and   operation like '%JOIN%'
```

Output from this query might resemble the following (note that it is possible for a single SQL statement to contain more than one Cartesian join):

```
CARTESIAN_STATEMENTS      TOTAL_CARTESIAN_JOINS
----------------------    ----------------------
                    3                         3
```

A DBA can then view the actual SQL statements containing the Cartesian joins, along with their performance metrics by using a query like the following:

```
select *
from sys.v_$sql
where hash_value in
(select hash_value
 from sys.v_$sql_plan
 where options = 'CARTESIAN'
 AND operation LIKE '%JOIN%' )
order by hash_value
```

Another area of interest for DBAs is table scan activity. Most DBAs don't worry about small table scans because Oracle can many times access small tables more efficiency through a full scan than through index access. Large table scans, however, are another matter. Most DBAs prefer to avoid those where possible through smart index placement or intelligent partitioning. Using the *v$sql_plan* view, a DBA can quickly identify any SQL statement that contains one or more large table scans. The following query shows any SQL statement containing a large table scan (defined as a table over 1 MB), along with a count of how many large scans it causes for each execution, the total number of times the statement has been executed, and then the sum total of all scans it has caused on the system:

```
SELECT sql_text,
       total_large_scans,
       executions,
       executions * total_large_scans sum_large_scans
FROM
(SELECT sql_text,
        count(*) total_large_scans,
        executions
FROM sys.v_$sql_plan a,
     sys.dba_segments b,
     sys.v_$sql c
WHERE a.object_owner (+) = b.owner
AND    a.object_name (+) = b.segment_name
AND    b.segment_type IN ('TABLE', 'TABLE PARTITION')
AND    a.operation LIKE '%TABLE%'
AND    a.options = 'FULL'
AND    c.hash_value = a.hash_value
AND    b.bytes / 1024 > 1024
group by sql_text, executions)
order by 4 desc
```

This query produces very interesting output. As a DBA, should you worry more about an SQL statement that causes only one large table scan, but has been executed 1000 times, or should you care more about an SQL statement that has ten large scans in it but has only been executed a handful of times? Each DBA will likely have an opinion on this, but regardless, you can see how such a query can assist in identifying SQL statements that have the potential to cause system slowdowns.

Oracle9.2 has introduced another new performance view — *v$sql_plan_statistics* — that can be used to get even more statistical data regarding the execution of SQL statements. This view can tell you how many buffer gets, disk reads, etc., each step in an execution plan caused, and even goes so far as to list the cumulative and last executed counts of all metrics. DBAs can reference this view to get a great perspective of which step in an SQL execution plan is really responsible for most of the resource consumption. Note that to enable the collection of data for this view, you must set the Oracle configuration parameter *statistics_level* to ALL.

Tune the Code/Database for Better Performance

Once you have your problem queries in hand, you can then start the tuning process. The two broad steps involved are:

1. Look for SQL rewrite possibilities.

2. Look for object-based solutions.

For problem systems, Step 1 above can consume a lot of a database professional's time. A chapter of this nature cannot possibly go into this vast subject as there are a plethora of techniques and SQL hints that can be used to turn a query that initially runs like molasses in winter into one that sprints as fast as a scalded dog.

Object-based solutions are another option for tuning specialists. These involve things like intelligent index creation, partitioning, and more. But to do this, you have to first find the objects that will benefit from such modification that, in turn, will enhance the overall runtime performance. Once again, the new 9i views can help. Continuing with the theme of finding large table scans on a system, the query listed in Exhibit 3 will identify the actual objects that are the target of such scans. It displays the table owner, table name, table type (standard, partitioned), table size in kilobytes (KB), number of SQL statements that cause a scan to be performed, number of total scans for the table each time the statement is executed, number of SQL executions to date, and then the total number of scans that the table has experienced (total single scans executions).

```
--  ****************************************************
-- Copyright © 2003 by Rampant TechPress
-- This script is free for non-commercial purposes
-- with no warranties.  Use at your own risk.
--
-- To license this script for a commercial purpose,
-- contact info@rampant.cc
--  ****************************************************

SELECT table_owner,
       table_name,
       table_type,
       size_kb,
       statement_count,
       reference_count,
       executions,
       executions * reference_count total_scans
FROM (SELECT a.object_owner table_owner,
             a.object_name table_name,
             b.segment_type table_type,
             b.bytes / 1024 size_kb,
             SUM(c.executions ) executions,
             COUNT( DISTINCT a.hash_value ) statement_count,
             COUNT( * ) reference_count
FROM sys.v_$sql_plan a,
     sys.dba_segments b,
     sys.v_$sql c
WHERE a.object_owner (+) = b.owner
AND   a.object_name (+) = b.segment_name
AND   b.segment_type IN ('TABLE', 'TABLE PARTITION')
AND   a.operation LIKE '%TABLE%'
AND   a.options = 'FULL'
AND   a.hash_value = c.hash_value
AND   b.bytes / 1024 > 1024
GROUP BY a.object_owner, a.object_name, a.operation, b.bytes
/
         1024, b.segment_type
ORDER BY 4 DESC, 1, 2 )
```

Exhibit 3. *Finding Large Table Scans*

The query in Exhibit 3 will help determine what tables might
benefit from better indexing or partitioning. However, a question
that might come up is: do these tables contain indexes and, if so,
why don't the queries that are scanning the tables make use of
them? While only examining the actual SQL statements can

---

answer the second part of that question, the first part can be answered through the following query:

```
SELECT DISTINCT a.object_owner table_owner,
                a.object_name table_name,
                b.segment_type table_type,
                b.bytes / 1024 size_kb,
                d.index_name
FROM sys.v_$sql_plan a,
     sys.dba_segments b,
     sys.dba_indexes d
WHERE a.object_owner (+) = b.owner
AND   a.object_name (+) = b.segment_name
AND   b.segment_type IN ('TABLE', 'TABLE PARTITION')
AND   a.operation LIKE '%TABLE%'
AND   a.options = 'FULL'
AND   b.bytes / 1024 > 1024
AND   b.segment_name = d.table_name
AND   b.owner = d.table_owner
ORDER BY 1, 2
```

Such a query can create a mini "unused indexes" report that you can use to ensure that any large tables that are being scanned on your system have the proper indexing scheme.

One final thing that a DBA might want to know is how much physical I/O, etc., a large table scan causes on a system. A new 9.2 performance view — *v$segment_statistics* — can come to the rescue here. It displays I/O and some wait metrics that can give a DBA more insight into what Oracle is doing behind the scenes to access the object. A query such as the following can be used to uncover this information:

```
SELECT DISTINCT a.object_owner table_owner,
                a.object_name table_name,
                b.segment_type table_type,
                b.bytes / 1024 size_kb,
                c.tablespace_name,
                c.statistic_name,
                c.value
FROM sys.v_$sql_plan a,
     sys.dba_segments b,
     sys.v_$segment_statistics c
```

```
WHERE a.object_owner (+) = b.owner
AND   a.object_name (+) = b.segment_name
AND   b.segment_type IN ('TABLE', 'TABLE PARTITION')
AND   a.operation LIKE '%TABLE%'
AND   a.options = 'FULL'
AND   b.bytes / 1024 > 1024
AND   b.owner = c.owner
AND   b.segment_name = c.object_name
ORDER BY 1, 2
```

Conclusion

Following the path of finding the problem sessions on a database and then identifying and tuning their SQL can be one quick way to turn around a poorly performing database. And with Oracle9i, the process of performing in-depth SQL analysis has been made much easier, thanks to the introduction of new V$ performance views. DBAs who become familiar with these new views can greatly increase their SQL troubleshooting abilities and accelerate the process of making things right in their database.

But, what can you do from the perspective of the code? Once you have used all the tools in Oracle to find the poorly performing code, and done what you can to determine what the issues are, how do you know what to change? Again, Robin Schumacher provides a step-by-step checklist to follow:

SQL Perfection Checklist:

Methods for Creating High-Quality Database Code

"Jeff" was a really nice guy but an absolute bare-boned novice at writing SQL code. So what does a company with a small IT staff do with someone like Jeff? Put him in a group of SQL developers who are charged with the task of writing decision support queries against a mammoth Teradata warehouse, of course! One day Jeff asked me to look at a query he had written against the warehouse, which really was an absolute monster. If you have never used Teradata, let me say that it is a true database junkie's dream come true. Infinitely scalable architecture, massive parallel processors, tons of RAM, and fast hashing algorithms used to distribute the tons of data among the many storage devices. Teradata also has a unique EXPLAIN plan that not only communicates the paths used to obtain a SQL result set, but also gives a time estimate of how long it believes the query will take to run. I asked Jeff if he had run his query through the EXPLAIN utility, and he said that he had not. So without reviewing his query, I sat down with him and put it through an EXPLAIN. Teradata went through its computations and issued its information back. My eyes widened as I focused on the time estimate. The year all this took place was 1993. Teradata estimated that Jeff's query would finish in the year 2049.

The story above is completely true and underscores how damaging and dangerous SQL can be in untrained hands. And, unfortunately, there are not only a lot of SQL novices out in IT shops right now, but their number is growing. At the same time corporations are increasing the number of projects that require database support, the number of seasoned database professionals available to do the work is shrinking. Faced with a terrible shortage of qualified database personnel, companies are throwing employees like Jeff into the meat grinder and are expecting them to produce systems that meet or exceed the difficult expectations of end users.

Writing high-quality SQL code isn't easy for a seasoned professional to do, let alone a rookie. But if you follow a judicious set of guidelines and work within a solid code framework that enforces certain standards, you stand a much higher chance of producing the types of response times needed for today's systems. This chapter won't teach you how to write optimized SQL code — books numbering into the hundreds of pages have attempted to do that (with some succeeding and many others failing). But what this chapter will do is offer a set of guidelines or checklist to follow when writing and testing SQL to ensure the best possible outcome. By adhering to what follows, you might just avoid a query like Jeff's that would still be running right now if we hadn't put the kibosh on it.

Start with the Basics

I am astounded at the number of developers who just paste SQL ad hoc into an application without first seeing if it is actually syntactically correct. Web folks are the worst at this because most of the tools they use do not provide a parser to check SQL code, so they just code or paste some SQL into their controls and hope for the best. Obviously, this is not the best way to work because syntax problems will come back to bite you continuously and your productivity will begin a downward slide.

Ideally, you want to do your work in an integrated development environment that offers the ability to quickly check the validity of — in other words, parse — your SQL code. Parsing validates security access to the underlying objects, ensures that object definition names or references are correct and in order, and confirms that the underlying syntax is valid and free of errors. This may seem terribly basic, but SQL validation is the first checkbox to mark in your SQL perfection checklist.

Know Thy Database

When writing efficient SQL, it is imperative to know the demographics and shape of the objects your code will bump up against. For most databases, all the information you will ever need can be found in the data dictionary. But when querying the dictionary for object statistics, make sure you are looking at accurate information. While some databases such as SQL Server 2000 have automatic updating of object statistics into the dictionary, other RDBMS engines require you to manually (and periodically) refresh the database catalog with upto- date object data. Fortunately, most make it pretty easy to accomplish. Oracle, for example, now offers packages to assist with the updating of objects. The *dbms_utility* package contains several procedures to help database professionals update their schema objects. To update the dictionary for a single schema, you can use the *dbms_utility.analyze_schema* procedure. Recently introduced is the *dbms_utility.analyze_database*. Just be careful when executing such a procedure up against a monolithic database like Oracle's applications!

However you choose to update your objects, you should make a practice of keeping data in the dictionary current, especially for databases that are very dynamic in nature. Scheduling the object updates in a nightly maintenance plan for such a database would likely be a good thing to do, especially if you use a cost-based optimizer in your RDBMS. Fresh statistics help the optimizer make more informed choices of what path to follow when routing queries to the data. Obviously, if your database thinks you only have 100 rows in a table that actually contains a million, the map used by the optimizer might not be the right one and your response times will show it.

So let's say you know (at least now) to keep your object statistics up to date. When tuning SQL, what are some things you should be looking for with respect to the objects used in your query to help make the right coding choices? Although this list is certainly not exhaustive, for tables you can start by eyeballing these items:

- **Row counts**. No heavy explanation needed for why you should be looking at this statistic. You will want to avoid full scans on beefy tables with large row counts. Proper index placement becomes quite important on such tables. Other reasons for reviewing row counts include physical redesign decisions. Perhaps a table has grown larger than anticipated and is now eligible for partitioning? Scanning a single partition in a table is a lot less work than running through the entire table.

- **Chained row counts**. Row chaining and migration can be a thorn in the side of an otherwise wellwritten SQL statement. Chained rows are usually the result of invalid page or block size choices (rows for a wide table will not fit on a single page or block). Migration is caused when a row expands beyond the remaining size boundary of the original block it was placed into. The database is forced to move the row to another block and leaves a pointer behind to indicate its new location. While chaining and migration are different, they have one thing in common: extra I/O is needed to retrieve the row that is either chained or migrated. Knowing how many chained or migrated rows your table has can help you determine if an object reorganization (or in extreme cases, a database rebuild with a larger block size) is needed.

- **Space extents**. For some databases, objects that have moved into multiple extents can be slower to access than same-size objects that are contained within a single contiguous extent of space. Later versions of Oracle, however, do not suffer from this multi-extent problem anymore, especially when objects are placed into new, locally managed tablespaces.

- **High water marks**. Tables that experience significant insert and delete activity can be special problem children. Oracle will always scan up to a table's "high water mark," which is the last block of space it "thinks" there is data. For example, a table that previously contained a million rows but now only has 100 rows may be scanned like it still has a million. You can determine if you need to reload a table (usually done by a reorg or truncate and load) by checking the high water marks of tables to see if they still are set to abnormally high values.

- **Miscellaneous properties.** There are several other performance-boosting properties that you may want to set for tables. For instance, large tables that are being scanned may benefit from having parallelism enabled so the table can be scanned (hopefully) much quicker. Small lookup tables may benefit from being permanently cached in memory to speed access times. In Oracle, this can be done by placing them into the KEEP buffer pool. The *cache* parameter can also be used, although it is not as permanent a fix as the KEEP buffer pool option.

Indexes have their own unique set of items that need to occasionally be reviewed. Some of these include:

- **Selectivity/unique keys.** Indexes by their nature normally work best when selectivity is high; in other words, the numbers of unique values are many. The exception to this rule is the bitmap index, which is designed to work on columns with very low cardinality (such as a Yes/No column). The selectivity of indexes should be examined periodically to see if an index that previously contained many unique values is now one that is losing its uniqueness rank. Complete unique-only indexes, of course, will not have this problem.

- **Depth.** The tree depth of an index will tell you if the index has undergone a lot of splits and other destructive activity. Typically, indexes with tree depths greater than three or four are good candidates for rebuilds, an activity that hopefully will improve access speed.

- **Deleted row counts.** Indexes that suffer from high parent table maintenance may contain a lot of "dead air" in the form of deleted rows in the leaf pages. Again, a rebuild may be in order for indexes with high counts of deleted leaf rows.

There are, of course, other items you can review on the table and index statistical front, as well as at the individual column level.

Understanding the current state and shape of the objects being used in the queries that you are trying to tune can unlock clues as to how you may want to restructure your SQL code. For example, you may realize that you have not indexed critical foreign keys that are used over and over again in various sets of join operations. Or, you might spot that your millionrow table is a perfect candidate for a bitmap index given the current WHERE predicate.

EXPLAIN and Understand

As someone who has worked in the database trenches for more than 15 years now, I have a terrible confession to make: I have never been really good at reading EXPLAIN plan output. Oh, I can do the basics like recognize table scans, spot Cartesian joins, and zero in on unnecessary sort operations; but when the EXPLAIN output "wave" starts rolling back and forth in large SQL EXPLAINs, I tend to get a little lost.

Some of the better SQL analysis tools are now sporting a new EXPLAIN format that makes following the access path trail a lot easier to read (see Exhibit 1). For people like me who were never good at traditional EXPLAIN output, it makes getting to the root of a bad SQL statement much simpler.

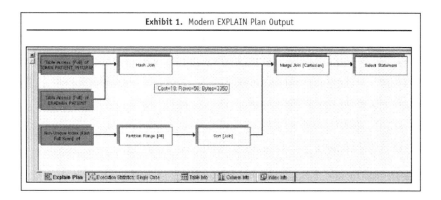

Exhibit 1. Modern EXPLAIN Plan Output

Whether you have access to the new, modern format shown in Exhibit 1 or still are forced to trudge through the standard EXPLAIN output, the EXPLAIN is the next stop on your SQL perfection checklist. The EXPLAIN is the tool to use in spotting obvious flaws in your code and brings to the surface what the database optimizer is doing underneath the covers to produce your desired result set. Remember, the EXPLAIN saved Jeff from launching the ultimate query from "you-know-where."

Correct Obvious Flaws

So what are some obvious red flags that can show up in an EXPLAIN? While such a large topic can not be covered in an chapter of this nature, we can go over some of the major items that should raise some eyebrows:

- **Cartesian product.** Jeff's query, which had an estimated response time of 56 years, suffered from a terrible case of Cartesian joins. His WHERE predicate did not contain a single correct join in the many million row tables he was trying to access. Although some optimizers will automatically try to rewrite SQL and will actually use a Cartesian product to accomplish its mission, seeing a Cartesian join in your EXPLAIN plan is usually not a good thing. If observed, check your WHERE predicate to ensure you are adhering to

---

Methods for Creating High-Quality Database Code

the N − 1 rule of thumb (for example, ten tables in a FROM clause will require nine proper join conditions).

- **Table scan**. So you thought you were using an index, did you? There are numerous conditions that can negate the use of an index (e.g., use of NOT, failing to use the starting column of a concatenated index, use of expressions such as WHERE PURCHASE_PRICE = LIST_PRICE * 1.2). Or perhaps the SQL is fine, but an improper indexing scheme is being used and needs to be changed. Remember, however, that you are really looking for table scans on large tables. Small lookup tables are often actually accessed faster when the database engine caches the whole table and scans it rather than using an available index.

- **Unnecessary sort**. Can your query do without the DISTINCT clause you have in the code? Can the UNION be replaced with a UNION ALL? Knowing when and how to yank sort activity out of an SQL statement can go a long way toward improving its response time.

- **Nonselective index scan**. If you've followed your checklist and understand the demographics of the objects used in your query, then you should know which indexes are selective and which are not. While cost-based optimizers should ignore indexes with poor selectivity, rule-based approaches may not. Be on the lookout for these types of scans because not every index scan is a good one.

Believe it or not, some of the good SQL tuning tools on the market actually can auto-correct your code for you. Finding missing join predicates and unindexed WHERE statements is just a mouse-click away in these tools.

Try Different Combinations

When the SQL is valid, your objects are in order, and you have eliminated noticeable flaws, it is now time to begin trying different code combinations in the hopes of improving your query's performance. This is where the use of hints can become a serious timesaver. The SQL language now contains a plethora of hints that you can embed in your query without really touching the actual code structure that exists. Using hints, you can, in effect, accomplish many iterations of rewrites in a short span of time.

Of course, one of the dangers of using hints is not coding them accurately. Unlike typical SQL code that will cough up a syntax error if you make a mistake, an invalid hint will not afford you that luxury. It will not do anything. Therefore, you need to make sure that you code your hints accurately.

Again, this is where a good SQL tuning tool comes in handy. Being able to visually add hints by selecting them from a pop-up list or other GUI dialog is really the way to go. That way, you know that your hint is syntactically correct and will have the intended effect.

What different coding approaches should you try through the use of hints? While there is no way to provide a complete rundown of everything that is open to you, there are a few mainstays to try:

- **The Four Horsemen**. These include RULE, FIRST ROWS, ALL ROWS, and CHOOSE. I cannot tell you how many times I have improved a query just by going back to the rule base optimizer. Even with all the progress made by cost based approaches, sometimes the old way is the best way.

- **Table Order Shuffle**. You may want to influence the order in which the optimizer joins the tables used in your query. The

ORDERED hint can force the database to use the right tables to drive the join operation and hopefully reduce inefficient I/O.

- **Divide and Conquer**. When databases introduced parallel operations, they opened up a whole new avenue in potential speed. The PARALLEL hint can be a powerful ally in splitting scans on large tables out into chunks that may be worked on separately in parallel and merged back into a single result set. One thing to ensure is that your database is set up properly with respect to having enough parallel worker bees (or "slaves") to handle the degree of parallelism you specify.

- **Index Now**. From the EXPLAIN plan, you may discover that the optimizer is not using an available index. This may or may not be a good thing. The only way to really tell is to force an index access plan in place of a table scan with an index hint.

Benchmark Your Rewrites

Once you have got a suite of new SQL combinations put together for your existing query, it is time to actually send them through the database and see if you have actually accomplished anything. Keep in mind that when you are performing these informal benchmarks, it is important to do them right. For example, do not just execute each query one time and record the measurements. First-time executions typically take longer than subsequent tries due to parse activity and data being read the first time from disk. At a minimum, I would send each new query through three to four times and throw out the high and low readings.

And just what measurements should you be looking at? If Oracle is your database, then there are quite a few excellent statistics that can be used to gauge the success of your rewrite prowess. A few of the more critical ones include:

- **Elapsed time**. What was the response time experienced?

- **Physical I/O**. Usually, the more physical I/O, the worse the query.

- **Logical I/O.** Consistent and block gets. Even in memory, less I/O is better.

- **Memory usage**. Shared, persistent, and runtime.

- **Sort operations**. Disk sort activity is usually many times slower than memory sorts.

- **CPU time**. How much of the server's "brain" did your query actually use?

- **Parse time**. How long did it take the database kernel to unwrap your query?

It is always exciting to see a rewritten set of SQL complete in a fraction of the time taken by the initial query. What a hero you will be! But what if the benchmarks aren't a no-brainer and you get a set of statistics back that are somewhat close? How do you decide whether or not to implement an altered set of code? There are really no hard-and-fast rules, but most people use a combination of elapsed time and I/O. Does the rewritten query show a somewhat better response time? Does it appear to use less I/O – both logical and physical? Are previously observed disk sorts eliminated? If so, you may have a new candidate to place into production.

Revisit When Necessary

If you are a database developer, you may think your job is over once you have delivered the SQL code into production. And in some shops, you might be right. Oftentimes, a database administrator then takes over and serves as the appointed sentry to monitor and identify SQL code that may be bottlenecking a system. But do not be surprised one day if your once well-running SQL is delivered back to you with the mandate to fix it again. Why might this happen? It is not uncommon for fast code to become sluggish in these circumstances:

- **Data volume changes**. Code that ran well with objects having small data volumes may turn into something that crawls along at a snail's pace when those same objects are a little heftier in size

- **Missing indexes**. Occasionally, a DBA will remove an index on a table that is causing slowdowns during INSERT, UPDATE, and DELETE operations. Unfortunately for you, that index may have been critical to your query success and you will have to come to a compromise with the DBA about what to do

There are plenty of other circumstances that can take the life out of what once was a good SQL query. You must always be ready to step back through your checklist and see what new miracle can now be delivered.

If you are a DBA, you may wonder how to quickly locate poorly running SQL in a production system. If an Oracle database is in question, then you can use the following code to find bad SQL running in an existing database. It combs through the Oracle shared pool and ranks SQL by one of the standard rules of thumb — disk reads per execution:

```
SELECT A.SQL_TEXT ,
       B.USERNAME ,
         ROUND((A.DISK_READS/DECODE
         (A.EXECUTIONS,0,1,A.EXECUTIONS)), 2),
       A.DISK_READS ,
       A.BUFFER_GETS ,
       A.PARSE_CALLS ,
       A.SORTS ,
```

```
         A.EXECUTIONS ,
         A.ROWS_PROCESSED ,
         A.FIRST_LOAD_TIME ,
         A.SHARABLE_MEM ,
         A.PERSISTENT_MEM ,
         A.RUNTIME_MEM
FROM     SYS.V_$SQLAREA A,
         SYS.ALL_USERS B
WHERE    A.PARSING_USER_ID=B.USER_ID
ORDER    BY 3 DESC
```

Epilogue

If Jeff is still out there writing SQL queries, I am sure his coding skills are much better today than they were back in 1993. To make sure you do not repeat some of his mistakes, follow the simple SQL checklist that we have covered in Exhibit 2. While certainly not exhaustive or all-inclusive, it will help serve as a reminder of some basic steps to follow when writing and troubleshooting database code.

- Validate the SQL

- Update and understand key object statistics

- EXPLAIN and understand the access path

- Correct obvious flaws

- Rewrite using various techniques and combinations

- Benchmark the rewrites

- Choose best option based on elapsed time and I/O consumption (normally)

Exhibit 2. *SQL Perfection Checklist*

Obviously, the goal is to find out what SQL is bogging the system down, and fix it. You can do this via poking around yourself, in the views as described above, running STATSPACK against the system, and retrieving the top SQL statements from that, or using the new 10g advisors to inform you where your SQL coding issues are.

This is extremely costly. STATSPACK can identify the most expensive, but the STATSPACK package at higher level is a real hog, and it may very well cause additional problems. The most expensive SQL on the system is best identified from *v$sqlarea* or using a 3rd party tool, like the ones from Quest Software (TOAD, SQL*Lab, SQL*Navigator).

Certainly, the next step is to run an explain plan on any poorly performing statement, to ensure that the access path is correct. Then you can move on to fixing the SQL statement.

And If You Can't Change The Code . . .

While system-wide tuning is not the best solution to SQL tuning, it can be extremely helpful in tuning systems with regular patterns of SQL processing, when you can't change the SQL (vendor delivered packages). It is not uncommon to see the Oracle DBA change the optimizer parameters depending on the time-of-day and day-of-week to accommodate changes in the type of SQL in the library cache.

Some of the More Common Changes:

- Changes to Oracle parameters - Changes to *optimizer_mode*, *optimizer_index_cost_adj* and *optimizer_index_caching* can make a huge difference in the execution plans of SQL.

- Changes to statistics - Using the *dbms_stats* package to import specialized statistics (geared to the current processing mode) can make a huge difference in SQL execution speed.

- Using automatic query re-write - Using Oracle Materialized Views you can pre-aggregate and pre-summarize data to reduce the amount of run-time table joins. For low-update databases, you can also pre-join tables together to improve processing speed.

Some of the Most Important Oracle Optimizer Parameters for tuning include:

- *optimizer_mode* - In Oracle9i there are many optimizer modes, all determined by the value of the *optimizer_mode* parameter. The values are *rule, choose, all_rows, first_rows, first_rows_1, first_rows_10* and *first_rows_100*.

  We need to start by defining the "best" execution plan. At any given time, all SQL statements in the library cache need to have the "best" execution plan. (Of course, this may change frequently because at any given time the processing demands may change). Is the best execution plan the one that begins to return row the fastest, or is the best execution plan the one that executes with the smallest amount of computing resources? Obviously, the answer depends on the processing for your database, and Oracle offers two optimizer modes that allow you to choose your definition of the "best" execution plan for you:

- *optimizer_mode=first_rows* - This *optimizer_mode* favors index access over full table scan access and is used when you want a query to start returning rows quickly, even if the overall amount of logical I/O is higher than a full-table scan. The *first_rows optimizer_mode* is generally used in online system where the end-user wants to see the first page of query results as quickly as possible.

- *optimizer_mode=all_rows* - This optimizer mode favors full-table scans (especially parallel full-table-scans) in cases where the server resources will be minimized. The *all_rows* mode is generally used during batch-oriented processing and for data warehouses where the goal is to minimize server resource consumption.

- *optimizer_mode=first_rows_n* - Starting with Oracle9i, we also have a new *optimizer_mode* to optimizer a query for a smaller result set. The values are *first_rows_1*, *first_rows_10* and *first_rows_100*, and you can use this parameter to ensure that Oracle optimizes the SQL

While the *optimizer_mode* parameter controls the overall behavior of the CBO, there are other Oracle parameters that have a great affect on CBO behavior. Oracle provides several important parameters to control the choices made by the CBO:

- *optimizer_index_cost_adj* - Adjusts the propensity of the CBO to favor index access over full-table scan access. The smaller the value, the more likely that the CBO will use an available index.

- *optimizer_index_caching* - Tells Oracle how much of your index is likely to be in the RAM data buffer cache. The setting for *optimizer_index_caching* affects the CBOs decision to use an index for a table join (nested loops), or to favor a full-table scan.

- *db_file_multiblock_read_count* - When set to a high value (with larger servers), the CBO recognizes that scattered (multi-block) reads may be less expensive than sequential reads. This makes the CBO friendlier to full-table scans.

This is no longer true, as of the version 9.2. System statistics, when computed, contains the value MBRC ("Multi Block Read Count"), which determines the price of the full table scan. What is more, Oracle 10g puts in some "platform defaults", which are rather bad. For the 9.2 version, please see Note: 149560.1 on Metalink.

- *parallel_automatic_tuning* - When set "on", full-table scans are parallelized on Oracle servers with many CPUs. Because parallelized full-table scans can be very fast, the CBO will give a higher cost to index access, and be friendlier to full-table scans.

- *hash_area_size* (if not using *pga_aggregate_target*) - The setting for *hash_area_size* parameter governs the propensity of the CBO to favor hash joins over nested loop and sort merge table joins.

- *sort_area_size* (only if you are not using the *pga_aggregate_target*) - The *sort_area_size* influences the CBO when deciding whether to perform an index access or a sort of the result set. The higher the value for *sort_area_size*, the more likely that a sort will be performed in RAM (thousands of time faster than the TEMP tablespace), and the more likely that the CBO will favor a sort over pre-sorted index retrieval.

Index Rebuilds

In an OLTP system, index space is often greater than the space allocated for tables, and fast row data access is critical for sub-second response time. Oracle offers a wealth of index structures:

- B-tree indexes –.This is the standard tree index that Oracle has been using since the earliest releases.

- Bitmap indexes – Bitmap indexes are used where an index column has a relatively small number of distinct values (low cardinality). These are super-fast for read-only databases, but are not suitable for systems with frequent updates

- Bitmap join indexes – This is an index structure whereby data columns from other tables appear in a multi-column index of a junction table. This is the only create index syntax to employ a SQL-like from clause and where clause.

```
create bitmap index
    part_suppliers_state
on
    inventory( parts.part_type, supplier.state )
from
```

```
        inventory i,      parts        p,      supplier   s
where
     i.part_id=p.part_id
and
     i.supplier_id=p.supplier_id;
```

In addition to these index structures we also see interesting use of indexes at runtime. Here is a sample of index-based access plans:

- Nested loop joins – This row access method scans an index to collect a series of ROWID's.

- Index fast-full-scans – This is a "multi-block read" access where the index blocks are accessed via a "db file scattered read" to load index blocks into the buffers. Please note that this method does not read the index nodes.

- Star joins – The star index has changed in structure several times, originally being a single-concatenated index and then changing to a bitmap index implementation. STAR indexes are super-fast when joining large read-only data warehouse tables.

- Index combine access – This is an example of the use of the *index_combine* hint. This execution plan combines bitmap indexes to quickly resolve a low-cardinality Boolean expression:

```
select /*+ index_combine(emp, dept_bit, job_bit) */
     ename,
     job,
     deptno,
     mgr
from
     emp
where
     job = 'SALESMAN'
and
     deptno = 30
;
```

Here is the execution plan that shows the index combine process:

```
OPERATION
-------------------------------------------------------------------
OPTIONS                                         OBJECT_NAME
POSITION
--------------------------- --------------------------- ---------
  SELECT STATEMENT

2
   TABLE ACCESS
BY INDEX ROWID                                  EMP
1
      BITMAP CONVERSION
TO ROWIDS
1
         BITMAP AND
            BITMAP INDEX
SINGLE VALUE                                    DEPT_BIT
1
               BITMAP INDEX
SINGLE VALUE                                    JOB_BIT
2
```

Inside Oracle b-tree Indexes

There are many myths and legends surrounding the use of Oracle indexes, especially the ongoing debate about rebuilding of indexes for improving performance.   Some experts claim that periodic rebuilding of Oracle b-tree indexes greatly improves space usage and access speed, while other experts maintain that Oracle indexes should "rarely" be rebuilt. Interestingly, Oracle reports that the new Oracle10g Automatic Maintenance Tasks (AMT) will automatically detect indexes that are in need of re-building. Here are the pros and cons of the issue:

- Arguments for Index Rebuilding – Many Oracle shops schedule periodic index rebuilding, and report measurable speed improvements after they rebuild their Oracle b-tree indexes.

- Arguments against Index Rebuilding – Some Oracle in-house experts maintain that Oracle indexes are super-efficient at space re-use and access speed and that a b-tree index rarely needs rebuilding. They claim that a reduction in Logical I/O should be measurable, and if there were any benefit to index rebuilding, someone would have come up with "provable" rules.

Index Information

The *dba_indexes* view is populated with index statistics when indexes are analyzed. The *dba_indexes* view contains a great deal of important information for the SQL optimizer, but there is still more to see. Oracle provides an analyze index xxx validate structure command that provides additional statistics into a temporary table called *index_stats*. But, the information needs to be saved, as each analyze validate structure command overlays the information

To get the full picture, you need both pieces. Also, there are certainly some columns that are more important than others:

- CLUSTERING_FACTOR – This is one of the most important index statistics because it indicates how well sequenced the index columns are to the table rows. If *clustering_factor* is low (about the same as the number of *dba_segments.blocks* in the table segment) than the index key is in the same order as the table rows and index range scan will be very efficient, with minimal disk I/O. As *clustering_factor* increases (up to *dba_tables.num_rows*), the index key is increasingly out of sequence with the table rows. Oracle's cost-based SQL optimizer relies heavily upon *clustering_factor* to decide whether or not to use the index to access the table.

- HEIGHT - As an index accepts new rows, the index blocks split. Once the index nodes have split to a predetermined maximum level the index will "spawn" into a new level.

- BLOCKS – This is the number of blocks consumed by the index. This is dependent on the *db_block_size*. In Oracle9i and beyond, many DBAs create b-tree indexes in very large blocksizes (*db_32k_block_size*) because the index will spawn less. Robin Schumacher has noted in his book Oracle Performance Troubleshooting notes,

"As you can see, the amount of logical reads has been reduced in half simply by using the new 16K tablespace and accompanying 16K data cache. Clearly, the benefits of properly using the new data caches and multi-block tablespace feature of Oracle9i and above are worth your investigation and trials in your own database. "

- PCT_USED – This metric is very misleading because it looks identical to the dba_indexes pct_used column, but has a different meaning. Normally, the pct_used threshold is the freelist unlink threshold, while in index_stats pct_used is the percentage of space allocated in the b-tree that is being used.

Are There Criteria for Index / Table Rebuilding?

The short answer is no, there is no 100% complete, definitive list. But, here are some things to start with:

- Index levels > 3

- Pct_used < 75%

- More than 20% of the rows have been deleted (space is not automatically reused)

- Index is becoming unclustered, and performance is degrading (causing increases in number of blocks to be read) – while unloading, resorting, and reloading the data in a table may provide better performance, this is an additional maintenance activity that needs to be performed, and can be difficult to keep the rows in their proper sequence, if the table gets a lot of insert / update / delete activity

Histograms

In some cases, the distribution of values within a column of a table will affect the optimizer's decision to use an index vs. performing a full-table scan. This scenario occurs when the value with a where clause does not have an equivalent distribution of values, making a full-table scan cheaper than index access in some cases. The problem is the optimizer can't tell when it is using a value with a few rows, and when it is using a value with a large number of rows.

A column histogram should only be created when we have data skew exists or suspected. In the real world, that happens rarely, and one of the most common mistakes with the optimizer is the unnecessary introduction of histograms into optimizer statistics. The histograms signals the optimizer that the column is not linearly distributed, and the optimizer will peek into the literal value in the SQL where clause, and compare that value to the histogram buckets in the histogram statistics.

While they are used to make a yes-or-no decision about the use of an index to access the table, histograms are most commonly used to predict the size of the intermediate result set from a multi-way table join.

For example, assume that we have a five-way table join whose result set will be only 10 rows. Oracle will want to join the tables together in such a way as to make the result set (cardinality) of the first join as small as possible. By carrying less baggage in the intermediate result sets, the query will run faster. To minimize intermediate results, the optimizer attempts to estimate the cardinality of each result set during the parse phase of SQL execution. Having histograms on skewed columns will greatly aid the optimizer in making a proper decision. (Remember, you can create a histogram even if the column does not have an index and does not participate as a join key.)

Because a complex schema might have tens of thousands of columns, it is impractical to evaluate each column for skew and thus Oracle provides an automated method for building histograms as part of the dbms_stats utility. By using the method_opt=>'for all columns size skewonly' option of dbms_stats, you can direct Oracle to automatically create histograms for those columns whose values are heavily skewed.

As a general rule, histograms are used to predict the cardinality and the number of rows returned in the result set. For example, assume that we have a product_type index and 70% of the values are for the HARDWARE type. Whenever SQL with where product_type='HARDWARE' is specified, a full-table scan is the fastest execution plan, while a query with where product_type='SOFTWARE' would be fastest using index access.

Because histograms add additional overhead to the parsing phase of SQL, you should avoid them unless they are required for a faster optimizer execution plan. But, there are several conditions where creating histograms is advised:

- When the column is referenced in a query — there is no point in creating histograms if the queries do not reference the column.

- When there is a significant skew in the distribution of columns values — this skew should be sufficiently significant that the value in the WHERE clause will make the optimizer choose a different execution plan.

- When the column values causes an incorrect assumption — if the optimizer makes an incorrect guess about the size of an intermediate result set, it may choose a sub-optimal table join method. Adding a histogram to this column will often provide the information required for the optimizer to use the best join method.

So how do you find those columns that are appropriate for histograms? There is a feature in *dbms_stats* that provides for the ability to automatically look for columns that should have histograms, and create the histograms. Multi-bucket histograms add a huge parsing overhead to SQL statements, and histograms should only be used when the SQL will choose a different execution plan based upon the column value.

To aid in intelligent histogram generation, Oracle uses the *method_opt* parameter of *dbms_stats*. There are also important new options within the method_opt clause, namely skewonly and auto (and others).

```
method_opt=>'for all columns size skewonly'
method_opt=>'for all columns size auto'
```

The first is the "skewonly" option, which is very time-intensive because it examines the distribution of values for every column within every index. If *dbms_stats* discovers an index with columns that are unevenly distributed, it will create histograms for that index to aid the cost-based SQL optimizer in making a decision about index vs. full-table scan access. For example, if an index has one column that is in 50% of the rows, a full-table scan is faster than an index scan to retrieve these rows.

Histograms are also used with SQL that has bind variables and SQL with cursor_sharing enabled. In these cases, the optimizer determines if the column value could affect the execution plan, and if so, replace the bind variable with a literal and performs a hard parse.

```
begin
 dbms_stats.gather_schema_stats(
    ownname         => 'SCOTT',
    estimate_percent => dbms_stats.auto_sample_size,
    method_opt      => 'for all columns size skewonly',
    degree          => 7
 );
end;
/
```

The auto option is used when monitoring is implemented (alter table xxx monitoring) and creates histograms based upon data distribution and the manner in which the column is accessed by the application (e.g., the workload on the column as determined by monitoring). Using method_opt=>'auto' is similar to using the gather auto in the option parameter of *dbms_stats*:

```
begin
    dbms_stats.gather_schema_stats(
        ownname         => 'SCOTT',
        estimate_percent => dbms_stats.auto_sample_size,
        method_opt      => 'for all columns size auto',
        degree          => 7
    );
end;
/
```

Finding the Poorly Running SQL

While complex queries may have extremely complex execution plans, most Oracle professionals must tune SQL with the following problems:

- Sub-optimal index access to a table — This problem occurs when the optimizer cannot find an index or the most restrictive where clause in the SQL is not matched with an index. When the optimizer cannot find an appropriate index to access table rows, the optimizer will always invoke a full-table scan, reading every row in the table. Hence, a large-table full-table scan might indicate a sub-optimal SQL statement that can be tuned by adding an index that matches the where clause of the query.

- Sub-optimal join methods — The optimizer has many join methods available including a merge join, a nested loop join, hash join and a star join. To choose the right join method, the optimizer must guess at the size of the intermediate result sets from multi-way table joins. To make this guess, the optimizer has incomplete information. Even if histograms are present, the optimizer cannot know for certain the exact number of rows returned from a join. The most common remedy is to use hints to change the join (use_nl, use_hash) or re-analyze the statistics on the target tables.

The *v$sql_plan* view can help locate SQL tuning opportunities. When searching for tuning opportunities, start by interrogating the *v$sql_plan* view to find these large-table full-table scans.

This is when business knowledge comes in handy. Very frequently, and I'm talking from experience, queries are monstrous because the developer doesn't understand what he goal is and what the data actually means. The old saying that there is no substitute for experience is confirmed here again.

Optimize Query Speed with the Clustering_factor Attribute

The cost-based optimizer (CBO) improves with each new release of Oracle, and the most current enhancement with Oracle9i is the consideration of external influences (CPU cost and I/O cost) when formulating an execution plan.

Rules for Oracle Indexing

To understand how Oracle chooses the execution plan for a query, you need to first learn the rules Oracle uses when it decides whether to use an index.

While important characteristics of column data within tables are known to the CBO, the most important characteristics are the clustering factor for the column and the selectivity of column values. Oracle provides a column called *clustering_factor* in the *dba_indexes* view that provides information on how the table rows are synchronized with the index. The table rows are synchronized with the index when the clustering factor is close to the number of data blocks and the column value is not row-ordered when the *clustering_factor* approaches the number of rows in the table.

To illustrate, consider this query that filters the result set using a column value:

```
select
   customer_name
from
   customer
where
   customer_state = 'New Mexico';
```

Here, the decision to use an index vs. a full-table scan is, at least, partially determined by the percentage of customers in New Mexico. An index scan is faster for this query if the percentage of customers in New Mexico is small and the values are clustered on the data blocks. But, there is one other piece of information that is relevant here. Are all the New Mexico rows stored together in one or more blocks next to each other, or are the New Mexico rows scattered all over all of the blocks in the table? This is referred to as clustering – are the New Mexico rows clustered together, or are they widely dispersed (non-clustered)?

Optimize Query Speed with the Clustering_factor Attribute

Why, then, would a CBO choose to perform a full-table scan when only a small number of rows are retrieved? Perhaps it is because the CBO is considering the clustering of column values within the table.

Four factors work together to help the CBO decide whether to use an index or a full-table scan: the selectivity of a column value, the *db_block_size*, the *avg_row_len*, and the cardinality. An index scan is usually faster if a data column has high selectivity and a low *clustering_factor*.

To maintain row order, the DBA will periodically resequence table rows or use a single-table cluster in those cases where a majority of the SQL references a column with a high *clustering_factor*, a large *db_block_size*, and a small *avg_row_len*. This removes the full-table scan, places all adjacent rows in the same data block, and makes the query faster, since it reads much fewer blocks.

On the other hand, as the *clustering_factor* nears the number of rows in the table, the rows fall out of sync with the index. This high *clustering_factor*, where the value is close to the number of rows in the table (*num_rows*), indicates that the rows are out of sequence with the index and an additional I/O may be required for index range scans.

Even when a column has high selectivity, a high *clustering_factor*, and small *avg_row_len*, there is still indication that column values are randomly distributed in the table, and an additional I/O will be required to obtain the rows. An index range scan would cause a huge amount of unnecessary I/O, thus making a full-table scan more efficient.

Use of Nologging

Often you have optimally coded SQL, but it still runs a long time, because it is doing a lot of work. Especially if you are loading a data warehouse or something, where the tables get reloaded on a regular basis – there is a huge effort to get the thing loaded, and then it stays stable for a while.

A great misnomer in the world of Oracle tuning is the use of nologging. It sounds really good – you don't care about the recoverability of what you are doing, so you just tell Oracle not to log it – which will reduce on your log switches, reduce on flushing buffers, reduce the work of the ARCH process, and in general, make things go a whole lot faster. And, Oracle even has clauses on the create table and alter table statement to make an object not log. Nologging is only useful on large objects – the benefit to be gained by using nologging on a small object is minimal.

If only it were as easy as it seems. The bottom line to nologging, is that it only works – sometimes.

First off, 'nologging' doesn't mean NO logging, it means a small amount of logging. Therefore, if you are watching a large load run, for example, you shouldn't expect to see NO redo activity at all. You will still see some, just not as much as you'd see if you hadn't set nologging. Any updates to the catalog for space management, and object management (minimized if you are using locally managed tablespaces) are still logged.

In general, the use of nologging only works when you are doing one of the following:

- direct loads via SQL*Loader
- direct loads via insert statements (insert with append hint)

- create table as select

- create index

- alter table move partition

- alter table split partition

- alter index split partition

- alter index rebuild

- insert, update, delete on LOBS in no cache nologging mode stored out of line (in their own table)

Nologging can be set at the table, index, or tablespace level, and can be done at object creation time, or later, via an alter:

```
create table emp_nologging
(empid number(8) not null,
 name char(40) not null,
 address char(50) not null)
tablespace bigtablespace
nologging;

alter table department nologging;

create index emp_ix_1
  on emp(empid_id)
nologging

alter tablespace USERDATA nologging;
```

SQL*Net Tuning

Once the SQL is tweaked, you should verify that the database is talking as efficiently as possible to its clients. Certainly, another aspect of tuning involves the network, as opposed to the actual code. While network tuning is certainly beyond the scope of this book, tuning SQL*Net is a critical piece of that. You can have the most efficient code in the world, but if you can't get it from the database to the user, who cares. Serg Shestakov and Dmitry

Petrov have summarized the major steps to tuning SQL*Net as follows:

SQL*Net Diagnostics and Performance Tuning

Network diagnostics and performance tuning are important issues to consider for savvy administrators managing complex distributed Oracle installations. Oracle has many powerful features for SQL*Net diagnostics, such as logging and tracing mechanisms, explanation tools, and statistics collection. To optimize network performance, administrators should accurately tune Oracle SQL*Net services. There are many external and internal factors influencing SQL*Net performance. We will consider how to tune SQL*Net buffer size, how to speed up connections for dedicated and multi-threaded servers, what is listeners load balancing, and we will learn new Net8 features affecting SQL*Net diagnostics and performance. We use the SQL*Net term to describe both Net8 software and older versions, starting with SQL*Net 2.3.x. We will also use Oracle utility names for UNIX systems.

SQL*Net is a transparent network interface provided for Oracle applications to connect to Oracle DBMS server software. Oracle SQL*Net hides the complexity of Underlying Network Protocol (UNP) and takes care of managing connections over distributed heterogeneous networks. Consider the protocol stack in detail. UNP consists of upper layer protocol (ULP) and lower layer protocol (LLP). To better understand the overall picture, take a look at the protocol stack in terms of the Open System Interconnection (OSI) model (see Exhibit 1).

Oracle applications can be Oracle Forms, SQL*Plus, etc. Oracle server software can be Oracle7, Oracle8 DBMS servers. SQL*Net software consists of several major components: Oracle Call Interface/User Program Interface (for client side), Oracle

Program Interface (for server side), Two Task Common, Transparent Network Substrate, and Oracle Protocol Adapters. The most popular ULPs are TCP/IP, and DECnet, IPX/SPX; and common LLPs are FDDI, Ethernet, Token Ring, and ARCNET. The physical layer deals with hardware sending and receiving data on a carrier.

Before starting the analysis, let's define what factors affect network performance and select evaluation criteria. We considered network stack and saw that SQL*Net performance is strongly influenced by underlying UNP parameters. On the other hand, SQL*Net performance is affected by upper-level Oracle software characteristics like administrator's choice on using multi-threaded server versus dedicated server, number of active server processes, time required to scan large tnsnames.ora files, level of SQL*Net tracing configured on client side and server side, security mechanisms used to authenticate connections, encrypt data being transferred, and checksumming models. And, of course, SQL*Net performance is influenced by external network factors like topology, throughput, domain name service configuration, etc. It is important to remember that the basic characteristics of SQL*Net performance for processing Oracle transactions are connect time and query time. We will see how to reduce network traffic and make data transfer fast and reliable by synchronizing UNP parameters with SQL*Net parameters.

Let's highlight some of the network problems related to SQL*Net software. Among these are: broken connections, bad load-balancing, too long response times at peak workloads, and automatic adjustment of Oracle server software causing excessive resources utilization. If an error arises, it affects many network components and error codes spread like wildfire through the protocol stack. It is difficult to locate the true reason causing the network problem; but fortunately, there are tools to help with SQL*Net diagnostics.

SQL*Net Diagnostics

To reduce administrator headaches because of network problems, Oracle offers tracing and logging features of SQL*Net and Trace Assistant tool to explain the trace codes. Tracing can provide very detailed information and it should be turned on to solve serious problems, that cannot be resolved by analyzing standard log messages. To locate what network component causes the problem, one should systematically run checks to reduce the search scope. First, check if the server node is accessible from the client machine. Then, make sure on the server side that the database is up and running. Third, check if the client has the appropriate network adapter installed. After that, run the Listener Control utility and see if listener required by client is running and can handle requests for target database. A good way to make sure that Oracle can establish client/server connection is *tnsping* utility. This utility takes the TNS service name as a first parameter, and the number of attempts as a second (optional) parameter. This utility returns response time if it manages to establish the connection. The *tnsping* utility can also be used to measure network throughput between client and server. If *tnsping* fails, check the configuration files syntax. If a problem persists, you can use logging and tracing mechanisms to get in-depth information.

Let's show how to turn on the SQL*Net logging and tracing. On the client side, one can define the directory where to put log and trace files in the *sqlnet.ora* file using the *log_directory_client* and *trace_directory_client* parameters, respectively. One can also define the log and trace file names with the *log_directory_client* and *trace_directory_client* parameters of the *sqlnet.ora* file. By default, trace on UNIX systems is written to $ORACLE_HOME/network/trace/sqlnet.trc, and log is written to *sqlnet.log* file under the same directory. On the server side, one can define log and trace destinations with the following parameters: *log_directory_<lsnr>*, *log_file_<lsnr>*, *trace_directory_<lsnr>* and *trace_file_<lsnr>*.

All these parameters should be configured in the *listener.ora* file. By default, server logs and traces are stored in *listener.log* and *listener.trc* files under the $ORACLE_HOME/network/trace directory. Note that, by default, logging is turned on and one can change this behavior with the *logging_<lsnr>* parameter of the *listener.ora* file. One can switch between different trace standards on the client side using the *trace_level_client* parameter of *sqlnet.ora*. At the server side, the trace level parameter is called *trace_level_<lsnr>* and it should be included into the *listener.ora*. Valid trace levels are: OFF, USER, ADMIN and SUPPORT for Oracle8.

Now let's discuss how to analyze network problem using log messages. First, scan the tail of SQL*Net log file and detect what is the latest error number caused by the application. It usually corresponds to the last line of log file. Remember that log files can grow to very large sizes, which makes it difficult to read. One should carefully filter the log information. For example, on UNIX systems, one can see the last 40 log lines issuing a tail -40 <log file name> command. The last non-empty message in the error stack usually indicates actual problem cause. If log analysis does not help to remove the problem, turn on the tracing at the desired level and repeat the sequence of events triggering the error. Trace information is generated according to the network layers participating in the data transfer. Do not forget to turn off the tracing once the problem is solved. Excessive tracing may slow down the overall network performance.

The mission-critical component of SQL*Net software is the listener. Let's take a closer look at most common listener error codes and workarounds for the corresponding problems. The ORA-12541 error "No listener," which appears at some client's logs while the listener is up and running, denotes that incoming connection requests are received too quickly and listener cannot handle it. To avoid this problem, increase the *queuesize* parameter at *listener.ora* file, restart the listener, and see if the new value is sufficient. Another listener- related error is ORA-12224 "TNS: No listener." It indicates that connection cannot be completed because listener is not running. One can try to bypass the problem by verifying if the client connects to the same address the listener actually uses, and that version compatibility is OK. One of the most frequent listener errors is ORA-12545 "TNS: Name lookup failure." This error indicates that the client cannot make contact with remote node. Check the correctness of the ADDRESS keyword syntax on the server and client. Next, make sure that the listener process on the remote node has been started. Log on to the server and run the Listener Control utility. Within this utility, issue a STATUS <lsnr> command; and if there are no listeners, run it with the START command. Common practice among administrators is to copy service descriptions on a client machine when target database changes or one more database should be added to those listed in the *tnsnames.ora* file. This can raise the ORA-12154 error "TNS: Could not resolve service name." Upon receiving this error, check if the service name supplied for connection exists in the configuration file and if all its parameters are correct. To avoid such problems, the administrator should take care of configuration files version control.

When turning on SQL*Net tracing, Oracle writes errors and warnings along with internal parameters and hex packet representations to trace files, which are not that easy to read and analyze. For better presentation and explanation of trace messages you can use Trace Assistant. Run Trace Assistant from the operating system environment, issuing a *trceval* command for SQL*Net 2.3.x or the *trcasst* command for Net8. Trace Assistant can evaluate SQL*Net packets; it can also present summary and detailed reports. Summary shows the total number of sent and received packets, and detailed report displays a bit-level picture. Valuable command-line options for Trace Assistant include:

- summary connectivity information (c)

- detailed connectivity information (d)

- detailed TTC information (t)

- summary Two-Task Common information (u)

- SQL commands (q) — which should be used together with (u) and overall trace statistics (s).

Command syntax is slightly different for SQL*Net 2.3.x and Net8.

To monitor network traffic carried by SQL*Net without resource-intensive tracing, you can use a third-party network analyzer that will collect statistics on SQL*Net listener ports. Another way is to use native Oracle statistics that can be accessed using the *v_$sysstat* view. There are six major parameters related to SQL*Net traffic statistics; these are number of bytes sent to client and database link via SQL*Net, number of bytes received from client and database link via SQL*Net, total number of SQL*Net roundtrips between client and database link. You can read current values by issuing the following SQL statement:

```
SELECT name, value FROM v_$sysstat
WHERE name LIKE '%SQL*Net%';
```

To avoid manual typing and get a better picture of network traffic dynamics you can decide to design a data schema for cumulative statistics, write a statistics collection procedure, and schedule it for regular execution. The entire process is described below in the "Optimizing Connect Time with MTS" section where a similar problem is solved.

Optimizing Query Time with SDU Buffer Size

SDU is an acronym for Session Data Unit. The SDU parameter can be included in the SQL*Net configuration files *tnsnames.ora* and *listener.ora*. SDU defines SQL*Net buffer size and it is a most important factor influencing SQL*Net query time. SDU buffer size varies from 2 K to 32 K. The goal is to synchronize SDU with buffer sizes of underlying UNP protocols and application-level buffer size. A wrong guess for SDU parameter may lead to traffic overhead and fragmentation, which may cause longer query times. If the SDU buffer size is insufficient for the application fetching mechanism, this causes fragmentation. And, of course, if the ULP buffer size is smaller than SDU buffer size, this also causes fragmentation. Following is an example on how one can overwrite the default SDU parameter in *listener.ora* file:

```
SID_LIST_LISTNER=
  (SID_LIST=
    (SID_DESC=
      (SDU=4096)
        . . . . . . .
    )
  )
```

And an example of configuring SDU buffer size for the *tnsnames.ora* file is:

```
oracle.world=
  (DEESCRIPTION=
    (SDU=4096)
      . . . . . . . .
  )
```

Let's show how to tune the SDU buffer size. Assume that ULP, LLP, and application fetch buffer sizes and header sizes are known. The best network performance will be gained if the buffer size for each underlying layer plus its header size is slightly greater than the data buffer size of the current layer. The administrator can model the data transmission for a wide range of

SDU parameters. The goal is to detect situations in which fragmentation occurs. Once fragmentation is detected, the data buffer should be split into parts according to the buffer sizes and header sizes of the underlying layer. Ideally the SDU buffer size should include the maximum application fetch size, possible and be less than or equal to the UNP buffer size minus SQL*Net header size.

Optimizing Connect Time with Dedicated Server

When working with a dedicated server, the SQL*Net connect time can be reduced using prespawned (prestarted) server processes. Thus, one can gain better performance during peak workloads. One can adjust the number of prespawned processes with *listener.ora* parameters: *prespawn_max, pool_size* and *timeout*. The first parameter restricts maximum number of prestarted Oracle server processes, the second parameter limits the number of prestarted server processes the listener can create for the selected protocol, and the third parameter can be used to make the server process wait for the net connect request before shutting down. Thus, one can get better connection times for next requests by increasing server resources utilization. The example below illustrates corresponding *listener.ora* syntax:

```
(SID_LIST=
  (SID_DESC=
    (SID_NAME=ORCL)
      (ORACLE_HOME=/opt/oracle)
      (PRESPAWN_MAX=70)
      (PRESPAWN_LIST=
        (PRESPAWN_DESC=
          (PROTOCOL=TCP)
          (POOL_SIZE=10)
          (TIMEOUT=2)))))
```

To tune the number of prespawned servers, one needs a thorough understanding of the connection request processing mechanism. When listeners process a request, it can either spawn a new server process and pass connection to it, or redirect the connection to an already allocated process. This mechanism is transparent to the user, but affects the connection time. One way to process the request is called a Bequeath session method, and a second method is called a Redirect session. When prespawned processes are not configured, the default method is Bequeath session. However, if one has configured the *prespawn_max* parameter, Oracle can use a Redirect session method. The client passes the request to the listener and the listener checks if any of prespawned processes are available. If yes, the listener returns a prespawned address to client, the client disconnects from listener and starts working with the prespawned process directly. If no prespawned processes are available, the listener refuses to process the client request. Best results can be achieved by experimenting with the parameters that control the prespawned processes' behavior and measuring connect time at different workloads.

Optimizing Connect Time with MTS

The multi-threaded server (MTS) has a major impact on overall SQL*Net performance — connect time first of all. The most important issues to consider when optimizing response times for a multithreaded server are balancing the number of shared server processes and number of dispatchers running. Oracle system dictionary views hold current performance indicators and values gathered since start-up; but server and network loads change all the time and there is a need for detailed time distributions to make correct decisions on performance tuning (i.e., how often indicators reach peaks and what are the average values). So, because of the need for cumulative statistics, simple select statements addressing the system dictionary views are not enough. Thus, step-by-step, additional data structures will be created to hold cumulative statistics and write a statistics collection procedure.

Statistics Collection for MTS

There are two adjustable parameters in the *init.ora* file related to shared server processes: *mts_servers* and *mts_max_servers*. The first parameter regulates the initial number of shared servers created at start-up, and the second parameter limits the maximum number of shared server processes. If the administrator sets an insufficient initial number of shared servers, Oracle dynamically creates additional shared servers up to *mts_mas_servers* and de-allocates when processes idle time exceeds a predefined threshold. If the administrator sets too high a number of initial shared servers, Oracle never de-allocates these processes created at startup. This may cause excessive usage of system resources. So, to optimize network performance without server overhead, one needs to set the *mts_servers* according to the calculated average number of active shared server processes. To avoid low connection times at peak server workloads, one needs to set the *mts_max_servers* parameter to not less than maximum number of required server processes. One way to tune these parameters is to experiment with different values and tracking the performance gains.

Now one can discuss how to collect, store, and view the statistics related to shared server processes. The Oracle system dictionary holds the current number of shared servers running at *v_$shared_server* view. (We prefer to directly address the *v_$* views to avoid addressing its public synonyms). To hold the history of this performance indicator, the *mts_server_statistics* table is defined by:

```
create table MTS_Server_Statistics (
  Timepoint DATE,        -- When statistics
    was collected
Server_count INTEGER     -- Number of shared
    servers running
  );
```

To regulate the number of dispatchers running, there are parameters in the *init.ora* file – *mts_dispatchers* and *mts_max_dispatchers* – that set the initial and maximum number of dispatchers, respectively. To tune these parameters one needs to calculate the dispatchers load ratio (i.e., the busy time divided by overall running time). One can monitor these statistics by querying the *v_$dispatcher*. To store cumulative statistics on dispatcher load, create the *mts_dispatcher_statistics* table. The corresponding DDL command is:

```
create table MTS_Dispatcher_Statistics (
      Timepoint DATE,     -- When statistics was collected
      Disp_name VARCHAR2 (5),         -- Dispatcher name
      Disp_network VARCHAR2 (128), -- Dispatcher Protocol
      Cumu_busy REAL,          -- Cumulative busy time
      Cumu_idle REAL,          -- Cumulative idle time
      Cumu_ratio REAL -- Cumulative dispatcher load ratio
);
```

Now we'll show how the administrator can fetch statistics to the tables using a PL/SQL procedure; call it *mts_statistics*. First, declare the procedure. Because one wants this procedure to gather cumulative statistics, there needs to be two parameters – the number of runs and the time delay between runs. (Assume that the time delay is indicated in minutes). The corresponding code is:

```
CREATE OR REPLACE PROCEDURE MTS_Statistics
    (Runs IN INTEGER, Time_delay IN INTEGER) AS
```

Now declare all the necessary variables. It is easy to gather cumulative statistics for shared servers because one must only fetch and store the number of running servers. No additional variables are necessary. But one needs several variables to calculate cumulative statistics on dispatcher loads. The *prev_busy* and *prev_idle* variables are used to keep information from the previous run — dispatcher busy time and idle time, respectively. The *intrv_busy* and *intrv_idle* will be used to store changes of corresponding parameters since the last run, and the *intrv_ratio* will be used to calculate the indicator of current dispatcher load. Once finished with the declarations, start procedure body defining the main loop, which calculates cumulative statistics several times as specified in the *runs* parameter.

```
        Prev_busy REAL;
        Prev_idle REAL;
        Intrv_busy REAL;
        Intrv_idle REAL;
        Intrv_ratio REAL;
BEGIN
FOR Counter IN 1 .. Runs LOOP
```

First, fetch statistics on the number of shared servers running from the corresponding system view and store it into the *mts_server_statistics* table along with current time. (Note that shared servers with QUIT status are not taken into account.

```
INSERT INTO MTS_Server_Statistics
   (Timepoint, Server_count)
   (SELECT SYSDATE, Count(*)
    FROM SYS.V_$SHARED_SERVER
    WHERE Status != 'QUIT');
```

The next section of code starts a loop for cursor *cur_status*, calculating the dispatcher load ratio for each network protocol being used. One obtains the dispatcher name, network protocol, total busy time, and total idle time from the *v_$dispatcher* system view. Once a loop starts, there are two possible situations. When the procedure is invoked for the first time, cumulative load ratio does not make any sense; thus, the situation is processed by analyzing the *counter* variable.

```
FOR Cur_Status IN (SELECT Name, Network,
Busy, Idle
        FROM SYS.V_$DISPATCHER)
    LOOP

    IF Counter = 1 THEN
        INSERT INTO MTS_Dispatcher_Statistics
```

```
                VALUES(SYSDATE, Cur_status.name,
Cur_status.network,
                Cur_status.Busy, Cur_Status.Idle, NULL);
        ELSE
```

However, each next time one enters the loop, one already has previous statistics; thus, one can calculate the current cumulative load ratio. The previous values are stored in the *mts_dispatcher_statistics* table; so one first needs to fetch previous values into memory variables *prev_busy* and *prev_idle*. To get these values, select a last recent row from the *mts_dispatcher_statistics* table:

```
SELECT Cumu_busy, Cumu_idle INTO Prev_busy,
  Prev_idle
    FROM MTS_Dispatcher_statistics
    WHERE Disp_name = Cur_Status.Name AND
      Timepoint =
    (SELECT max(Timepoint)
      FROM MTS_Dispatcher_Statistics
      WHERE Disp_name = Cur_Status.Name);
```

Detect changes in busy time and idle time since last run and store it into *intrv_busy* and *intrv_idle* variables. Then calculate the cumulative dispatcher load ratio as the percentage of busy time since last run divided by the time elapsed since last run. Now one can store the cumulative ratio into the *mts_dispatcher_statistics* table along with system time, dispatcher name, network protocol, total busy, and total idle time. The processing of statistics for dispatchers is over, so the inner loop is closed.

```
  Intrv_busy := Cur_Status.Busy - Prev_busy;
  Intrv_idle := Cur_Status.Idle - Prev_idle;
  Intrv_ratio := Intrv_busy / (Intrv_busy +
    Intrv_idle) * 100;
  INSERT INTO MTS_Dispatcher_Statistics
    VALUES(SYSDATE, Cur_status.name, Cur_status.network,
      Cur_status.Busy, Cur_Status.Idle, Intrv_ratio);
END IF;
END LOOP;
```

SQL*Net Diagnostics and Performance Tuning   **327**

To save the inserted statistics, issue a COMMIT statement and then call the SLEEP procedure from the *dbms_lock* package to suspend the procedure execution for a given period, thus converting the parameter *time_delay* given in minutes to seconds. Now, at last, one can close the main loop and end the procedure body. The corresponding statements are:

```
    COMMIT;
    DBMS_LOCK.SLEEP(Time_delay*60);
  END LOOP;
END MTS_Statistics;
```

One can run the statistics collection procedure manually from the SQL*Plus console, issuing the EXECUTE statement, or schedule it for regular execution in crontab file (on UNIX systems). If the statistics collection procedure is to be run under an Oracle user different from SYS, do not forget to grant necessary access rights for system views and *dbms_lock* package .

Tuning Methodology Based on MTS Statistics

Remember that the multi-threaded server performance indicators discussed above are strongly related to SQL*Net connection times. Now we show the tuning methodology based on statistics collected into the *mts_dispatcher_statistics* and *mts_server_statistics* tables using the *mts_statistics* procedure. The methodology consists of three major steps.

1. **Initialization**. We need to assign initial values to the MTS parameters influencing SQL*Net performance. A good starting point for *mts_dispatchers* is one integer higher than the maximum number of concurrent sessions, divided by the number of connections per dispatcher. The number of connections per dispatcher can be extracted from the MAXIMUM_CONNECTIONS field of *v_$mts* system view. The initial *mts_servers* value should be set so that each shared server is related to 20 users. Oracle recommends setting

mts_max_dispatchers and *mts_max_servers* to the upper limit applicable for your particular system.

2. **Statistics collection**. We need to run our *mts_statistics* procedure issuing the below listed SQL*Plus command. Note that, to reduce the influence on statistics being collected, the procedure should be run via dedicated session:

```
EXECUTE MTS_Statistics(<Number of runs>, <Time delay>);
```

Ideally, the number of runs multiplied by the time delay should be equal to the application running time — 24 hours for non-stop systems. Statistics should be collected each working day for at least one week. To improve the statistics quality, one can run the collection procedure according to the following recommendations. First-day statistics collection should be run as frequently as possible because parameters are not tuned. Each evening, statistics should be analyzed and parameters should be adjusted (according to Step 3). Each next day, increase the time delay and decrease the number of runs. If by the end of the tuning period (the analysis shows that no changes are necessary, then one has a well-tuned multi-threaded server. Otherwise, tuning should be continued.

3. **Analysis**. This step is broken into two parts:

   ▪ **Servers performance analysis**. To see the overall distribution, one can select the last recent rows, filtering by collection time, thus one can screen peak workloads. To adjust the shared server tuning parameters, issue the following SQL statement:

```
SELECT avg(Server_count), max(Server_count)
   FROM MTS_Server_Statistics
   WHERE Timepoint like SYSDATE;
```

We recommend setting the *mts_servers* equal to the average number of shared servers running. Respectively, we recommend setting the *mts_max_servers* equal to the maximum number of shared servers running.

- **Dispatchers load analysis**. One can analyze overall distribution as done for the shared servers. But now we need to detect the average dispatcher's workload ratio and its standard deviation:

```
SELECT Disp_name,
    avg(Cumu_ratio) "Avg ratio",
    stddev(Cumu_ratio)"Std.dev."
 FROM MTS_Dispatcher_Statistics
 WHERE Timepoint like SYSDATE GROUP BY
    Disp_name;
```

If the average workload is greater than 50 per- cent, we significantly increase the number of *mts_dispatchers*. If the average workload is less than 50percent, this means that there are too many dispatchers; thus, one should decrease *mts_dispatchers* and *mts_max_dispatchers*. Standard deviation indicates how often the workload changes. The closer the standard deviation is to zero, the better the statistics obtained. Note that the administrator can add more dispatchers and shared servers running the appropriate ALTER SYSTEM command.

Improving the Interface

The best way to avoid manual typing of SQL commands to view the statistics gathered into our data structures is to build a Web interface. For example, one can use the Oracle application server and write PL/SQL procedures, generating dynamic HTML pages on-the-fly. Thus, information can be presented in a very convenient way; for example, one can highlight performance indicators exceeding the threshold.

Listener Load Balancing

One good way to increase SQL*Net performance is listener load balancing. This has major impact on connection time for heavily loaded systems. With several listeners configured for a single database or several database instances and load balancing, there are more chances to bypass the bottlenecks when establishing a connection. This works for both dedicated servers and multi-threaded servers. One can configure multiple listeners configuring *init.ora* and *listener.ora* files on the server side, and *tnsnames.ora* on the client side. To enable load balancing between multiple listeners with multithreaded server one should assign TRUE to *mts_multiple_listeners* parameter of *init.ora* file. If we need to run several listeners for single multithreaded server, we should add several addresses to init.ora file like shown below:

```
MTS_LISTENER_ADDRESS=
  (ADDRESS=(PROTOCOL=tcp)(HOST=myhost)
    (PORT=1521))

MTS_LISTENER_ADDRESS=
  (ADDRESS=(PROTOCOL=tcp)(HOST=myhost)
    (PORT=1522))
```

If each listener is to serve several ports, one should include the *address_list* keyword. Note that, for dedicated servers, one does not need to change *init.ora* parameters at all. Now go to the client side and see how to configure the *tnsnames.ora* file. To gain the increased performance from load balancing, one should enable the random connection between listeners. This can be done by providing each listener coordinates with a separate *description* keyword.

```
oracle.world=
(DESCRIPTION_LIST=
  (DESCRIPTION=(ADDRESS_LIST=
    (ADDRESS=
      (PROTOCOL=tcp)(HOST=myhost)
        (PORT=1521))))
  (DESCRIPTION=(ADDRESS_LIST=
```

```
(ADDRESS=
  (PROTOCOL=tcp)(HOST=myhost)
    (PORT=1522))))
(CONNECT_DATA=(SID=mysid)))
```

For many listeners to communicate with many database instances, one should indicate the *connect_data* keyword for each description and skip the final *connect_data* for all listeners. If there are equal replicated databases, one can create a service name that maps to several database instances with different global names.

To make sure that load balancing works, you can run the Listener Control utility (*lsnrctl*) and issue the SERVICES command. From its output, you will then learn current listener configuration. Also, turn on SQL*Net tracing and monitor how clients connect to database instances.

Net8 New Features

The administrator can use multiplexing and connection pooling. The connection pooling feature helps to maximize the number of physical links to MTS. To increase network performance by multiplexing sessions across a single physical link, one can install Connection Manager software. Another important feature of Net8 is Raw Transport — the ability of Net8 to work without headers whenever possible. Tracing functionality is also extended and supplied with better explanation capabilities. Trace Assistant for Net8 can display error information at three decoding levels.

Connection Pooling: How It Works

With connection pooling, Oracle opens up new connections to the multi-threaded server until a maximum number of connections is reached. Next connection requests will wait until the dispatcher temporarily disconnects some idle connection and becomes available. Note that when the idle session (disconnected temporarily) requests service from dispatcher, the connection will be re-established as soon as possible. This mechanism gives significant SQL*Net performance gains for OLAP applications. To configure the connection pooling, one must specify four additional attributes for the *mts_dispatchers* parameter of the *init.ora* file. The first attribute is POOL. Valid values are ON, OFF, IN, and OUT. Simply turn on the pooling mechanism setting POOL=ON. The second attribute is CONNECTION; it controls the maximum number of connections to database per dispatcher in terms of pooling. The third attribute is SESSIONS; it regulates the maximum number of sessions per dispatcher. The fourth attribute is TICKS; it is given in 10-second ticks and defines the time limit for a connection to wait. One can use brief attributes to name up to three characters. An example for connection pooling configuration:

```
MTS_DISPATCHERS=
"(PROT=tcp)(CONN=4)(DISP=1)(POOL=ON)(SESS=5)
  (TICKS=3)"
```

Now let's discuss how to make sure that connection pooling works. For the above listed configuration, upon restarting the database, we can sequentially open and leave idle five SQL*Plus sessions. If connection pooling works, we notice that the fifth connection will hang for 30 seconds according to the *ticks* parameters.

Summary

To summarize, Oracle network problems can be caused by numerous internal and external factors. SQL*Net diagnostics are based on trace files analysis. Trace Assistant is a tool aimed to ease the diagnostic codes filtering and explanation. SQL*Net performance is measured by connection time and query time. The best query time obtains if we manage to synchronize SQL*Net buffer size with application fetching buffer and UNP buffers. We discussed how it could be tuned by adjusting the SDU parameter. Connection time can be decreased by tuning Oracle server software and configuring the SQL*Net client. We demonstrated how to enable load balancing between multiple listeners, how to prestart Oracle server processes for dedicated server, and how to tune a multi-threaded server by collecting and analyzing the statistics on shared servers and dispatchers. Finally, we outlined the Net8 new features affecting network performance and discussed how the connection pooling mechanism works.

Conclusion

This chapter provided a summarization of SQL Coding, tips and tricks to obtain high performance, as well as tuning SQL*Net. Using the checklists provided, a DBA should be well on the way to obtaining an optimally performing system. However, statistics need to be up to date and accurate, to start with. Without that, any tuning effort will be destined to fail. Certainly, focus on the init.ora parameters, as well as indexes and histograms, which are crucial. If nologging is an option, that's great. Unfortuntately, very often you aren't using one of the 'chosen commands' upon which nologging works, so you have no choice but to log.

Index

M

N

O

P

Q

R

S

T

U

V

X

About Kimberly Floss

Kimberly Floss has over 15 years of experience in the Information Technology Industry, with specific focus on relational database technology, including Oracle, DB2, Microsoft SQL Server, and Sybase. Kimberly has extensive experience performing as a DBA on Mainframe, UNIX and Windows based systems, as well as managing DBA teams supporting multiple database platforms. She also works as an Adjunct Professor, teaching SQL Programming / Database Administration at a local community college.

Kimberly Floss is the current President of the International Oracle Users Group (IOUG). With more than a decade of experience, Kimberly specializes in Oracle Performance Tuning and is a respected expert in SQL tuning techniques. She is an active member of the Chicago Oracle User Group, and the Midwest Oracle User Group, in addition to the IOUG. She is also a frequent contributor to Oracle Magazine and Select Journal.

She holds a Bachelors of Science Degree in Computer Information Systems from Purdue University, specializing in Systems Analysis and Design, and an MBA with emphasis in Management Information Systems from Loyola University.

Kimberly lives in the Chicago-land area, with her husband, son, and two cats.

The Oracle In-Focus Series

The *Oracle In-Focus* series is a unique publishing paradigm, targeted at Oracle professionals who need fast and accurate working examples of complex issues. *Oracle In-Focus* books are unique because they have a super-tight focus and quickly provide Oracle professionals with what they need to solve their problems.

Oracle In-Focus books are designed for the practicing Oracle professional. Oracle In-Focus books are an affordable way for all Oracle professionals to get the information they need, and get it fast.

Expert Authors – All *Oracle In-Focus* authors are content experts and are carefully screened for technical ability and communications skills.

Online Code Depot – All code scripts from *Oracle In-Focus* are available on the web for instant download. Those who purchase a book will get the URL and password to download their scripts.

Lots of working examples – *Oracle In-Focus* is packed with working examples and pragmatic tips.

No theory – Practicing Oracle professionals know the concepts, they need working code to get started fast.

Concise – All *Oracle In-Focus* books are less than 200 pages and get right to-the-point of the tough technical issues.

Tight focus - The *Oracle In-Focus* series addresses tight topics and targets specific technical areas of Oracle technology.

Affordable – Reasonably priced, *Oracle In-Focus* books are the perfect solution to challenging technical issues.

http://www.rampant-books.com

Free!
Oracle 10g Senior DBA Reference Poster

This 24 x 36 inch quick reference includes the important data columns and relationships between the DBA views, allowing you to quickly write complex data dictionary queries.

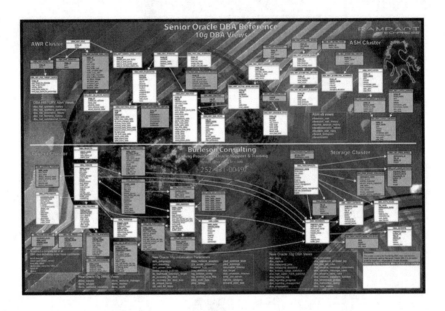

This comprehensive data dictionary reference contains the most important columns from the most important Oracle10g DBA views. Especially useful are the Automated Workload Repository (AWR) and Active Session History (ASH) DBA views.

WARNING - This poster is not suitable for beginners. It is designed for senior Oracle DBAs and requires knowledge of Oracle data dictionary internal structures. You can get your poster at this URL:

www.rampant.cc/poster.htm